# ENERGY
# AND
# SOCIETY

## TIMOTHY J. HEALY

*University of Santa Clara*

# ENERGY
# AND
# SOCIETY

## TIMOTHY J. HEALY

*University of Santa Clara*

# BOYD & FRASER PUBLISHING COMPANY

*3627 Sacramento Street, San Francisco, California 94118*

2nd ed.

93

*Timothy J. Healy*: ENERGY AND SOCIETY

Library of Congress Catalog Card Number: 75-1781

ISBN: 0-87835-049-7

1  2  3  ·  8  7  6

# CONTENTS

# DEDICATION

This book is dedicated to the four billion people who inhabit the earth.

• • •

I am most grateful to Mr. Arthur Weisbach, who edited this book, and who contributed so much during the months we have worked on the material. I received valuable information and assistance from the Pacific Gas and Electric Company, the Exxon Corporation, and a large number of other groups in government, industry, and private life. Finally, I am most pleased to acknowledge the continuing support of Dean Robert J. Parden of the School of Engineering at the University of Santa Clara.

# PREFACE

About 10,000 years ago mankind began to emerge from the chaos of unwritten history. For the previous 500,000 years, give or take a few dozen millenia, evolving humans had roamed the earth in search of food. They were hunters and gatherers. Their needs were simple. They used little of nature's energy.

Then quite suddenly, from our viewpoint, the human creature changed. It turned from gathering wild grains to the formalism of agriculture, from hunting wild animals to taming and breeding. The foundations were laid for a new kind of human life which would in time lead to the birth of cities (civilization), to the industrial revolution, and to the atomic age.

It was a curious transition. Our forebears began with a life which was intensely linked to nature. They then used the gifts of nature, energy and materials, and that uniquely human spark called genius to move ever further from the land. The trick became to isolate one's self from the capriciousness of nature, from flood and famine, disease and cold. Mankind has been largely successful. Some ask today if humans have succeeded too well—if, in fact, it is time now to retreat.

The answer is that one cannot go back to the teepee by the stream, or to the log cabin. There are too many humans. They do not know the life of their forgotten ancestors. Largely by choice, and perhaps more by necessity, mankind must live the life of civilization. That is a life which still evolves, still changes as I write, as you read.

Like the earth, mankind is always a part of change because humans are in and of time and space, where change takes place. The human's task is always to take the matter and space that are the clay of his time, and to mold from them a world as he would have it. He does not have complete freedom to mold in any way he chooses. He has constraints. They are physical and political, economic and ethical. But with the freedom which remains, mankind has tremendous potential—extraordinary opportunities.

This book is about mankind and energy. It is mostly factual, though some philosophy occasionally surfaces. It is meant to be neutral, to present both sides of the issues, though biases probably are evident on occasion.

In the chapters ahead we present the important facts and issues relating to energy production and use. The primary objective of the book is to give the reader sufficient knowledge to assess, and perhaps vote on, the critical energy problems of our time intelligently.

Virtually no mathematical sophistication is necessary to understand the text. A reader can skip the few equations without substantially affecting his or her understanding. Readers should, however, learn the basic terminology; the units of energy and power, the sizes of fuel conversion plants and electric power plants, and the energy required to do certain jobs. At first this may seem to be unnecessary memorization. Later, however, it should become clear that to know, appreciate, and use this material effectively requires some acquaintance with terms and magnitudes.

To accommodate a variety of reader interests and abilities, we have developed three types of problems at the end of each chapter. The first are *General Problems*. These require at the most simple arithmetic. The second kind of problems are *Advanced Mathematical Problems*. They are designed to challenge the student with a background in advanced mathematics, including calculus. Finally, there are *Advanced Study Problems* for the more serious student. They sometimes require some mathematical sophistication, but more commonly they simply require critical study beyond the content of the book.

Drafts of this text and its predecessor, *ENERGY, ELECTRIC POWER AND MAN*, have been tested in classroom use for four years. Students have ranged from freshman humanities majors to senior engineers. The author (and teacher) has not observed a significant difference in the interest or ability to learn the material among such diverse groups.

A last and cautionary note: The reader will not find in the chapters ahead any simple or direct solutions to the energy problems we face today. We hope, however, that the reader will gain that knowledge necessary for finding solutions to the energy problems we all face.

# 1

# ENERGY IN HUMAN HISTORY

> To have dragons one must have change; that is
> the first principle of dragon lore. Otherwise
> everything becomes stale, commonplace, and
> observed.
>
> Loren Eiseley
> *The Night Country*

This chapter is a very brief history of the long evolution of
mankind and human life on earth. Where do we start a history?
The farther back we go, the less we know. Therefore our history
must begin in speculation. And, if we consider history as one
continuum from man's past into his future, then we must end in
speculation also. We live in the present with a sometimes-dim
picture of mankind's past, needing to anticipate or plan
mankind's future.

1

We start our story with a few milestones. It all began a long, long time ago.

4,000,000,000 B.C. - The earth is born. We believe today that our planet is at least four billion years old. For those first few billion years the lands evolve slowly, and the first simple cellular forms appear.

200,000,000 B.C. - The continents move. There begins an extraordinary migration of continents over the face of the earth. It continues today. (In Chapter 10 we shall see an interesting part of our energy future which relates to this curious phenomenon.) In the meantime the first fishes and animals have evolved. Vegetation appears.

100,000,000 B.C. - Oil begins to form from decaying vegetation—nature's organic wastes. As continents shift and animal life evolves to successively higher stages, the trees of 100 million years ago gradually become the oil that humans consume today.

50,000,000 B.C. - Coal begins to form from later types of vegetation. In many parts of what is today the United States, this evolving mineral is particularly abundant.

3,000,000 B.C. - Mankind emerges from the animal world. There begins to appear a new animal, with a highly developed brain structure. As the earth continues to evolve beneath this animal, its brain gradually grows, and the creature turns its brain toward the mastery of nature's goods for its own security and convenience.

10,000 B.C. - Agricultural humans make their appearance, and with them come the first hesitant steps into the Energy Age.

5,000 B.C. - Citizen mankind begins to move from tribal units to larger and more complex societies. Cities are born. The need for control of natural energy sources increases, though still slowly.

1,750 A.D. - Industrial mankind begins in the West to build the great industrial complex which so largely governs life today, at the same time freeing humans from nature's whims and tying them to the very tools which give them freedom.

1,975 A.D. - Contemporary mankind sees the good and the bad of the energy-rich life. Humans face an uncertain transition, groping as they must into an unknown tomorrow.

It is fascinating to look back to mankind's beginnings, particularly to the use of energy in those uncharted eons before written history began. We know something of human prehistory. On the rest we must speculate. Our motivation for starting this text with mention of our long-dead ancestors is simple. Our present uses of energy have much in common with the first human uses. From a study of the past we understand better the present, and these lessons must help us shape our futures.

Over a million years ago man or near-man emerged as a new species in the animal kingdom. At first, like its animal ancestors, the human was a hunter-gatherer, gathering vegetation from the land and eventually hunting small animals. As humans depleted the land about them, they moved on. Primitive humans were wanderers, nomads. Their first use of energy was that of metabolic energy gained from their food, necessary to sustain their vital functions, and to move in search of new food. Thus sustenance of life and self-propelled transportation were mankind's first uses of energy. As we shall see in Chapter 2, these two elements are still near the top of the human list of energy uses.

At some time in their evolution, the hunter-gatherers discovered a new source of energy—fire—that provided heat, light, and perhaps food preservation. It is interesting that these were mankind's first luxuries. They were not absolutely essential to the sustenance of life. But they must have made life a little easier, perhaps a little less terrifying. All else that mankind has done since has been in a sense an extension of those luxuries that go beyond just staying alive. So, long before the emergence of so-called civilization, mankind had already discovered those major energy uses that still dominate its life.

In summary, primitive humans used energy sources for:

1) Sustenance of life
2) Transportation
3) Comfort heating
4) Light
5) Food preparation and preservation

About ten to fifteen thousand years ago the hunter-gatherers gradually became farmers. They domesticated the animals they had hunted and the grains they had gathered. They became sowers, reapers, storers. But these activities required land and buildings. So mankind gave up the nomadic life and turned to the ownership of land in a search for security—for the guarantee of tomorrow's meal. (It has been suggested that perhaps mankind's Garden of Eden was the natural garden in which man and woman first wandered, and that their first sin was to wed themselves to a garden they had made in a futile and unending search for perfect security.)

With the farm came new sources and uses of energy. Animals and other men were harnessed to help build farms, to plant and to reap, and to serve. The water cycle was harnessed for irrigation, and later to turn water wheels to perform other tasks.

First wood and then fossil fuels were burned to provide more energy, more intense heat. Having learned to multiply its own weak power by controlling and directing natural sources of power or energy, mankind will continue to do so through the rest of history.

To make the farm operate more efficiently, tools and storage containers were made. Mankind invented pottery and manufactured bronze and iron tools. Industry arrived. (The industrial revolution would not flower until the eighteenth and nineteenth centuries, even though it had been born in a dim past a hundred centuries earlier.)

About 5,000 years before Christ, the growth of agriculture, a new diversity of labor, and the expanding trade of goods combined to induce the development of cities. Civilization was born. Citizen humans emerged. For the first time some people did not work to produce food or tools used for agriculture. Some traded goods. And some acquired sufficient power and wealth that they did not need to contribute directly to society's tasks. The capacity to control the energy of nature or of others gave some the freedom to spend their time on idle thoughts—some of which were the genius which would give birth to new industry.

This was a strange period in mankind's life. For perhaps five to ten thousand years the human capacity to control energy did not change a great deal. Transportation, always one of man's major uses of energy, is an excellent example. Consider the speed at which mankind travels. Until he tamed the horse, a man's own top speed was about 20 miles per hour (mph). With the taming of horses and other animals to carry people and pull them in wagons or carriages, the top speed rose to about 50 mph. And there it stayed through the Egyptian dynasties, the Asian empires, the Greek state, the Roman Empire, the dark ages, the renaissance, and up to the invention of the steam locomotive—essentially coincident with the flowering of the Industrial Revolution. And then mankind's capacity for speed suddenly began to grow at a fantastic rate. By 1850, one could travel 60 mph in a train; by 1900, a car could go 70 mph; in

1930, commercial aircraft traveled at 150 mph; in 1960, jet travel at 600 mph was common. And in the late 1960s, mankind turned away from the earth and toward the moon —perhaps someday beyond—at speeds greater than 25,000 mph. With greater speed, people traveled not only faster but also farther. And their use of energy for travel grew at extraordinary rates.

Transportation was only one of industrial mankind's major uses of energy. The development of steel permitted new tools, new structures, new devices. All required energy for fabrication. Many required energy for operation too. Heating and cooling standards rose. Electricity emerged as a highly versatile, convenient new form of energy. The industrial revolution was a success. Mankind had harnessed nature's energy to multiply many-fold his own capacity to do work.

But in the waning decades of the twentieth century, we realize that difficulties exist with energy use. It is now our turn to anticipate, and perhaps to plan, the future. We face growing shortages of energy sources, and at the same time we face growing demands for energy. We are increasingly aware of the pollution that is a necessary part of our supply and use of energy. In light of these problems, mankind today faces serious decisions about its own supply of energy, and about energy for mankind tomorrow.

The knowledge we have today about energy must facilitate a reasonable and just evolution into the energy world our children will inherit.

## GENERAL READING FOR CHAPTER 1

1. E. Ayres and C. A. Scarlott, *Energy Sources—The Wealth of the World*, McGraw-Hill Book Co., New York, 1952.

   Much of this book is dated, as are all books on energy, but it is still one of the best available references in many areas. Chapter 2 is a very interesting review of the history of energy resources and man's use of energy.

2. P. Sporn, *Energy—Its Production, Conversion, and Use in the Service of Man*, Pergamon Press, New York, 1963.

This is an interesting short monograph which includes some good material on energy history. It stresses modern history, including the growth of electric energy.

3. L. White, *The Science of Culture*, Farrar, Straus and Giroux, New York, 1949.

There are many books on anthropology which the reader might study. This book is particularly concerned with man's technological growth. There is an interesting chapter entitled "Energy and the Evolution of Culture." It is qualitative rather than quantitative. (I am not aware of any quantitative estimates of man's energy uses in pre-history.)

4. J. Bronowski, *The Ascent of Man*, Little, Brown and Co., Boston, 1973.

Bronowski's brief survey of the life of man gives much food for thought about man's first uses of energy. The answers about energy use are not here, but the reader should be able to deduce many of the right questions.

## PROBLEMS FOR CHAPTER 1

### General Study Problems

1. Read a book on anthropology. Estimate how man probably used energy at different stages in his evolution. See, for example, Chapter 13 in General Reading 3.
2. Write a short history of the industrial revolution, noting dates of important inventions or developments which affected energy.

# 2

# HOW MANKIND USES ENERGY

*He saw the cities of many men, and knew their mind.*

Homer

What is energy? How much energy do we use? For what tasks? In what amounts? What about future use? What is the nature of growth? Are there alternate ways to grow? These are the questions we next consider. In this chapter we ask what energy is and how mankind uses it. In later pages we will investigate present and future sources of mankind's energy needs.

## 2.1  WHAT IS ENERGY?

Energy is a very fundamental concept which resists simple definition. A really deep and meaningful understanding of this concept requires extensive study of thermodynamics. However, it is possible to develop some intuitive ideas which will be useful in our study of energy.

We start with a related concept called *work*. Work is formally defined in mechanics as the product of the force acting on a body and the distance which the body moves in the direction of this force. Beyond this formal definition we shall rely upon the reader's intuitive sense of physical work. Work is done when an object is lifted from the ground, or when an automobile is driven along a road, or when a lamp lights a room.

We define *energy* as the available capacity of a body to do work because of its position or condition. The extent to which energy is available depends on the nature of the process.

Finally, we define *power* as the time rate at which energy is made available, or work is done. An example should help you understand these terms.

Suppose you push a block up a frictionless plane, as in Figure 2–1. The energy stored, when the block is at the top, equals the work you did to get it there. This stored energy depends on the weight W and the height H, and not on how fast you push. But the power you generate in order to move the block does depend on how fast you push it. If you push slowly, and hence take a long time to do the work, the power is low. But if you push the block up rapidly the power is greater.

As another example, consider a lump of coal. The lump has a certain amount of energy—a certain capacity to do work —which depends on its nature or condition, and on the process used to make the energy available. If we specify these two factors, we can give the amount of energy which can be made available. But we cannot talk sensibly about the power contained in a lump of coal. Power depends on how fast the lump burns and hence how fast the energy is made available.

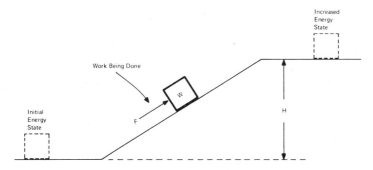

**Figure 2-1.** Work, Energy, and Power.

Another approach to the understanding of the concept of energy is through two extremely important statements, called the First and Second Laws of Thermodynamics. There are many ways to express these laws. The following expressions are useful for our viewpoint.

1) **The First Law of Thermodynamics:** Whenever a process undergoes a cyclic change, energy is always conserved.

2) **The Second Law of Thermodynamics:** It is impossible to construct an engine which, when operating through a complete cycle, will convert all of the heat supplied to it into work.

Neither of these laws is obvious; neither can be proved. They are based on observations. There is no confirmed evidence that either has ever been violated. We accept them because they have proved thus far to be true.

The First Law of Thermodynamics is sometimes called the Law of Conservation of Energy. It tells us that energy can be neither created nor destroyed. It can only be transformed from one form to one or more other forms. All of the energy we introduce into a system must go somewhere. Suppose that we decide to burn a certain amount of coal to produce electric energy. Some energy will remain as unburned coal particles, some will be lost as heat in the stacks, or dissipated as heat radiated from the boiler or from steam pipes. Some energy is lost (due to the Second Law) as waste heat; some goes into friction losses, and some (about 40 percent) is converted to electric energy. All of these energies must add up to the total initial energy released in the coal combustion process.

The implication for all energy systems is that we cannot get energy out unless we put some kind of energy in, or that if we put in a certain amount of energy, all of it must be accounted for. Since our systems have inherent inefficiencies, we conclude that *every energy system will produce waste heat.* The percentage of waste heat in the case of thermal power plants is quite large, and it poses major engineering and environmental problems. We discuss these in some detail in Chapters 8, 14 and 15.

The Second Law of Thermodynamics tells us that we cannot transform all of the heat input to an engine into mechanical work. Some heat must be wasted. There are many forms of the Second Law, but this one seems particularly relevant to our studies because of its emphasis on waste heat. This waste heat is inevitable in any heat-work conversion process. In Chapter 14 we pursue this question quantitatively to see just how much waste is inevitable in a thermal power plant.

## 2.2 THE UNITS OF ENERGY

Before we can begin our discussion of energy use, we need to define a *unit* (or a basic quantity) of energy. Many different units of energy are used by persons working in different fields. The units used by a theoretical physicist will not generally be the same as those used by an electric power plant supervisor.

Of the many available units of energy, we have chosen to define four. The first two will be used extensively in this textbook. The second two are not of direct use to us here.

However, they are important, and it is of interest to show how they relate to the units we will be using.

1. The *British Thermal Unit* (BTU). This is approximately the energy which must be added to one pound of water to increase its temperature by one degree Fahrenheit. This unit is commonly used in the United States to specify the energy content of primary fuels or energy sources, and the total amount of energy used for some specified purpose. For example, each gallon of gasoline has a heating value of about 136,000 BTU. (Heating value is the maximum amount of energy released when fuel combines with oxygen in a combustion process.) If a particular automobile gets ten miles per gallon of gas, then it takes about 13,600 BTU to drive the car each mile.

2. The *Kilowatt-Hour* (KWH). This is the amount of energy used to run a 1,000 watt (one kilowatt) lightbulb for one hour. This unit is very commonly used in connection with the generation and use of electric energy. A 2 KW water heater uses 6 KWH of electric energy in 3 hours. A 200 KW electric generator produces 1,000 KWH of electric energy in 5 hours. A perfect (100% efficient) energy conversion system, which lost no energy, would require 3,413 BTU to produce one KWH. (In practice a good modern fossil fuel electric power plant wastes as much as 60% of its input fuel energy, requiring about 9,000 BTU to produce a single KWH.)

3. The *joule*. This unit is the energy used by a one-watt light bulb in one second. This is a metric unit. It will probably be used to an increasing degree as the metric system gains wider adoption.

4. The *calorie*. This is approximately the amount of energy that must be added to one gram of water to increase its

temperature by one degree Celsius (or centigrade). One thousand calories is a *kilocalorie*, or *kcalorie*, or *Calorie* (with a capital C). The kcalorie or Calorie is the familiar dietetic unit of food energy. The average American takes in about 3,000 Calories each day.

Table 2–1 summarizes a few of the most important and interesting numerical relations between energy units.

Before closing this section we must briefly define the two important units of *power* we will be using. You will recall that power is the time rate of doing work or making energy available. The basic unit of electric power is the *watt*. This unit is a bit small, so we often use the *kilowatt* or KW (1,000 watts). When we are discussing the power capacity of a large electric power plant, even the kilowatt is small, so we use the *megawatt* or MW (1,000,000 watts or 1,000 kilowatts). A small electric lightbulb may require 50 watts, a large stove about 10 KW. A large nuclear power plant may generate 1,000 MW. The total electric power capacity in the United States in 1975 was about 500,000 MW.

The power capacity of an engine or motor is often given in units of horsepower. (One horsepower = 746 watts = 0.746 KW.) The power of the motor which drives an electric clock is a very small fraction of one horsepower. An automobile engine may generate as little as 50 horsepower or as much as 400 horsepower. Huge water pumps may have a power rating greatly in excess of 10,000 horsepower.

## 2.3  HOW MANKIND USES ENERGY

In 1968 the total primary energy used in the United States was about 60,526,000,000,000,000 BTU. That number is so large that it is convenient to invent still another unit. We express yearly energy use in quintillions of BTU. One quintillion ($10^{18}$) BTU is called one $Q$. In 1968 we used about

## TABLE 2–1

### Energy Unit Equivalents

| | | |
|---|---|---|
| 1 KWH | = | 3,413 BTU |
| 1 KWH | = | 3,600,000 joules |
| 1 BTU | = | 1,055 joules |
| 1 Cal. | = | 4,186 joules |

0.06Q; by 1972 it was 0.07Q; in 1975 it will probably be close to 0.08Q. But we shall return to 1968 figures, since that is the last year for which we have rather detailed data on how this total energy use is divided among various economic sectors.

Table 2–2(1) shows how energy was used in 1968. It divides the economy into four major sectors: residential, commercial, industrial, and transportation. The table shows how the 0.06Q was divided in percentages of the total. Also shown are average annual growth rates, which indicate which uses are growing most rapidly.

Table 2–2 contains much information and is well worth some detailed study. First, we note that we use about 20% of our energy in private residences—our homes. Over half of that is for space heating. Because this use is so large, it received major attention in the fuel-oil shortage of 1973–4, when the plea came to turn the thermostat down to 68°. Food-related energy use in homes adds up to a relatively small 2.2%. However, much more energy is used in the industrial sector for processing food, in the transportation sector for delivering food, and in the commercial sector for selling food. Air conditioning is an extremely important factor, not because of its percentage of the total, which is small, but because of its very high growth rate. Air conditioning was once considered a luxury. Today, in many regions, it is considered a necessity. Because it is so energy-intensive (that is, it uses large quantities of energy), it will be a major source of growth for some time to come.

About 15% of our energy is used in the commercial sector. (See Figure 2–2.) This sector includes stores, businesses, shops and offices for lawyers, insurance agents, dentists, accountants, and many more. Again, space heating is the major use of energy. Air conditioning is number two but growing rapidly. One of the absurdities that came from the days of cheap-energy planning was the sealed office building that had so much lighting that air-conditioning was needed even in the winter to remove the heat radiated by the lights. Today's energy-conscious society is beginning to pay much more attention to the energy design of its commercial office buildings.

## TABLE 2–2

### Energy Consumption in the United States—1968

| Sector and End Use | Annual Growth Rate | Percent of Total |
|---|---|---|
| Residential | | |
| Space Heating | 4.1% | 11.0% |
| Water Heating | 5.2 | 2.9 |
| Cooking | 1.7 | 1.1 |
| Refrigeration | 8.2 | 1.1 |
| Air Conditioning | 15.6 | 0.7 |
| Other | 6.1 | 2.4 |
| Total | 4.8 | 19.2 |
| Commercial | | |
| Space Heating | 3.8 | 6.9 |
| Air Conditioning | 8.6 | 1.8 |
| Feedstock | 3.7 | 1.6 |
| Water Heating | 2.3 | 1.1 |
| Refrigeration | 2.9 | 1.1 |
| Other | 26.0 | 1.9 |
| Total | 5.4 | 14.4 |
| Industrial | | |
| Process Steam | 3.6 | 16.7 |
| Direct Heat | 2.8 | 11.5 |
| Electric Drive | 5.3 | 7.9 |
| Feedstock | 6.1 | 3.6 |
| Electrolytic Processes | 4.8 | 1.2 |
| Other | 6.7 | 0.3 |
| Total | 3.9 | 41.2 |
| Transportation | 4.1 | 25.2 |
| National Total | | 100.0 |

**Figure 2–2.** Industrial use of energy. Industry uses over 40% of all energy in the United States. In the end, of course, the consumer is the final though indirect user of all energy, whether it be industrial, residential, or commercial. Transportation uses 25% of all energy resources in the United States for propelling vehicles. Another 15% is used to build vehicles, roads, and shops, and to provide required transportation sales and maintenance service.

The industrial sector uses nearly 41% of our energy to produce the materials and products used by society. An important and often misunderstood relation exists between the energy used to make a product and the energy used to operate it when it is delivered to one of the sectors for use. Consider some examples. Clothes dryers probably use more energy in a lifetime than was required to build them. Automobiles require somewhat more energy to operate them than to build, sell, maintain, and insure.(2) A chair will require much more energy to build than to maintain. Considerations such as these are an important part of the energy evaluation of the products of industry.

At first glance the transportation sector, at 25%, is number two in the energy-use list. However, the 25% includes only fuel energy. Recent studies have shown that an additional 15% of our energy comes from the other three sectors to support the transportation complex. This energy is required to build vehicles and roadways, and to sell, insure, maintain and park vehicles. Thus, in the United States we use about 40% of all our energy on transportation. About 20%, or 1/5 of all our energy, goes to the private automobile. The remaining 20% is used for planes, buses, trains, and ships. The very large amount of energy used by cars permitted that sector to absorb a major part of the fuel shortage of early 1974. The long lines and rising gas prices were successful in cutting gasoline use during those months.

It is often claimed that this nation is quite wasteful in its use of energy. This is a complex issue; an individual's position on the matter depends on his definition of waste, and also perhaps on the relation of waste to the economy. (This author is of the opinion that much waste exists, and that it should be cut significantly. We shall return to this question in Chapter 15, on energy conservation.) Regardless of one's view of waste, it is a curious fact that the existence of this waste permits us to absorb sudden cuts in energy supply with relatively minor disruptions in our way of life.

This last point brings us back to our observations in Chapter 1 about the minimum requirements for the sustenance of life. We argued that only metabolism (food) and transportation are vital. Today these two areas require about 50% of all our energy, although with a degree of sophistication well beyond the necessary minimum. If we add the first basic luxuries of heat, light and sanitation, we are probably close to 75% in energy use. In fact, the great majority of our energy still goes to the basic needs of life, as it did for our prehistoric ancestors. Of course we cannot forget that our standards in these areas are far higher than those of our parents, let alone our ancestors of pre-history. We use much more energy than we require for mere survival. Most of us want to keep things that way, although some would argue that we could afford to lower our standards.

## 2.4  USING ELECTRIC ENERGY

We use energy in many different forms. Gasoline is used to fuel most automobiles. Other oil products are used for transportation, space heating, and process heating in industry. Natural gas is used for cooking and heating in homes and for process and space heating. Coal is used for many industrial purposes. All of the above can be used to generate electric energy. Because electric energy use is so common and familiar to us, and because its use is growing at a greater rate than total energy use, we devote this section to a brief look at how we use this electric energy.

We consider first the total electric power capacity and total annual electric energy use in the United States. In 1973 United States electric power capacity was about 440,000 MW. The energy produced and used amounted to approximately 1,850,000,000,000 KWH. Electric power and energy use both have an historic growth rate of about 7% per year. With a population of about 210,000,000 people, each individual had, on the average, about 2,100 KW of capacity available, and used about 9,000 KWH of electric energy in 1973. Next we ask how we use our electric energy. The data will not be for 1973, since it is not yet available, but the percentages will be quite accurate.

Table 2–3 shows how electric energy was used by major economic sectors in 1972.(3) Transportation does not appear on this list because it uses so little electric energy.

Now we look behind these gross numbers to find some specific

**TABLE 2–3**

**Electric Energy Use By Major Sectors—1972**

| Classification | KWH (Billions) | Percent |
|----------------|----------------|---------|
| Industrial | 639 | 40 |
| Residential | 539 | 34 |
| Commercial | 359 | 23 |
| Other | 51 | 3 |
| | 1,588 | 100 |

examples of energy use within the groups. First take residential use, since it is familiar to most of us.

Table 2–4 gives the power required and the average energy used by some residential energy consumers.(4) The reader will no doubt find it interesting to spend some time looking at these numbers, and perhaps looking for some characteristic patterns or significant points hidden among the raw statistics. You may wish to interrupt your reading of the text at this point to look for such points for yourself before we make some observations of our own below.

The average *household* in the United States uses about 8,000 KWH each year. (This is consistent with our earlier figure of 9,000 KWH per *person*, combined with a household occupancy of a little over three persons and the 30 percent residential use figure above.) It is apparent that any household with all of the devices in Table 2–4 is using much more energy than one might expect from the average. In fact, the figure for electric heating is 16,000 KWH by itself. Most homes do not use electric heating; perhaps this is fortunate.

An important fact apparent from Table 2–4 below is that the major energy-consuming devices tend to be those which intentionally produce heat or cold, such as the air conditioner, clothes dryer, freezer, refrigerator, range and water heater. Devices which drive motors or fans tend to require less power and use less energy than others mentioned above. More economical devices include the washing machine, furnace fan, and vacuum cleaner.

## TABLE 2-4

## Typical Household Appliance Power and Energy Requirements

| Appliance | Power (Watts) | Annual Energy (KWH) |
|---|---|---|
| Air Conditioner (Window) | 1,566 | 1,389 |
| Broiler | 1,439 | 100 |
| Carving Knife | 92 | 8 |
| Clock | 2 | 17 |
| Clothes Dryer | 4,856 | 993 |
| Deep Fat Fryer | 1,448 | 83 |
| Dishwasher | 1,201 | 363 |
| Electric Blanket | 177 | 147 |
| Fan (Circulating) | 88 | 43 |
| Fan (Furnace) | 292 | 394 |
| Food Blender | 386 | 15 |
| Food Freezer (Frostless 15 cu. ft.) | 440 | 1,761 |
| Food Mixer | 127 | 13 |
| Food Waste Disposer | 445 | 30 |
| Frying Pan | 1,196 | 186 |
| Heat Pump (Electric Heating System) | 11,848 | 16,003 |
| Heater (Radiant) | 1,322 | 176 |
| Hot Plate | 1,257 | 90 |
| Iron | 1,088 | 144 |
| Oil Burner or Stoker | 266 | 410 |
| Radio | 71 | 86 |
| Radio-Phonograph | 109 | 109 |
| Range | 12,207 | 1,175 |
| Refrigerator (12 cu. ft.) | 241 | 728 |
| Refrigerator (Frostless 12 cu. ft.) | 321 | 1,277 |
| Refrigerator-Freezer (14 cu. ft.) | 326 | 1,137 |
| Refrigerator-Freezer (Frostless 14 cu. ft.) | 615 | 1,829 |
| Sewing Machine | 75 | 11 |
| Shaver | 14 | 18 |
| Television (BW) | 287 | 362 |
| Television (Color) | 332 | 502 |
| Toaster | 1,146 | 39 |
| Toothbrush | 7 | 1 |
| Vacuum Cleaner | 630 | 46 |
| Washing Machine (Automatic) | 512 | 103 |
| Washing Machine (Non-Automatic) | 286 | 76 |
| Water Heater (Standard) | 2,475 | 4,219 |
| Water Heater (Quick Recovery) | 4,474 | 4,811 |
| Water Pump | 460 | 231 |

We see that it costs far less to run a carving knife than a clock even though the clock is much less powerful. The reason, of course, is that the clock is always "on," whereas the knife is seldom used. The refrigerator uses about the same amount of energy as the range, although it demands far less power. We shall see later that this condition makes the refrigerator a much more desirable consumer than the range from the standpoint of

**Figure 2–3.** Use of electricity in the home. The residential sector accounts for about 30% of electric energy used in the United States. Cooking is a major user of electric energy. Using gas is more efficient, but gas may not be available in all locations. Such devices as television sets and refrigerators are nearly saturated; that is, nearly all homes contain both a television set and a refrigerator. The dishwasher is an example of an appliance that will probably grow significantly in use. Smaller appliances use some power, but cooking, heating, and air-conditioning require the major amounts of power in residences. (Courtesy of the Tennessee Valley Authority.)

the electric utility which must provide for both energy and power demand.

Recently a number of groups have proposed that every appliance sold should clearly state the power it requires. From the discussion above it is clear that it may be just as desirable to state the average energy required per year by the device. This information should be of interest to the consumer, since it will provide him with a measure of the cost of operating the device and the relative effect of the device on the environment.

Finally, most of the large energy users on our list provide for basic human needs such as food, heat and cleanliness. Few of the commonly-discussed frills use much energy. To summarize this question of residential usage, we have selected some representative devices to use in a 10,000 KWH/year residence which has an electric water heater and non-electric heating. This summary is given in Table 2–5.

Next we ask how industry uses its large share of energy. Table 2–6 gives the energy used by the major industries in this country for 1963. Also shown is the cost of purchased power as a percent of the total product value. The latter figure is interesting because it shows that very little of the cost of manufacturing things is in the electric energy consumed. It is sometimes argued that low-cost electric energy is the essential ingredient in stimulating the growth of an industry in an undeveloped area. The figures in Table 2–6 suggest that it takes much more than the availability of energy to cause industrial growth. This point is discussed in some detail by Sporn.(5)

### TABLE 2–5

#### Residential Use of Electric Power

| Use | KWH | Percent |
|---|---|---|
| Cleanliness (includes hot water) | 5,200 | 52 |
| Food Storage and Preparation | 2,800 | 28 |
| Lighting | 1,000 | 10 |
| Service Appliances: Iron, Vacuum, etc. | 500 | 5 |
| Entertainment | 500 | 5 |

We have seen how various sectors of society use electric energy.
Now we consider how society presents its demands for power as
a function of time. The demand or use of energy is often called
the *load* on the system.

If everyone demanded a constant level of power at all times,
the task of meeting this demand would be much simpler than it
is. Unfortunately, our demands vary from hour to hour, day to
day, and season to season. A curve of typical diurnal (daily)
demand in a large metropolitan area is shown in Figure 2–4.
There is a minimum power level at all times, even late at night.
This minimum demand comes from street-lighting, heating,

## TABLE 2–6

### Industrial Uses of Electric Energy, 1963

| Industry | Electric Energy Consumption: Millions of KWH | Cost of Purchased Power: Percent of Product Value |
|---|---|---|
| Chemicals and allied products | 109,494 | 2.0 |
| Primary metal industries | 100,264 | 1.9 |
| Fabricated metal products | 9,412 | 0.6 |
| Paper and allied products | 39,572 | 2.2 |
| Food and kindred products | 22,149 | 0.5 |
| Stone, clay and glass products | 18,052 | 1.5 |
| Transportation equipment | 18,898 | 0.4 |
| Petroleum and coal products | 17,781 | 0.8 |
| Textile mill products | 15,427 | 0.9 |
| Machinery, except electrical | 11,730 | 0.5 |
| Electrical machinery | 13,070 | 0.5 |
| Rubber products | 7,637 | 1.0 |
| Lumber and wood products | 6,055 | 0.9 |
| Printing and publishing | 4.099 | 0.4 |
| Apparel and related products | 2,509 | 0.3 |
| Furniture and fixtures | 1,848 | 0.5 |
| Instruments and related products | 2,122 | 0.5 |
| Leather and leather products | 1,019 | 0.4 |
| Tobacco manufactures | 511 | 0.1 |
| Miscellaneous manufactures | 1,880 | 0.5 |
| Ordnance and accessories | 2,091 | 0.4 |
| ALL MANUFACTURING | 405,932 | 0.86 |

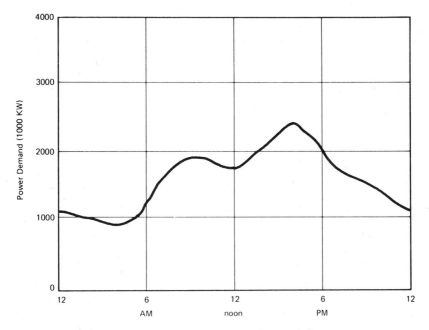

**Figure 2–4.** Typical Daily Power Demand Curve.

all-night businesses and factories, etc. About dawn the demand begins to grow as people get up, turn up the heat, cook breakfast, and open offices. There is usually a dip around noon, perhaps 11 A.M. to 2 P.M., and then a second and usually greater peak around 4–6 P.M. as people begin to cook evening meals and businesses remain open. After 6 P.M. the peak gradually diminishes into the night.

This same basic demand curve shape applies to all weekdays. On weekends, the curve tends to be generally lower, with less-pronounced peaks. Seasonal variations are also quite important. Figure 2–5 shows the monthly United States energy demand since 1968.(6) Pronounced seasonal peaks from heating loads in the winter and air-conditioning loads in the summer are apparent. Both diurnal and annual curves will be affected by such factors as weather conditions and the state of the economy.

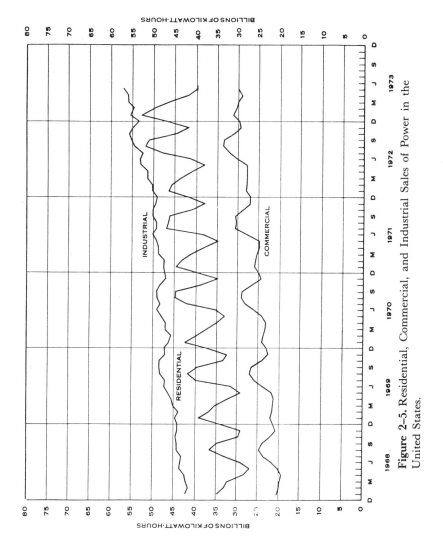

**Figure 2-5.** Residential, Commercial, and Industrial Sales of Power in the United States.

26

It is the responsibility of the power industry to meet the peak power demands of its customers. Since the industry cannot know exactly what demands will occur or when, companies generally try to maintain a fairly comfortable excess of capacity beyond peak demand. This excess is called a "margin." It usually amounts to at least 15 to 20 percent of the peak. This margin allows for excessive or unexpected demands and for breakdowns or "outages." When a company or a region has a low margin and some bad luck with equipment or weather, demand may exceed capacity. The results are blackouts (loss of power to some or all customers) or brownouts (decrease in voltage to customers). The area in and around New York City has experienced this problem during recent summers.

Since it costs money and requires land to build plants to meet power demands, we must have a demand whose peaks are as little above the base load (minimum demand) as possible. Because of the importance of the relation of peak demand to base load, a ratio, called a *load factor*, has been developed to tell us how "peaked" a load demand is. The load factor is the ratio of the average load over a designated period to the peak load occurring in that period.

## Example 2–1

Assume that the United States generating capacity has a margin of 25%. Use the figures given in Section 2.4 to find the load factor for the United States in 1973.

Since the margin was 25%, the peak power demand was 440,000/1.25 MW or 352,000 MW. The average load was:

$$\frac{1,850,000,000,000 \, \text{KWH}}{24 \times 365 \, (\text{hours})} = 211,000 \, \text{MW}.$$

Hence the load factor was $\dfrac{211,000}{362,000} = 0.60$

The nature of the load or demand curve dictates not only the total capacity which a company must install but also the kind of equipment which will be used for generation. We discuss this problem in more detail in a later chapter. At this point, we distinguish between "base load," which is always present, and "peak load," which occurs only at certain times. Base loads tend to be supplied by large fossil-fuel or atomic plants which should run continuously because of the rather long times required to start them. Peak loads tend to be supplied by hydro facilities where available; or increasingly by pumped-storage plants; or by gas turbines, smaller fossil-fuel plants (often older units), or by internal-combustion engines.

## 2.5  ENERGY FOR TRANSPORTATION

As we noted earlier, we use a large share of our energy budget on transportation in the United States. Table 2–7 gives an approximate summary of how transportation energy is used as a percent of all energy use in the country. The figures for total energy use are subject to some dispute, since it is not obvious exactly how much indirect energy should actually be charged to transportation. Nonetheless, the data are reasonably meaningful.

The fact that a large percentage of our energy is used for transportation has a number of important implications for our energy plans. As we noted earlier, our large demand for gasoline could be (and was) damped very quickly when our supplies of petroleum were cut. On a longer range, it has been observed for many years that the standard of a 4,000 pound

### TABLE 2–7

**Transportation Energy—Percent of the United States Total**

| Use | Percent |
| --- | --- |
| Fuel for private automobiles | 12 |
| Total for private automobiles | 20 |
| Fuel for all transportation | 25 |
| Total for all transportation | 40 |

automobile for almost every driver is unnecessary if not absurd. Two basic solutions are commonly proposed. One is to decrease car size and to make more effective use of cars through car pooling, for example. The second proposal is to replace many of the cars now on the roads with some energy-efficient mode of mass transit. (See Figure 2–6.)

We begin our discussion of these proposals by considering the four basic physical reasons for which energy must be supplied to vehicles.

1. *Rolling resistance.* As a vehicle rolls there are friction losses because of the wheel or tire contact with the surface. This energy-loss is proportional to vehicle weight.

2. *Grade resistance.* This is the energy required to lift a vehicle against the earth's force of gravity as the vehicle goes up hills. It is proportional to weight.

3. *Acceleration.* This is the energy required to increase the speed of a vehicle. It is proportional to weight.

4. *Aerodynamic drag.* This is energy required by the vehicle to push through the air. It is not dependent on weight, but does increase a great deal as speed increases.

Note that the first three loss terms are weight dependent. In fact, for most vehicles including automobiles, energy intensiveness (*e.g.*, in units of BTUs/vehicle-mile) is nearly proportional to weight. This is clearly illustrated by the empirical data shown in Figure 2–7.(7,8) No other single item is as important for energy conservation in automobiles as reducing the weight. This is one of the major factors leading to the increased interest in small cars in recent years. They use less gas per mile primarily because they are light.

The grade-resistance factor can be reduced by using radial tires, which have less frictional heat losses (and which last longer) than conventional tires.

The aerodynamic drag loss is reduced by streamlining the

**Figure 2–6.** The Bay Area Rapid Transit (BART) System. When BART began operations in 1972, it was the first completely new rapid-transit system under construction or in planning stages in the United States. Much electric energy is needed for such systems. However, this energy is small compared with the total demand for electric energy. Also, mass transit systems tend to be more energy-efficient than the automobile. (Courtesy of Pacific Gas and Electric Company.)

vehicle or by reducing its speed. This was a major impetus behind the move to 55 mph highway speeds in the United States in 1974.

If automobiles use too much energy, do we have alternatives in public transit systems? It is very difficult to present meaningful comparative data, because there are so many different modes of transit and ways of operating these systems. Table 2–8 is a very brief comparative survey of some typical systems.(9) (The reader is cautioned not to use these data without studying the assumptions and considerations upon which they are based. See the referenced literature.)

From the data of Table 2–8 and a knowledge of the

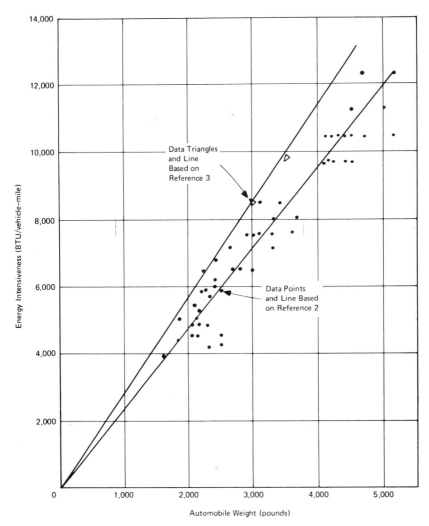

**Figure 2–7.** Automobile Fuel Consumption as a Function of Vehicle Weight (1971 and 1972 cars).

**TABLE 2–8**

**Comparison of Energy Demand of Vehicles**

| Vehicle | Weight | Seats | BTU/VM[a] | BTU/SM[b] |
|---------|--------|-------|-----------|-----------|
| Gas auto (small) | 2,000 lbs | 4 | 4,750 | 1,187 |
| Gas auto (large) | 4,000 | 5 | 9,500 | 1,900 |
| Personal rapid transit | 2,000 | 4 | 3,000 | 750 |
| Commuter rail | 180,000 | 150 | 154,500 | 1,030 |
| Rapid rail transit | 58,000 | 72 | 58,500 | 812 |
| Fixed route bus | 20,000 | 50 | 37,750 | 755 |
| Express bus | 20,000 | 50 | 29,600 | 592 |

[a] BTU/VM: British Thermal Units per vehicle-mile
[b] BTU/SM: British Thermal Units per seat-mile

assumptions behind them we can make a few general statements about energy for transportation.

1. A well-loaded bus or commuter train, particularly if it operates in an express mode, can be considerably more energy efficient than a poorly loaded automobile.

2. On the other hand a small automobile with four or five passengers can be extremely efficient, probably more so than most mass transit systems operating under average load conditions.

3. Nothing is as important in reducing energy use per passenger-mile as increasing the loading, regardless of the type of the vehicle. Conclusion: Car-pooling and well-loaded buses are excellent ways to save energy.

## 2.6  THE GROWTH OF ENERGY USE

In the preceding sections of this chapter we have considered the ways in which man uses energy. In this section we turn to the question of how these uses add up over time to present a history of growth.

Many phenomena in life, both natural and man-made, roughly follow an S-shaped growth curve, as shown in Figure 2–8.

Growth curves of this type are found in populations of people; in the number of fruit flies in a jar, of bacteria in a culture; and perhaps in one's knowledge about a particular field.

In the beginning, growth is often quite rapid. It is commonly *exponential*, which means that the growth rate at any time is a fixed percentage of the size at that time. This type of growth leads to rapid increases in size if the fixed percentage is high. We shall look at exponential growth in more detail shortly.

In all practical systems, forces eventually begin to operate to limit growth. It ceases to be exponential and approaches saturation. In the case of fruit flies in a jar, growth is eventually constrained by crowding and the exhaustion of nutrients. After

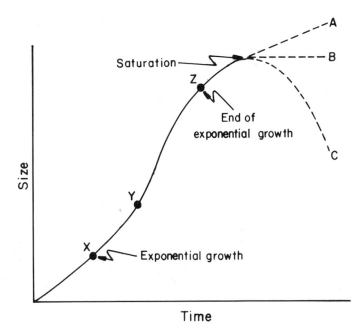

**Figure 2–8.** Typical Growth Curves.

the growth curve has begun to saturate, it can follow three paths. It may continue to rise quite slowly (dashed curve A) for some time. The curve for population in the United States is following such a curve at this time, with a declining growth rate presently a little less than 1% per year. A growth curve might totally saturate (curve B). This form is sought by "zero-growth" advocates in fields such as population, annual energy use, resource use, the national economy, and many more. Finally, the curve may pass saturation and turn downward (curve C). This happens to fruit flies in a jar if they exhaust their nutrients, or to other populations which fail to stabilize their demand and supply for any vital need.

In the field of energy use it is very difficult to know where we are on the curve of Figure 2–8. Energy use still appears to be growing rapidly. But are we near X on the curve, with much growth ahead of us, or are we closer to Y, which would presage the end of exponential growth? Or, finally, are we near Z, close to saturation? We don't know. We don't have sufficient evidence to suggest we are nearing saturation. But we do recognize some elements which could lead toward saturation. These include: shortages of energy supply; increased prices; pollution control needs; a slowing of the population growth rate; and some demand for governmental control of energy growth. We are not sure where we are or where we are going, but the evidence we have today suggests that energy use growth rate may be starting to decline.

Just what is exponential growth, and how does it operate? As we said earlier, it is growth which is proportional to size. In the discussion below we are actually going to talk about something called *geometric growth*. But it is so similar in nature to exponential growth (which is mathematically more complex) that we will limit our discussion to geometric growth. Suppose that energy use at the beginning of a given year is $E_O$, and that during the year energy use grows by the fraction r of $E_O$. (Currently r is about 0.035, corresponding to 3.5%, in the United States. It has been near 3.5% on the average, for many decades.) Then energy use at the end of the first year is:

$$E_1 = E_O + rE_O = (1 + r) E_O$$

At the end of the second year energy use is:

$$E_2 = E_1 + rE_1 = (1 + r)E_1 = (1 + r)^2E_O$$

And at the end of the 17th year it is:

$$E_r = (1 + r)^{17}E_O$$

The annual energy use, assuming $E_O = 0.07Q$ in 1972, and assuming a constant growth rate of 0.035 per year, is plotted in Figure 2–9. The lower curve, with its scale on the left, is the projected annual energy use. The upper curve, scaled on the

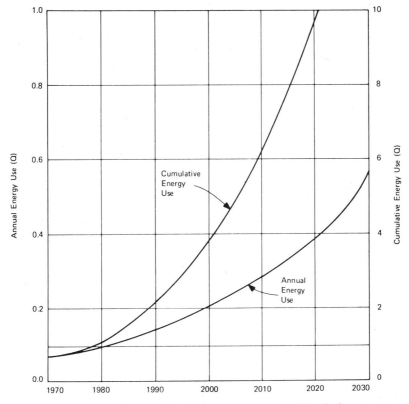

**Figure 2–9.** Projected future United States energy needs. This display assumes an annual growth rate of 3.5%.

right, is the cumulative energy use—that is, the total summed energy required from 1970 until the year given.

The reader is cautioned to note that these curves are not predictions. They are projections based on the *assumption* of continued exponential growth at 3.5% per year. If the factors mentioned earlier tend to saturate energy growth, these curves will be too high.

The mathematics required to arrive at the curves above is a little complex for those who do not regularly work with mathematics. There is, however, a very simple concept which can be easily used to measure growth. If growth is exponential, the time required for the size of the variable to double is given quite simply and fairly accurately by the expression:

$$t_D = \frac{70}{r}$$

Where doubling time is $t_D$, and the annual growth rate is r, expressed as a percentage. For example, if a population has 100,000,000 members and a growth rate of 2% per year, in 35 years it will have about 200,000,000 members. In 70 years it will have about 400,000,000 members.

## 2.7  CONCLUSIONS ON ENERGY USE

In this chapter we have traced the patterns of energy use and growth in the United States. The basic dilemma we face is the growing demand for energy, compared with the growing difficulties in supplying energy. We have looked at the demand or use side of the equation. In the chapters ahead we will turn our attention to the problems of meeting demand, and then of reducing demand.

### REFERENCES FOR CHAPTER 2

1. "Patterns of Energy Consumption in the United States," Executive Office of the President, U.S. Government Printing Office, Washington, D.C., January, 1972.

2. E. Hirst, "Direct and Indirect Energy Requirements for Automobiles," Oak Ridge National Laboratory, Oak Ridge, Tennessee, February, 1974.

3. *Statistical Abstract of the United States—1974*, U.S. Department of Commerce, Washington, D.C., 1974.

4. Edison Electric Institute, Marketing Division, New York, 1969.

5. P. Sporn, *Technology, Engineering, and Economics*, MIT Press, Cambridge, Mass., 1969.

6. "Electric Power Statistics," Federal Power Commission, U.S. Government Printing Office, Washington, D.C., May, 1973.

7. Data obtained from various *Consumer Reports* automobile surveys.

8. W. D. Ruckelshaus, speech at the Highway Research Board, Washington, D.C., January 24, 1973.

9. T. J. Healy, "Energy Use of Public Transit Systems," for the Department of Transportation, State of California, Sacramento, Cal., August 1, 1974.

## GENERAL READING FOR CHAPTER 2

1. *Patterns of Energy Consumption in the United States*, Stanford Research Institute, Office of Science and Technology, U.S. Government Printing Office, January, 1972.

    This is a recent comprehensive government report on how energy in all forms is used by different sectors of society. It has about 200 pages of important data on energy use. It is not light reading.

2. O.L. Culberson, *The Consumption of Electricity in the United States*, Oak Ridge National Laboratory, ORNL-NSF-EP-5, Oak Ridge, Tenn., June, 1971.

    This is a good general study of how electric energy is used. It is interesting and easily read.

## PROBLEMS FOR CHAPTER 2

*General Problems*

2.1. Recall that the total energy use in the United States in 1968 was about 0.06Q. Using Table 2–2, determine the number of BTU used for residential water heating. About how many pounds of water could this energy raise ideally by 80° F? (1.74 × 10¹⁵ BTU, 21.75 trillion pounds or 10.875 billion tons. This is about 51.8 tons for each person in the United States in 1968.)

2.2. Using the data in Table 2–2 and the definition of doubling time in Section 2.6, find the doubling time for energy use by: a) residential cooking; b) industrial electric drive; c) residential refrigeration; d) residential air conditioning. (41, 13, 9, 4.5 years.) What do these calculations of doubling time assume?

2.3. What are "Industrial feedstocks," mentioned in Table 2–2?

2.4. About 12% of all energy is used as gasoline in the private car. Total energy use in 1975 should be about 0.08Q. Gasoline has about 136,000 BTU per gallon. About how many gallons were used in the United States in 1975? Assuming there were about 90 million cars, what was the average use per car? (71 billion gallons, 790 gallons per car.)

2.5. Let us assume that the total power of the light bulbs in your home is 2000 watts and you operate them an average of 5 hours per day. If electric energy costs you $.024/KWH find the daily cost of lighting your home.($.24)

2.6. What percentage of the time are clothes dryers in operation? (See Table 1–4.) (2.33%)

2.7. Estimate the amount of electric energy used in your home each year and the cost of that energy.

2.8. How does the cost of operating a device compare with the cost of buying the device? To find out, select an appliance, estimate its cost and its lifetime, average the cost over the lifetime to get an approximate cost per year, and compare this with the operating cost per year. Assume an energy cost of $.025/KWH. Try this for a clothes dryer, a television, a shaver, and others. Any observations?

2.9. The "operation factor" is defined as the ratio of the total time of actual service, of a machine or equipment, to the total period of time considered. What is the operation factor of a a) clothes dryer; b) furnace fan; c) 12 cu. ft. refrigerator; d) clock? (0.023; 0.154; 0.345; 1.000)

2.10. Find the approximate energy used per day corresponding to the demand curve of Figure 1–6. Do this by considering the demand constant over a one-hour period and finding the energy for each of the 24 hours during the day. Those familiar with calculus may wish to think in terms of using the trapezoidal integration rule. Also, find the approximate load factor. (37,000,000 KWH; 0.67)

2.11. Consider the data in Table 2–8. The energy demand in BTU per passenger miles is approximately equal to the BTU per vehicle mile divided by the number of passengers. If a small gasoline automobile carries 3 people, and a fixed route bus carries 20 people, which uses less energy per passenger mile?

2.12. Why do you suppose express buses tend to use less energy than fixed route buses?

2.13. Assume that the population growth rate was reduced to zero and the per capita energy-use growth rate remained at about 5.5%. What is the doubling period? That is, in how many years will energy use double? (13 years)

*Advanced Mathematical Problems*

2.14. Use a mathematical proof by induction to show that the equation for $E_n$ in Section 2.6 is valid. This requires that you: 1) show that it is valid for $n = 1$; and 2) assume it is valid for $n = k$ and show that it is then valid for n = k + 1. (Hint: To see how you get from n = k to n = k + 1, recall that the increase in energy is just r times the energy in year k.)

2.15. Look up the expression "geometric series" in a mathematics text, and relate it to the problem of exponential growth.

2.16. The value of differential calculus is that it allows us to study phenomena which change over differentially small periods of time. The student of calculus can study exponential growth through the simple differential equation dE/dt = kE which says that the instantaneous rate of change of energy is directly proportional to the present level of energy. Show that

$$E = E_O e^{kt}$$

is a solution to the above differential equation by substitution of this proposed solution into the differential equation.

2.17. Compare the solution to the differential equation given in Problem 2.16 with the equation for $E_n$ in Section 2.6. Let one year be represented by a time t = T. Find the relation between k and r. If r = 0.07. what is k? (k = 0.0677/year)

2.18. Suppose that the population of the United States continues to grow at 1.5% per year. What will the population be in a) 20 years; b) 100 years; c) 200 years; d) 500 years? Assume it is 205 million now. (275 million; 910 million; 4 billion; 350 billion)

2.19. Suppose that energy-use growth rate per capita is 5% per year. Draw a curve of the growth assuming an initial energy $E_O$ if the population growth rate is a) 0%; b) 2%. Consider a 20 year growth interval.

2.20. Plot the number of years required to double energy use as a function of the yearly percentage growth rate.

## Advanced Study Problems

2.21. Find the power required to run as many devices, appliances, etc. as you can, and make a list of them. You can usually find this data stamped on a nameplate somewhere on the device. Compare this with the list given in this chapter. Why should there be any differences?

2.22. Why is energy of value to man? Outline its history of use. What would happen to our present society if a) energy growth was stopped so that the amount used became constant; b) energy use was halved; c) energy use was cut to zero?

2.23. If energy is a *sine qua non* for industrial development, is it also sufficient for development? See P. Sporn (Reference 5). Explain!

# 3

# SOURCES OF ENERGY

*The resources of civilization*
*are not yet exhausted.*

William Gladstone

Is there an energy shortage? Of course not! There are hundreds of billions of tons of coal in the United States. We know where there are billions of barrels of oil, and we suspect that our known reserves may be dwarfed by those we have not yet found. Huge amounts of solar energy reach the earth hourly. The sea contains enough energy, which may be tapped from the hydrogen isotope deuterium, to give man all the energy he can use for millions of years. We are literally surrounded by vast sources of energy. The answer to the question "Is there an energy shortage?" is no! But that's the wrong question.

The question we need to ask is this: Are there available sufficient energy resources to meet our present and expected future demands in a form we can use at a price we are willing to pay? The key words are *form* and *price*. And price includes the environmental as well as the dollar cost. We have limited amounts of available resources that we know how to use, and their price is increasing—in some cases very rapidly. As for prospective future sources such as the sun (in large amounts), or fusion power from deuterium, we do not as yet have the technology or know the price.

Our purpose in this chapter is to consider how nature stores or offers us energy, and to study the prospects for undeveloped as well as existing sources. We conclude the chapter with a discussion of the gap between energy use in the United States and the supply of domestic energy.

## 3.1  HOW NATURE STORES ENERGY

In Chapter 2 we defined energy as the capacity to do work. A major factor in man's technological evolution has been his finding of ways to use nature's energy. Nature stores or offers energy in many different forms. Table 3–1 gives the forms of storage and the primary resource available. In parentheses are the percentage contributions to the total U.S. energy use in 1972.

We turn now to a brief discussion of some of the most important of these energy forms.

*Potential energy* is energy which a body has solely by virtue of its position in space. More particularly, gravitational potential energy is energy which a body has by virtue of its position in a space dominated by a gravitational field, such as the earth's. Consider Figure 3–1. The rock at the top of the hill (point A) has a potential energy *relative* to points B, C and D. (We cannot associate a potential energy with the rock except in relation to some point in space.) The rock has the same potential energy with respect to points B and C because these points are at the same elevation. The distance in the *direction* of the earth's gravitational field from A to B or C is the same. But the distance *down* to D is greater, and therefore the rock has a greater potential energy with respect to D than with respect to B or C.

The statements above should be intuitively appealing. Suppose the rock rolled down the hill. We know that as it rolled it would gain speed and would be capable of doing more work

### TABLE 3–1

### Forms of Natural Energy

| Form of Energy | Associated Energy Resource |
| --- | --- |
| Gravitational potential | Hydroelectric (4%) |
| | Tidal* |
| Chemical | Coal (17%) |
| | Oil (46%) |
| | Gas (32%) |
| | Wood and other burnable fuels* |
| | Magnetohydrodynamic (MHD) |
| | Fuel cells* |
| Nuclear | Fission (1%) |
| | Fusion |
| Heat | Geothermal* |
| Kinetic | Windmills* |
| Wave | Wave-driven (ocean or lake) |
| Radiation | Solar* |

Other forms of energy: Strain (spring); spin (rotational kinetic); latent heat (evaporation and melting); electromagnetic-wave; electric; magnetic.

* Indicates small contribution—much less than 1%.

(such as smashing other rocks or denting the earth) at point D than at points B or C. We also know that the rock's capacity to do work will depend on its weight. The gravitational potential energy of a body of weight W located at an elevation H greater than some point will have a potential energy with respect to the reference point.

Potential Energy = Weight × Height

We make use of this form of energy in hydroelectric power plants by storing rain and snow water behind dams, and then allowing it to fall through hydraulic turbines to generate electric energy. We explore potential energy and its application to hydroelectric plants in Chapter 7.

Most substances, including those which we use as fuels in

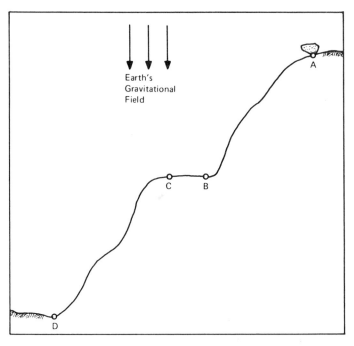

**Figure 3–1.** Gravitational Potential Energy.

fossil-fuel power plants, can be said to store *chemical energy*. They store energy in the sense that when they enter into a chemical reaction with oxygen to form a new chemical compound, they release energy as heat. For example, when carbon combines with oxygen to form carbon dioxide, two molecules come together because of atomic forces of attraction, causing a new chemical bond. The result is that the new molecule of carbon monoxide has some additional energy which appears as heat. Coal, oil, and natural gas are commonly used as sources of chemical energy or fuels for many industrial and commercial processes and in electric power plants. (Because of their development over millions of years as fossilized vegetation, oil, gas and coal are called *fossil fuels*.) The way in which the heat from fossil fuels is used to generate electricity will be explained briefly in the next section and in detail in Chapter 8.

*Nuclear energy* is associated with the mass of the nuclei of atoms. A part of this energy is released when nuclei disintegrate during an atomic reaction. There is a loss of mass when nuclei break up into new components, and a corresponding gain in energy equal to $E = \Delta mc^2$ where $\Delta m$ is the change of mass and c is the velocity of light. The energy released in a nuclear chain reaction can then be used in essentially the same way as the energy released from burning fuel. We shall consider nuclear power plants in detail in Chapter 9.

## 3.2  ENERGY SOURCES IN PERSPECTIVE

Before we begin our detailed study of energy resources, we should stop for perspective. In Table 3–2 we show some typical energy levels for a wide range of phenomena or activities. The Table is written in units of Q, each of which, as we saw in Chapter 2, is one quintillion ($10^{18}$) BTU.

## TABLE 3–2

### Typical Energy Levels in Units of Q

| Source | Energy in Units of Q |
|---|---|
| Annual solar energy incident on earth | 5,300 |
| Estimated uranium reserves | |
|     With breeder reactor | 200 to 2,000 |
|     With conventional reactors | 2 to 20 |
| Estimated fossil fuel reserves (U.S.) | 15 to 120 |
| World energy use (1970) | 0.2 |
| U.S. energy use (1970) | 0.07 |
| U.S. electric energy use (1970) | 0.005 |
| One-megaton nuclear bomb | 0.000004 |

Start by noting that, as we saw earlier, total energy use in the United States in 1970 was about 0.07Q. Next, note that this is 35% of world energy use. We use this portion with only 6% of the world's population. Many people question whether this disproportion is morally acceptable or politically wise.

Moving up the table, we see that we have very substantial fossil fuel reserves. Most of these reserves are in coal and in oil shale. We will have serious difficulties in developing these resources in the years ahead, as we shall see in detail later. Recall from Table 3–1 that about 95% of our present energy use comes from the depletable fossil fuels. We are eating away fuels which began to form as much as 100 million years ago, and which cannot be replaced over any time period useful to man. This steady erosion of a resource base which cannot be replaced has led man to seek alternatives to the fossil fuel economy which carried him so successfully through the industrial revolution.

Nuclear energy offers an alternative with two important advantages over fossil fuels. First, it extends very significantly the lifetime of depletable fuels, particularly if the breeder reactor is successfully developed. Second, it does not have the serious air pollution problems associated with the burning of fossil fuels. For these two reasons many people feel that nuclear energy is an excellent answer to man's energy needs for hundreds of years to come. Unfortunately, nuclear energy has a number of disadvantages, which we will discuss in detail in Chapter 9. It suffices to say now that these disadvantages have resulted in vocal opposition to nuclear development, and have caused much interest in looking for still further alternatives.

Tremendous amounts of solar energy are incident on the earth each year. This form of energy has two major advantages. It is abundant and widespread, and it is non-depletable. For these reasons many see it as the most desirable solution to our energy needs. In fact, it is quite common to hear people ask why we do not simply harness the "free" energy of the sun. The answer, of course, is that solar energy, like all other forms of energy, is *not* free. Before it can be used it must be harnessed. Harnessing solar energy requires large amounts of capital (or construction) costs, and possibly significant operating costs. We have just begun the task of seriously studying the widespread converstion of solar energy for our needs. We don't know what the future holds, but we do know that the energy won't be free.

Not listed in Table 3–2 are the essentially limitless potential resources of fusion energy. Fusion may be a nearly ideal long-term answer. But before we have any significant amounts of fusion energy available, we will have to solve tremendous scientific and technological (engineering) problems.

So we conclude this overview with the observation that there is energy "out there." We have yet to determine when we can make it available, and whether we can do so at an acceptable price.

Our next step is to consider in more detail the prospects for some particular sources of energy. We start with a discussion of non-depletable resources; then we turn to the depletable sources.

## 3.3  NON-DEPLETABLE ENERGY RESOURCES

When we quantify resources that are not depleted, it is not useful to try to talk about the total quantity of energy available, since this is theoretically unlimited. We are interested, however, in the rate at which these resources can be used. Hence we use the dimensions of power in this section, and then return to dimensions of energy in the following sections on depletable resources.

For reference purposes we start by reviewing in Table 3–3 the total energy use rate and the electric power capacity and electric energy use rate for the year 1972. We express energy use rate in units of BTU per hour. (There are 8,760 hours in a year.)

Of the non-depletable energy sources only two presently produce an appreciable amount of commercial power in the United States:

| | |
|---|---|
| Hydroelectric | 55,000 MW |
| Geothermal | 500 MW |

We now briefly review the prospects for each of the non-depletable sources in the future.

**1. Hydroelectric.** The Federal Power Commission has estimated that there is an additional hydroelectric potential of about 126,000 MW which could conceivably be developed.(1) Much, however, would be far too expensive, or more desirable for other uses, and will never be developed. It is estimated that by the year 2000 the hydroelectric capacity in the United States will have increased by about 70,000 MW to a total of 125,000 MW. This will be a small fraction (probably less than 10%) of the electric power needs of the year 2000. It should be noted that much of this hydroelectric potential will be in pumped storage (see Chapter 7.) This implies a depletable resource,

## TABLE 3–3

### Power and Energy Use Rates (1972)

| | |
|---|---|
| Total energy use rate | $8 \times 10^{12}$ BTU/HR |
| Electric energy use rate | $0.57 \times 10^{12}$ BTU/HR |
| Electric power capacity | 410,000 MW ($1.4 \times 10^{12}$ BTU/HR) |

since the stored water is pumped "uphill" by power from a thermal power plant which ordinarily uses depletable fuels. (See Chapter 7.)

**2. Geothermal.** The most optimistic estimates suggest that geothermal power may reach 25,000 MW in the foreseeable future.(2) This would be about one percent of our electric power needs in 2000. Actually it is very difficult to predict how big a role geothermal power may play in the future. There are huge heat resources inside the earth. Whether we will find a way to tap substantial quantities of this heat is something only time will tell. (See Chapter 10.)

**3. Solar.** An average of 2,500 MW or $8.5 \times 10^9$ BTU/Hr is incident on each square mile of earth where the skies are usually free from clouds. Clearly, if an efficient and economical solar conversion scheme can be developed, and if enough square miles of land can be dedicated to the project, any portion of our power needs of 2000 can be met by solar power. It is not clear today whether we can develop an acceptable system or whether we wish to dedicate the necessary land. Solar electric power appears to have some prospects for major development, but it is again too early to be sure of its future.

Much more attractive for development in the near future are proposals for solar heating and cooling in relatively small residential and commercial situations. (See Chapter 11.)

**4. Tidal.** There will probably be many proposals to develop one site or another in the years ahead. Capital cost will be a very strong deterrent to development. It is difficult to believe that any substantial amount of our energy needs will ever be met by tidal power. (See Chapter 13.)

**5. Fusion.** Fusion power, along with solar power, offers the major hope for significant quantities of electric power from non-depletable resources. It seems likely that physical and technological problems will prevent or delay major development at least until around the year 2000. But there is a real prospect that fusion power may provide a long range solution to the energy crisis. (See Chapter 12.)

**6. Wood.** Although the burning of wood can provide a great deal of power for short periods, the time required to replace trees makes the realization of large amounts of average power unfeasible.

**7. Refuse.** Recently a number of new proposals for burning solid wastes have been made. Some small plants are in operation or under design. One plant in St. Louis burns 300 tons of numicipal waste per day to generate 12.5 MW.(3) It has been estimated that if 10 percent of the 1970 solid waste had been incinerated, 25 billion KWH could have been generated; that is about 1.8 percent of the total 1970 electric energy consumption.(4) Refuse can also be used to make alternate fuels such as methane or methanol. The latter could be a partial or complete substitute for gasoline. (See Chapter 5.)

We conclude this section with the observation that some non-depletable energy resources offer hope for significant future exploitation. Today, however, about 95% of our energy comes from depleting fossil fuel resources. We turn our attention now to these resources.

## 3.4   DEPLETABLE ENERGY RESOURCES

To gain perspective for our study of depletable energy resources, we consider first the amount of energy of each major type used in the United States in 1972. This is summarized in Table 3–4.(6)

### TABLE 3–4

### Use of Energy Resources in 1972

| Energy Source | Amount | Energy (Units of Q) | Percent of Energy |
|---|---|---|---|
| Petroleum | 5,960 million barrels | 0.0328 | 46 |
| Natural Gas | 22,607 billion cu. ft. | 0.0233 | 32 |
| Coal | 517 million short tons | 0.0124 | 17 |
| Hydro | 280 billion KWH | 0.0029 | 4 |
| Nuclear | 57 billion KWH | 0.0006 | 1 |

More detailed data than those given in Table 3–4 are not yet available on how the major energy sources were used in 1972. We can get a rather accurate general picture of energy use, however, by returning to 1969 figures.(6) Table 3–5 shows how each of the three major fuel forms were used in 1969 in percent of total use of that resource.

## TABLE 3–5

### Uses of the Three Major Fossil Fuels (1969)

| | | |
|---|---|---|
| Petroleum | Automobiles | 27.7% |
| | Other transportation | 25.2 |
| | Space heating | 20.0 |
| | Process heat | 10.9 |
| | Petrochemicals | 10.5 |
| | Electric energy generation | 5.7 |
| | | 100.0 |
| Natural Gas | Process heat | 40.2% |
| | Space heat | 22.0 |
| | Electric energy generation | 17.1 |
| | Water heating cooking | 10.1 |
| | Petrochemicals | 2.6 |
| | Losses | 8.0 |
| | | 100.0 |
| Coal | Electric energy generation | 56.0% |
| | Process heat | 21.7 |
| | Iron and steel production | 17.2 |
| | Space heat | 3.9 |
| | Petrochemicals | 1.2 |
| | | 100.0 |

Finally, Table 3–6 shows how energy resources were used in the generation of electric energy in 1972.

In Chapter 2 we saw how energy was used by consumers. In the three tables above we have seen where our energy originates and how the major sources are distributed to the economy. Next we look at the prospects for these major resources: coal, oil, natural gas, and uranium. We begin with a brief look at the phenomenon of depletion.

The world has only a finite supply of its depletable resources. In time our coal, oil, natural gas, and every other resource we

**TABLE 3–6**

**Resource Use for Electric Energy Generation, 1972**

| Resource | Percent |
|----------|---------|
| Coal | 46 |
| Natural gas | 23 |
| Hydro | 16 |
| Petroleum | 11 |
| Nuclear | 4 |
| | 100 |

use must be exhausted or become too expensive to extract from the earth. The phenomenon of depletion is discussed in an outstanding essay, by M. King Hubbert, recommended to every reader of this text. Hubbert develops in mathematical and historical detail the concept of a *resource production cycle*.

An idealized example of such a cycle is shown in Figure 3–2. The rate of production of a resource, such as barrels of oil per year, or ounces of silver per year, etc., is plotted against the year of production. If a certain finite amount of a resource exists, it is hypothesized that its production rate will follow, approximately, the curve shown in dark in Figure 3–2. If a greater amount of the resource exists, then the dashed line is more accurate. In practice, production rate curves are not smooth as shown here but are somewhat jagged. Nonetheless, the examples shown by Hubbert fit the pattern in general shape quite well.(7)

Production begins in year $Y_O$. In some cases, such as that of coal, $Y_O$ is lost in antiquity. In other cases, such as the California gold rush of 1849, or the production of Uranium, $Y_O$ is known accurately.

The year of maximum production is $Y_M$. In some cases, such as that of natural gas, we may have already reached $Y_M$. For oil it is probably some years into the future. For coal or Uranium it may be generations from today.

$Y_D$ is the year of depletion. It is not a well-defined date, since small pockets of material may continue to be found almost

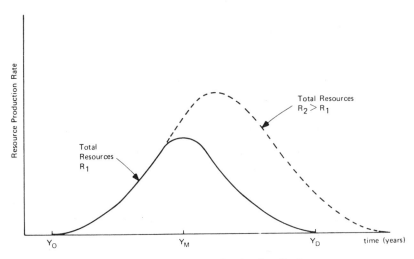

**Figure 3–2.** Resource Production Cycle.

indefinitely. In the foothills of the Sierra Nevada, campers, weekend miners, or small mining companies still find an occasional nugget or a few flakes of gold even though the peak production of gold occurred over 100 years ago.

The logic of the resource production cycle is basically quite simple. In the early years of the cycle, production grows almost exponentially as demand increases continually. Eventually a point is reached where the cost of extraction begins to go up. Growth rate slows. Eventually, with ever increasing costs of extraction as the easy "near-surface" resources are used up, the production rate reaches a maximum, and then decreases toward zero. This does not mean that all of the resource has been used, but rather that it is no longer economically feasible to extract the remaining resource.

The symmetry of the ideal curve of Figure 3–2 is upset by the discovery of new reserves. The Alaska oil find is an excellent example of an unexpected new reserve. It is common to classify reserves in terms of estimates of the ease of extraction and the state of knowledge about the existence of the reserves. There are a number of degrees of refinement of these estimates.(6) We shall consider briefly a fairly simple model and then further reduce the complexity of the estimation problem for our study of specific fuels. Figure 3–3 suggests one way of considering resources.

The reader should realize that the lines suggested are very flexible, if not amorphous. What is possible or undiscovered today may be known tomorrow. What is financially infeasible at one time may become feasible in a new economic environment.

The relatively simple model of Figure 3–3 is valuable conceptually but is still a little bit complex for the estimates we shall be making in the sections to follow. Accordingly, we reduce the model to a very simple two-part form. The lower left block, called *Known and Economically Feasible* (resources), will be called *Proved Reserves*. The remaining three blocks will be referred to as *Possible Resources*.

Changes in knowledge about resource availability and feasibility of recovery tend to make the right side of the curve in Figure 3–2 irregular and unpredictable. The ideal model is a first order representation of how the production rate tends to

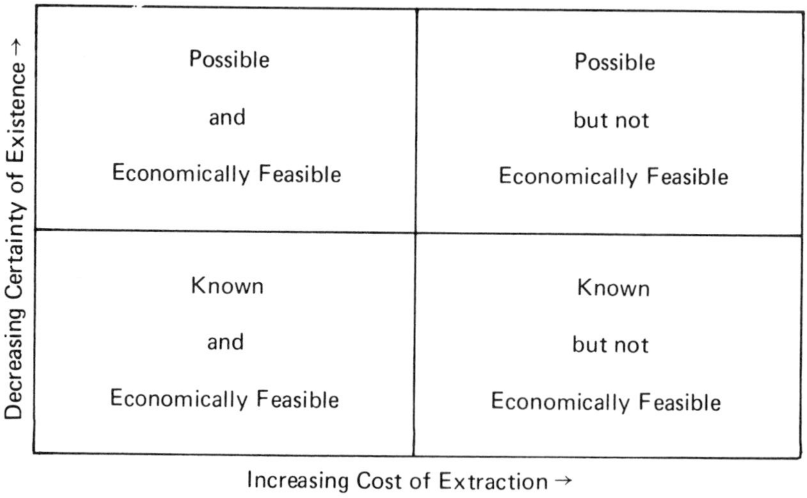

| Decreasing Certainty of Existence → | Possible and Economically Feasible | Possible but not Economically Feasible |
|---|---|---|
| | Known and Economically Feasible | Known but not Economically Feasible |

Increasing Cost of Extraction →

**Figure 3–3.** Estimates of Resources.

vary with time. To get a more detailed picture of what the future may hold we must look at specific fuels and try to estimate what reserves may exist and the costs of these reserves.

We conclude this section with an important implication of the argument above. The reader should understand that we will *never* exhaust any of our natural fuels. There will always be more oil and gas and coal in the ground. But the rate at which we produce these fuels may decrease very significantly in the future. For 75 years it has been said that we have had only ten years worth of oil left. There is nothing inconsistent in such a statement, given the definition of proved reserves. In fact, we could have only ten years of oil left for hundreds of years to come. The important statistic will be the resource production rate, and that may well decline in the near future for at least some of our resources.

In the sections to follow we consider in detail the proved reserves and possible resources of petroleum, natural gas, coal, and uranium in the United States. This is the order of their present use level as energy resources.

## 3.5 PETROLEUM

In this text we use the word *Petroleum* as a generic term to include crude oil, natural gas liquids, and petroleum products. The latter are products obtained by processing or refining crude oil or natural gas liquids. Dry natural gas is not included here, but is discussed in Section 3.6. Natural gas liquids are obtained by processing natural gas at special processing plants. Natural gas liquids include ethane, butane, propane, natural gasoline, jet fuels, petrochemical feedstocks, and many more. They are often classed as petroleum liquids because their products are similar to crude oil products, and are often blended with these products. The reader who wishes to study energy statistics in detail is cautioned to determine whether the petroleum data under study include natural gas liquids. Reporting agencies are not consistent in this classification. Natural gas liquids are an important element in petroleum energy use. In 1972 a little more than 10% of domestic petroleum consumption came from natural gas liquids. (See Reference 8 for additional details on natural gas liquids.)

The place of petroleum as an energy source in the United States for the year 1973 is shown in Table 3–7.(9) Total petroleum consumption is 46% of all energy consumption. However, of all the petroleum used in the United States, only 64% comes from domestic sources. The remaining 36% is imported as crude oil or oil products from a number of countries around the world. Most of the energy imported into the United States is in the form of petroleum. We shall return to this highly important issue of petroleum imports in Chapter 6 when we discuss the international energy market.

In 1973, as Table 3–7 indicates, domestic production of petroleum was about 4 billion barrels. This number has not changed very much since about 1969. It is likely that this production rate will not change significantly in the immediate future. Further into the future the production rate will depend on such uncertainties as price, availability of international petroleum, governmental actions, and environmental concerns. Approximate petroleum resources in the United States are given in Table 3–8. These figures must be used cautiously. The proved reserves figure changes constantly as reserves are used

## TABLE 3–7

### Petroleum in the U.S. Energy Market—1973

| Energy form | Energy (trillions of BTUs) | Percent of petroleum consumption | Equivalent crude oil (billions of barrels) |
|---|---|---|---|
| Total U.S. energy consumption | 75,561 | | 12.80 |
| Total petroleum consumption | 34,689 | 100 | 6.19 |
| Domestic petroleum production | 22,165 | 64 | 3.96 |
| Net crude oil imports | 6,589 | 19 | 1.17 |
| Net oil products imports | 5,943 | 17 | 1.06 |

and new reserves are found. The possible-resources figure has a very wide range because a number of different sources have made different estimates. The most optimistic estimate of possible resources assumes much success in seeking oil offshore on the Outer Continental Shelves (OCS). But little actual data can be obtained for these regions, particularly for the shelf off the East Coast. The general conclusion is that we simply do not know how much oil is left.

### TABLE 3–8

### United States Petroleum Resources

| Region | Proved Reserves (Billions of barrels) | Possible Resources (Billions of barrels) |
|---|---|---|
| Continental U.S. | 30 | 420—2,700 |
| Alaska | 15 | 30—35 |

As we discussed at the end of the last section, it is not meaningful to divide proved reserves by annual production rate to determine how many years oil will be available. As time passes, possible resources become proved reserves, even as other proved reserves are consumed. We don't know how much oil is down there, and we don't really care. We will continue to use oil until the cost of producing it exceeds the price we are willing to pay for it. "Proved reserves" is an economic definition, not a geological phenomenon. Possible resources are unknown and probably unknowable. There will always be oil in the ground, as there will always be gold in the hills. But eventually a time will come when costs drive the production rate down so far that petroleum is no longer a major source of energy in the United States. This may be 20 years, or 50, or 200. We don't know.

An important new addition to domestic crude oil production will be the recently discovered Alaskan North Slope oil. An 800-mile pipeline is now being built from the oil fields near Prudhoe Bay in Northern Alaska to the port of Valdez in Southern Alaska. From there oil will be shipped by tankers, probably to West Coast ports in the United States. The line should be completed in 1977, with an initial capacity of 440 million barrels per year. By 1980 capacity might be increased to 725 million barrels per year. This would probably be about 10% of U.S. petroleum demand in 1980, and about 20% of domestic petroleum production. There is some thought that additional discoveries might justify additional pipelines.

Oil exploration will also take place in various parts of the Continental United States, and probably on the continental shelves off the coast. The latter explorations and production will no doubt be opposed on environmental grounds by many groups and individuals. Eventually, the American people will have to decide whether they wish to pay the additional cost of environmental damage (or suffer its threat) in order to obtain the oil that is off the coasts. The alternative to tapping this resource will be conservation or an alternate fuel which may or may not be more costly or more polluting or both. There will never be a clear solution; there will only be sets of advantages and disadvantages to compare.

In 1973 the cost of a barrel (42 gallons) of domestic oil was about $3.50. By early 1975 the average price was close to $7.50, and was expected to rise still further. For the immediate future the price will tend to be set by the price of imported oil. In the longer term the price of oil may be set largely by the cost of alternatives to oil, such as shale oil. In any event, the price incentives to drill for new oil should be somewhat greater than they were in 1973. We should expect to see increased oil exploration in at least the immediate future. Only time will tell what effect this work will have on United States petroleum resources.

## 3.6  NATURAL GAS

Of the 75.6 quadrillion BTU of energy consumed in the United States in 1973, about 23.5 quadrillion BTU (or 31%) came from natural gas. This represents a little more than 22.5

trillion cubic feet (TCF). The proved reserves of natural gas are close to 200 TCF. Hence if we had only these resources, and continued our use rate, we would nearly exhaust our natural gas supplies in about nine years. However, in the past our possible resources have been estimated to range from 800 to

**Figure 3–4.** Offshore oil. Most of the world's supplies of oil are found off-shore. This North Sea platform must withstand the great North Atlantic storms which buffet Europe. Offshore oil will be expensive, and extracting it from undersea beds will cause pollution. However, we must pay the price to the oil we need for the decades ahead. (Courtesy of the Exxon Corporation.)

2,100 TCF(2.6). Some recent estimates have been as low as 450 TCF. Hence, our range of estimates is from 450 to 2,100 TCF, representing a present-use-rate lifetime of 20 to 100 years.

The same fundamental arguments hold for natural gas resources as for petroleum resources. We will never run out of natural gas, but it may become so expensive that we are not willing to continue to produce it. We cannot say with confidence whether natural gas will continue to be a major part of our energy production for 10 years, or 20, or 50, or perhaps more.

Price has long been a major factor in the life of natural gas as an energy resource. For more than two decades the Federal Power Commission has regulated the price of natural gas destined for interstate sale. At first this price was close to $0.15 per million BTU, rising to $0.25 by 1973, prior to the so-called energy crisis precipitated by the October, 1973 Arab oil embargo.

This was the price at the wellhead where the gas was produced. After shipment through pipelines for as far as a thousand or more miles, and distribution by a local gas company, the final price to the consumer is much higher than $0.25. A doubling in the wellhead price would not imply a doubling in the price to the consumer.

The decision to regulate gas prices was a political decision intended to keep the price to the consumer as low as possible. Unfortunately, it also had the effect of greatly encouraging the use of natural gas for a number of purposes for which it was perhaps not best suited, such as the generation of electric energy. (See Figure 3–5.) In addition, producers of natural gas argue that the price was not sufficiently high to justify or encourage substantial new exploration. The result of overuse and underdevelopment was not surprising. In 1968 the amount of proved reserves declined for the first time. It has been gradually decreasing since then; this decrease has led to the familiar statement that we are running out of natural gas.

The problem of declining reserves led a wide range of people, in and out of the natural gas industry, to urge that natural gas be deregulated. In June of 1974 the FPC raised the price of interstate gas to $0.42 per million BTU. By December of 1974 it was $0.50, with at least one FPC commissioner calling for further deregulation. To get some perspective on the price of natural gas, we compare the approximate prices of a number of fuels in early 1975 in Table 3–9.

### TABLE 3–9

### Comparative Fuel Prices (January, 1975)

| Fuel | Per Million BTU |
| --- | --- |
| Natural gas (wellhead), regulated | $0.50 |
| Natural gas (wellhead), unregulated, for intrastate use | 1.60 |
| Coal (at $10 per ton) | 0.50 |
| Domestic crude oil (average) | 1.35 |
| Imported crude oil | 2.05 |
| Heating oil (No. 2 oil) | 2.00 |

These costs will change, perhaps rather rapidly. An additional increase in the price of regulated natural gas would not be surprising. Coal prices vary from place to place, and will probably increase as the demand for coal increases. Domestic crude oil should approach the price of imported crude, but the price of the latter is very uncertain in a highly volatile international petroleum market. However, these prices do give us some reference against which to compare proposed alternate fuels. For example, it has been estimated that the cost of imported liquified natural gas (LNG) may be from $2.00 to $2.50 per million BTU. This is somewhat above present market prices. However, it might well be competitive if prices continue to rise.

If all energy markets were free markets—with no government price regulation—it might be expected that prices of the various fuels would equalize. In fact this would probably not happen, at least not fully. Fuels are not always interchangeable. Where some can be used, others cannot, and hence they are not competitive. Nonetheless, to the extent that markets are freed (e.g. natural gas prices rise toward other fuel prices) we should expect to see some tendency of fuel prices to equalize.

We conclude this section with the observation that we do not know how long natural gas will be an important source of

**Figure 3–5.** Fossil-fuel plant at Moss Landing, California. At 2,100 MW, the Moss Landing Power Plant, on the Pacific Ocean 100 miles south of San Francisco, is one of the largest in the United States. It was completed in 1969 at a capital cost of $214 million; its cost per kilowatt is a very attractive $100. Moss Landing provides an excellent example of a two-fuel fossil plant. It has had to switch from natural gas to residual oil because of the growing shortage of natural gas. In 1970, 98% of Moss Landing energy came from natural gas. Only 2% came from oil; the use of oil occurred during cold spells in the winter when demands for gas for heating purposes normally increase. By 1975, Moss Landing had converted almost entirely to residual oil. With the conversion, unfortunately, will come increased air pollution. (Courtesy of Pacific Gas and Electric Company.)

energy. Increasing prices will encourage production, on the one hand. On the other hand, increased production will hasten the day when natural gas can no longer be produced economically.

## 3.7  COAL

Coal is by far the most abundant fossil fuel in the United States. Unfortunately, it is also the dirtiest of fuels, so it requires extensive and costly measures to make its use environmentally acceptable. The problem with coal is not to find it but to use it cleanly.

In 1972 the United States consumed 517 million short tons of coal. Proved reserves are estimated at about 400 billion tons.(2) Possible resources are as much as 3,200 billion tons, with perhaps half of that recoverable.(10) This suggests resources which might last for many hundreds or perhaps thousands of years. But before we can talk about this magnitude of use we must consider the problems associated with using coal.

Coal is found in the eastern United States along the Appalachians, in some Midwestern states (Illinois, Ohio, Indiana and others), and in or near the Rocky Mountain states (Montana, Wyoming, Colorado, New Mexico). Many other states have lesser reserves, though often enough to justify some power development. An example is Washington State with its new Centralia plant. (Chapter 8)

Roughly half of the coal in this country is on each side of the Mississippi. Eastern and Midwestern coal in states such as West Virginia, Pennsylvania, Kentucky, Illinois and Ohio has been mined extensively for many years because of its proximity to large concentrations of industry and population. Unfortunately, coal in the eastern part of the United States tends to have rather high sulfur content. Western coal has much less sulfur on the average. With increasingly strict air pollution control laws, interest in coal is shifting from east to west.

States such as North Dakota, with 50 billion tons of low

sulfur strippable coal, Montana with 15 billion tons, and Wyoming with 10 billion tons all appear to be ideal sources of fairly clean energy, with lots of open space and few neighbors to object to a local power plant.(11) But the lessons of Four Corners are not easily forgotten.(12) The air pollution which coal-fueled power plants brought to the Southwest could become a fact of life in the northern Rocky Mountain states. Such moves will probably be opposed by some local residents.(13) Stripping and burning the coal of Montana for the energy needs of Chicago will no doubt meet increasing opposition in Montana if not in Illinois.

Air pollution is not the only concern in coal-rich states. Most of the coal under consideration for development would be strip mined. An overburden of dirt up to perhaps 100 feet in thickness is removed. The coal seam is then removed by huge stripping machines. Strip mining has two major advantages over deep mining. It is easier and less expensive, and it is far less dangerous to miners. But it has very important disadvantages. If the exhausted coal seam is left exposed, the result is an ugly scar on the land. Also, rain may drain mine wastes into local watersheds and rivers, causing severe pollution in many cases. Much of this problem is eliminated by returning the overburden of dirt which was originally stripped off, and replanting the land. However, it is necessary that the topsoil of the replaced overburden be good growing ground.(14)

Coal need not be used directly, as it is found, for energy production. One alternative which should produce a much cleaner and easily transported fuel is coal gasification. This process converts coal into a gas which has many of the advantages of natural gas, and which could replace it as supplies of natural gas diminish. El Paso Natural Gas and Texas Eastern Transmission Corporation are planning plants which would each produce about 250 million cubic feet per day. This represents a little less than one percent of the natural gas consumption rate in 1974. This gas should cost about $2.00 per million BTU, although continued inflation may increase

**Figure 3–6.** After the strip-mining. When the overburden is removed and coal is stripped from the earth, the land should be restored by re-seeding and planting of new trees. This helps prevent erosion and leaching of mine wastes into streams, and it can restore some of the natural appearance of the land. Here a crew following a strip-mining bench plants loblolly pine seedlings. (Courtesy of the Tennessee Valley Authority.)

this figure. We shall turn to a more detailed look at coal gasification in Chapter 5.

Many people see the tremendous reserves of coal as a major part of the answer to our energy problems. Some call for coal use instead of nuclear power, or in place of increased petroleum imports. For many years the use of coal declined, reaching a low of about 420 million tons in 1961. Today coal production continues to rise, with more than 600 million tons produced in 1974. Most estimates of coal use in 1985 are in the range from 750 to 1,125 million tons.(15)

Coal may be an important element in the energy picture of tomorrow, but it will not be a panacaea. It will be expensive to mine and to burn or process cleanly. The mining process will draw environmental opposition.

The abundance of coal is a major factor in its favor. But many problems must be solved before the energy promise of abundant coal can be realized.


## 3.8  URANIUM

Reserves of uranium in terms of remaining years of supply are very difficult to estimate for a number of reasons. First, the nuclear industry is small but growing rapidly. Nuclear power may provide as much as 50% of our electric energy needs by the year 2000. Second, uranium can be extracted at a wide variety of price ranges. The maximum feasible extraction cost is very difficult to estimate today. Third, successful development of the breeder reactor would make fuel costs almost meaningless, and it also should extend fuel lifetime into the thousands of years.

Uranium ore is mined and processed into $U_3O_8$, which is the form for which costs are generally stated. The cost of $U_3O_8$ is presently about $15 per pound. In 1973 the price was usually quoted as $8 per pound. Table 3–10 shows the effects of

**TABLE 3–10**

**Estimated U.S. Uranium Reserves—January 1, 1970**

| $U_3O_8$ Price Per Pound | Reasonably Assured (Cumulative) (Tons) | Estimated Additional (Cumulative) (Tons) | Total (Cumulative) (Tons) | Increase in Energy Cost Due to Higher Fuel Cost (Mills/KWH) |
|---|---|---|---|---|
| $  8.00 | 204,000 | 390,000 | 594,000 | 0.0 |
| 10.00 | 340,000 | 600,000 | 940,000 | 0.1 |
| 16.00 | 500,000 | 950,000 | 1,450,000 | 0.4 |
| 30.00 | 640,000 | 1,600,000 | 2,240,000 | 1.3 |
| 50.00 | 6,000,000 | 4,000,000 | 10,000,000 | 2.5 |
| 100.00 | 12,000,000 | 13,000,000 | 25,000,000 | 5.5 |

uranium price on energy cost. Since $U_3O_8$ now costs more than $8, the estimates in dollar terms are dated. However, the point made by the Table has not changed.

It is sometimes suggested that we have only about 30 years of uranium left. But, as Table 3–10 suggests, the amount of $U_3O_8$ available is highly dependent on the cost of extraction. We use here the terminology of the original document.(16)

The column on the right in Table 3–10, giving the incremental cost of energy due to increased $U_3O_8$ cost, assumes an average energy cost increment of 0.06 mills per dollar per pound of $U_3O_8$. The message of Table 3–10 is that much fuel is available at prices which are probably not prohibitively high.

For example, the total supply of uranium increased by about four times for an energy cost increase of about 1 mill/KWH. It seems likely that other factors in the complex and changing energy market will override this relatively small change.

If the breeder reactor is developed, the situation changes dramatically, since the fuel-use factor goes up by about 100 times with the utilization of $U^{238}$. (See Chapter 9.)

## 3.9  THE ENERGY GAP

There are many ways in which we might analyze or study the so-called energy problem. One approach is to consider the gap or difference between energy use in the United States and domestic energy production. Now that we have completed our study of energy use and our study of energy resources we are in a position to consider the gap viewpoint.

In Figure 3–7 we show the history of United States energy use and production from 1950 to 1973. In the early 1950s the United States was an energy exporting nation. By the end of that decade we had begun to use somewhat more energy than we produced. The gap did not begin to widen significantly until about 1970. By 1973 the difference between energy use and production was more than 13.5 quadrillion BTUs. This means that our net imports in 1973 were almost 18% of our demand.

One way to view the energy problem is to consider the ways in which we can fill the gap between use and production in this country. The gap, of course, must be filled in one way or another, since we must either produce or import as much as we use, except for the relatively small amounts of stored energy. There are at least five ways in which we might fill or eliminate the gap.

**1. Free the energy market.** The first approach is essentially economic. We could ban any imports of energy and free the domestic energy market. This means we would remove all governmental restrictions on energy prices. The price of energy

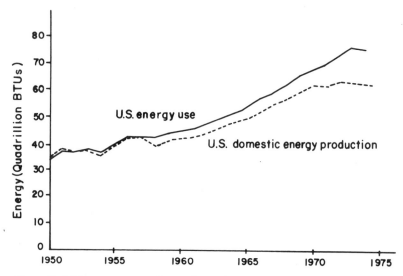

**Figure 3–7.** The energy gap. Some alternative methods of filling the gap are:

    1. Allow a free market for energy
    2. Increase conventional domestic sources
    3. Develop alternative domestic sources
    4. Increase imports
    5. Conserve resources

would be whatever the buyer and seller mutually accept. Proponents argue that this approach is more efficient than government control and would eliminate surpluses or shortages. (See Additional Reading 3 for Chapter 4.) Opponents argue that this approach would lead to inequities. It is not likely that the United States will seriously consider a totally free market in the near future. However, the degree of government regulation is certain to change with time.

**2. Increase conventional domestic sources.** As we have seen in this chapter, we will have difficulty increasing our fossil fuel production. We may be able to increase our coal production significantly, but natural gas will probably go down. We are increasing our production of nuclear energy, and this will no doubt help fill the gap unless we encounter more problems with nuclear development. (We will discuss nuclear energy in Chapter 9.)

**3. Develop alternative domestic sources.** In place of, or in addition to, our conventional sources, we can attempt to develop major new sources of energy such as oil from shale, gas from coal, solar energy, fusion energy, and a number of others. A major factor here will be the time to develop a new source as a large contributor to our energy needs. We will be discussing many of these alternatives in the chapters ahead, particularly Chapters 5, 11, and 12.

**4. Continue or increase energy imports.** Certainly one strategy is to continue to import energy. The instability and economic stress of this approach has caused much concern in recent years. At this time (1975), the United States is attempting at least to limit imports of energy. We discuss the international energy market in Chapter 6.

**5. Conserve or reduce our use of energy.** Obviously, one way to eliminate the gap is to reduce consumption until it equals domestic production. This would no doubt hurt our economy, and would not be accepted by many people. In Chapter 16 we discuss energy conservation as a way of closing at least part of the gap.

Which of these approaches will we take? We will almost certainly use all of them in some undetermined mix. We will probably loosen the market in some areas, as we have in the case of interstate natural gas, and we may tighten the market in other areas. We will seek additional supplies of oil and coal and natural gas, and at the same time we will continue to search for alternative energy sources. We will import and export energy, and we will conserve energy, because its price is increasing, or because its availability will be restricted by rationing or allocation. No one can predict what combination of approaches we will see. We are in the midst of a rapid evolution, if not a revolution, in the way in which we supply and use energy. We do not know where these changes will lead us.

## 3.10   A FINAL NOTE TO THE READER

On the day I completed writing this chapter, my local newspaper headlined, "Oil, Gas Reserve 'In Error.'" A report from the National Academy of Sciences suggests that the government has overestimated the supply of undiscovered oil and natural gas resources in the United States. My first inclination was to rewrite Sections 3.5 and 3.6 to add these alternative estimates. As it turns out the report's natural gas estimate (530 TCF) is near the low end of the range I give and the petroleum estimate is somewhat less than the low end of the estimate in Section 3.5. The report's estimate of petroleum resources is 113 billion barrels.

I finally decided that changing my estimates, or reporting these new estimates within the original text, would be inconsistent with my argument that the energy market is changing very rapidly. No book or paper can be up-to-date on the most recent figures on use or estimates of resources. And it doesn't have to be, because the underlying principles are more important than today's updated estimates. The principles do not change; the estimates do. I chose to write this final section to stress this point.

## REFERENCES FOR CHAPTER 3

1. "Hydroelectric Power Resources of the United States—Developed and Undeveloped," Federal Power Commission, January 1, 1968.
2. *U.S. Energy—A Summary Review*, Department of the Interior, Washington, D.C., January, 1972.
3. *Energy Recovery from Waste*, U.S. Environmental Protection Agency, 1972.
4. E. Hirst and T. Healy, "Electric Energy Requirements for Environmental Protection," *Public Utilities Fortnightly*, Vol. 91, No. 10, May 10, 1973, pp. 52–60.
5. "The President's Energy Message, Summary Outline—Fact Sheet," Office of the President, Washington, D.C., April 18, 1973.
6. *Reference Energy Systems and Resource Data for Use in the Assessment of Energy Technologies*, for Office of Science and Technology, Associated Universities, Inc., Upton, N.Y., April, 1972.
7. M. King Hubbert, "Energy Resources," in *Resources and Man*, National Academy of Sciences—National Research Council, W.H. Freeman and Co., San Francisco, Calif., 1969.
8. *Minerals Yearbook—1972*, Vol. 1, Metals, Minerals and Fuels, U.S. Department of the Interior, U.S. Government Printing Office, Washington, D.C., 1974.
9. *Statistical Abstract of the United States, 1974*, U.S. Dept. of Commerce, U.S. Government Printing Office, 1974.

10. P. Averitt, *Coal Reserves in the United States, Geological Survey Bulletin 1275*, U.S. Government Printing Office, 1969.
11. *The Economy, Energy, and the Environment*, Joint Economic Committee, Congress of the United States, U.S. Government Printing Office, Sept. 1, 1970.
12. A. Wolff, "Showdown at Four Corners," *Saturday Review of the Society*, June 3, 1972, pp. 29–41.
13. S. Jacobson, "The Great Montana Coal Rush," *Science and Public Affairs*, April 1973, pp. 37–42.
14. W. Greenberg, "Chewing it up at 200 Tons a Bite: Strip Mining," *Technology Review*, February, 1973, pp. 46–55.
15. *Project Independence Report*, Federal Energy Administration, U.S. Government Printing Office, Washington, D.C., Nov. 1974.
16. *Potential Nuclear Power Growth Patterns—WASH 1098*, Atomic Energy Commission, U.S. Government Printing Office, Washington, D.C., December, 1970.

## GENERAL READING FOR CHAPTER 3

1. See Reading No. 1 in Chapter 1.
2. *Resources and Man*, National Academy of Sciences—National Research Council. W.H. Freeman and Co., San Francisco, 1969.

    This is an outstanding book on resources in general and on their relation to man's life. The chapter written by Hubbert (Reference 7) is one of the classic references on energy resources.
3. *Reference Energy Systems and Resource Data for Use in the Assessment of Energy Technologies*, for Office of Science and Technology, Associated Universities, Inc., Upton, N.Y., April 1972.

    This is a very complete and up-to-date summary of energy sources and energy use. It is not meant for casual reading, but it contains a wealth of important data.
4. *Mineral Facts and Problems—1970 Edition*, Bureau of Mines,

U.S. Department of the Interior, U.S. Government Printing Office, Washington, D.C., 1970.

This document has much information and data concerning the nature and use of fuel minerals. It is excellent for students who wish to study fuels in more detail than can be provided in this text.

## PROBLEMS FOR CHAPTER 3

### General Problems

3.1. Discuss in what sense the following energy sources may or may not be considered non-depletable: geothermal, tidal, wood.

3.2. About how much energy, expressed in units of equivalent barrels of oil, were used in the world in 1970? Assume that a barrel of oil has an equivalent energy value of 5,600,000 BTU. (35.7 billion barrels)

3.3. Explain why it is not very meaningful to talk about the "free energy" of the tides.

3.4. It can be seen in Table 3–3 that the electric power capacity in the United States is more than twice the average electric energy use rate. Explain why capacity must be so much greater than average use rate.

3.5. Consider the fairly common expression: "We have only ten years of natural gas left." What is the justification or reason for this statement? Why is the statement not meaningful?

3.6. Use Tables 3–4 and 3–5 to determine the approximate number of barrels of petroleum used to fuel automobiles in 1972.

3.7. Make a list of the most important natural-gas liquids and indicate their use. (See, for example, Reference 8.)

3.8. Make a sketch of the general shape of a resource

production cycle curve if a major, new, easily-extracted
reserve is located some years after $Y_m$.

3.9. Estimate the volume in cubic miles of coal used in the
United States in 1972.

3.10. What percentage of total energy consumption in the
United States in 1973 came from petroleum imports?
(16.5%)

3.11. If the domestic production of oil in the United States
(excluding Alaska) continued at the level shown in Table
3–7, how long would our *proved reserves* last? (7.6 years)

3.12. List the major advantages and disadvantages of coal as a
source of energy.

### Advanced Mathematical Problems

3.13. Assume that an ideal resource production cycle can be
accurately modeled by a Gaussian probability law of
mean $Y_M$ and standard deviation $Y_S$. Write the equation
for the production rate. Draw the curve of the cycle. If $Y_S$
is 40 years, how many years after $Y_M$ is the resource 90%
depleted?

3.14. For the assumptions made in Problem 3.13, when is the
production rate changing most rapidly?

3.15. Write an equation for the increase in nuclear energy cost
*versus* $U_3O_8$ under the assumption made for Table 3–10.
Find the cost of $U_3O_8$ which corresponds to an energy
increase of 2 mills/KWH. ($41)

3.16. Suppose that the natural gas use rate of 1972 held
constant for a number of years but the total energy use
rose at 4% per year. Write an equation for the percentage
of United States energy supplied by natural gas in the
year Y, where Y is greater than 1972. What would be the
percentage supplied in 1985; in 2000? (19%; 10%)

## Advanced Study Problems

3.17. Make a map of the United States indicating where coal deposits are located, what their heating value and sulfur content are, and what the implications are for the electric energy industry.

3.18. Determine when and how oil from Alaksa's North Slope will begin to come to the lower 48 states. What is the project timetable? Where will tankers off-load oil?

3.19. Determine from appropriate literature which sources of energy are considered most desirable, or least harmful, by one or more so-called environmental groups. Why are these sources considered best? Repeat this exercise for a major energy company, such as an electric power company.

3.20. Make a careful study of which groups support extension of coal mining and which groups do not in a Rocky Mountain state, such as Wyoming, for example.

# 4

# ENERGY AND ECONOMICS

*He is well paid that is well satisfied.*

William Shakespeare

The purpose of the economic study of any project is to determine if the project *ought* to be carried out. At one time this study was restricted mostly to factors relating to income and expenses in dollars. Today, however, there is growing concern for the consideration of less tangible factors, such as the effect on the environment. It is necessary that we find a way to include these factors, although not necessarily in precise dollar values.

A recent government document breaks the economic justification of a project into two parts:(1)

1) Economic analysis
2) Financial feasibility

## 4.1  ECONOMIC ANALYSIS

The economic analysis compares all of the benefits of a project with its costs. The benefit-to-cost ratio must exceed one. Financial feasibility is determined by comparing the income or revenues in dollars with the estimated costs in dollars (usually on an annual basis). Some projects meet one criterion but not the other. In some cases a project which is economically justified but not financially feasible may actually be carried out. As an example, the United States space program was judged to be economically justified for complex reasons including scientific discovery, national prestige, military development, and others. It is not, however, financially feasible, as the projected "income" is negligible. On the other hand, damming Yosemite Valley for a hydroelectric project might well be financially feasible, but we hope it would never be considered economically justified because of the value of the magnificent scenery. We shall now consider these two parts of the justification study in detail.

As the government report mentioned above states, "A project is properly formulated and economically justified if:

1) Project benefits exceed project costs

2) Each separable segment or purpose provides benefits at least equal to its costs

3) The development provides maximum net benefits compared to alternatives

4) There is no more economical means of accomplishing the same purpose which would be precluded from development if the project were undertaken."

The first of the criteria above requires that *all* benefits exceed *all* costs. The difficulty, of course, is that it is extremely hard to assess the value of some benefits and costs, such as a lake to swim in, a stream to fish in, homesites, local weather effects, and many more. For the time being, perhaps, we shall have to be content to consider such benefits and costs in our evaluation, without attempting to ascribe dollar values to them. It may be that in the future we can quantify these values; it may also very well be that man will choose not to attempt to put numbers on such values. Perhaps it would be a mistake to try to quantify them. This problem will not be resolved easily. There is, of course, increasing interest in these intangibles. In large measure we consider such factors in a political framework with final project decisions being made or accepted by a state legislature or commission, or Congress, or the President, or a body such as the Federal Power Commission. The existence of final decision-making bodies does not free either citizens or engineers from pointing out and evaluating all possible benefits and costs, both tangible and intangible.

The second criterion above requires that each separable part of the project be justified. Many parts of a project are not separable. The building of a storage reservoir and the formation of a fishing lake cannot be separated. However, the building of a fish hatchery on the lake could probably be separated. This criterion simply says that if parts *can* be separated, they should be justified independently. This makes it possible to develop justifiable parts of a project and omit parts which cannot be justified.

The third criterion concerns scale. The scale or size of the project should be such that the net benefits are as large as possible. Scale is critical to the success of a project. A hydroelectric facility which is very small for a given site will be uneconomical since little power can be generated, and certain initial and fixed costs will exist even though the cost of the plant may be low. On the other hand, too large a plant will be very expensive and unable to work close to its capacity with a limited supply of water.

An interesting example of trade-offs related to scale arose during the construction of the San Onofre Nuclear Power Generating Plant between San Diego and Los Angeles, California. The site of the plant is a bluff about 100 ft. high overlooking the Pacific Ocean. It was decided that part of the bluff would be excavated to permit the plant to be built close to the ocean. One reason for doing this was to reduce the pumping head required for pumping ocean water to the plant's cooling condensers. The power required to pump a fixed rate of water is proportional to the height it is pumped. This power costs the power plant money (because it cannot be sold), so it is quite desirable to minimize the pumping head. However, decreasing the head means increasing the amount of excavation and also increasing the possibility of damage from the ocean. In the case of the San Onofre plant it was determined that an optimum plant elevation was about 20 feet above the ocean.

The last of our four criteria requires that there not be any *more economical* means of accomplishing the same purpose. That is, it must be demonstrated that the project supplies the type of load required better than any of the alternatives, such as a fossil-fuel plant, an atomic plant, or perhaps internal combustion or gas turbine units.

## 4.2  FINANCIAL FEASIBILITY

We move now from the problem of economic evaluation to a determination of financial feasibility. Here we must compare the dollar cost of producing energy with the expected income from the energy. The cost of energy from any type of conversion process is usually expressed as the sum of two costs, namely *fixed charges* and *operation and maintenance charges*.

Fixed charges include taxes and insurance, amortization or depreciation, and interest or cost of money. These charges relate to the presence or existence of a plant or facility regardless of how much energy is being produced. They do not vary with production and are hence said to be fixed. We shall discuss them in detail shortly. Operation and maintenance charges include fuel or material costs (if any), supplies, expenses, supervision, maintenance engineering and labor.

An excellent analogy can be made between the costs of a conversion plant and the cost of a home. The latter has taxes and insurance. Amortization and interest charges are accounted for in paying off the mortgage obtained from the lender (usually a bank). These fixed costs do not depend on use of the home. However, variable charges for heating, electricity, upkeep (repairs, painting, etc.) do depend at least partially on the use of the home.

One of the most important costs for an energy conversion plant is the original cost of acquiring property and constructing a facility. The scale of such plants is such that this requires a relatively large amount of capital investment. (See Figure 4–1.) It is necessary to have this money available at the beginning of the life of the facility to pay for its construction. The necessary capital is usually borrowed from an investor. It is necessary then to repay the money borrowed plus interest charged for use of the money. For example, this repayment or amortization period is usually 50 years for a hydroelectric facility. Such facilities typically have an expected lifetime close to 100 years. However, Federal Power Commission licenses extend only 50 years or less. At the end of this time the company must apply for a new license.

A distinction should be made here between amortization and depreciation. Assume that we borrow money to build some facility (of any type) with an expected lifetime of 50 years. Each year we pay an interest charge for using the money plus an amount necessary to pay off part of the capital. At the end of 50 years we have paid off the loan, and theoretically our plant's value has decreased to zero (due, perhaps, to deterioration, obsolescence, or other factors). Since the plant's value has decreased to zero, we design a new plant, borrow some more money and start over. Suppose, however, that at the beginning of the life of the plant we had sufficient cash on hand to pay for all construction costs; that is, we owned the capital. We might argue that we could therefore forget about the cost of money and cut our expenses sharply for the 50 year life of the plant. But that would not be good economics, because at the end of

**Figure 4–1.** Morrow Point Dam on the Gunnison River in Colorado. The primary factor in the cost of hydroelectric power is the cost of the dam and powerhouse. The Morrow Point Dam cost $60 million. The spectacular 360 foot waterfall illustrates another economic consideration. This water is wasted as far as electric energy generation, because it does not pass through the turbines. More turbines could have been installed to handle the overflow during the short periods when the dam cannot contain all the water of the Gunnison. But more turbines cost more money. So we must seek an economic compromise between turbine cost and the value of the additional energy which could be generated. (Courtesy of Bureau of Reclamation, U.S. Department of the Interior.)

the 50 years, we would have lost both our plant *and* our capital. We could have loaned out our capital and borrowed some more capital as before. At the end of the 50 years we would have our capital back plus interest. Of course we might also find a way to lend ourselves the money and pay ourselves back. One way to do this is to pay for the plant ourselves and then pay a fixed amount each year into a fund established to counteract the depreciation of the plant. This can be called a depreciation fund, or sinking fund. It is a fund into which payments are "sunk" to produce a desired amount at the end of a set period.

It should be clear from the above that a project must pay for the capital investment, one way or another, whether we borrow the money from an outsider or from ourselves. If it does not, the payments are not a true reflection of the cost. Sometimes people might wish to pay into both amortization *and* depreciation funds. This would be an abuse in the other extreme. In this case the ratepayer would be paying not only for the present plant but also for its replacement, simultaneously. This would be an unfair burden.

The Soviet Union once attempted to ignore the problem of capital cost by assuming capital belonged to the state and need not be accounted. The result was an incorrect decision on development of a project, and later the decision had to be reversed. This case is discussed in an interesting short book on engineering economics by Sporn.(2)

What is interest? Interest is money we must pay for the privilege of borrowing money. It is usually expressed as a percentage rate per year. An interest rate of 5% means that we must pay $5 for every $100 we borrow for each year we have the "capital." People lend money because they have it and are willing to forego the use of it temporarily in order to acquire more money (interest), and set aside "savings" for some future need. People borrow money and pay interest because they expect to produce goods (such as tennis rackets or electric power) which return an income greater than the cost of the investment. If they fail to do so they will go out of business.

How much does it cost to borrow money? Suppose you wish to borrow $100,000,000 (a fairly reasonable price) to build a 300 MW hydroelectric plant, paying off the loan over 50 years. How much should you pay each year? The answer depends on the interest rate and the method of repayment chosen. There are a number of methods of repaying a loan. The most common is to make equal payments at the end of each of n years so that the loan is completely paid off after n years. What should these equal payments be? Let's call the original loan value P. We have borrowed P dollars at an interest rate i. At the end of the first year the value of the money has become:

$$P + iP = P(1 + i)$$

Now we make a payment toward paying off the loan. If we decide to pay it off in one year we simply let our payment (call it R) be $P(1 + i)$. Suppose, however, we choose to pay off our loan in two years. Then we make a payment R, which, when subtracted from the value of the money at the end of one year, leaves a loan balance:

$$P(1 + i) - R$$

At the end of the second year we pay i interest on this balance. Again we subtract the same R, and the result must be zero to pay the loan off in two years.

$$[P(1 + i) - R](1 + i) - R = 0$$
$$P(1 + i)^2 - R(1 + i) - R = 0$$

The equation above can be solved easily to find the repayment R. It is also possible to show that the payment R for any value P and any interest rate i is:

$$R = P\frac{i(1 + i)^n}{(1 + i)^n - 1}$$

This equation can be solved with many modern hand calculators. It is also quite convenient to construct a table of the multiplier of P in the above equation. This multiplier, called r, depends only on n and i. The multiplier is given in Table 4–1.

**TABLE 4–1**

**Values for the Fraction** $r = \dfrac{i(1 + i)^n}{(1 + i)^n - 1}$

| $\frac{i}{n}$ | 1 | 2 | 4 | 5 | 6 | 7 | 8 | 10 |
|---|---|---|---|---|---|---|---|---|
| 1 | 1.010 | 1.020 | 1.040 | 1.050 | 1.060 | 1.070 | 1.080 | 1.100 |
| 2 | 0.507 | 0.515 | 0.530 | 0.538 | 0.545 | 0.553 | 0.561 | 0.576 |
| 3 | 0.340 | 0.347 | 0.360 | 0.367 | 0.374 | 0.381 | 0.388 | 0.402 |
| 5 | 0.206 | 0.212 | 0.225 | 0.231 | 0.237 | 0.244 | 0.251 | 0.264 |
| 10 | 0.106 | 0.111 | 0.123 | 0.130 | 0.136 | 0.142 | 0.149 | 0.163 |
| 15 | 0.072 | 0.078 | 0.090 | 0.086 | 0.103 | 0.110 | 0.117 | 0.132 |
| 25 | 0.045 | 0.051 | 0.064 | 0.071 | 0.078 | 0.086 | 0.094 | 0.110 |
| 30 | 0.039 | 0.045 | 0.058 | 0.065 | 0.073 | 0.081 | 0.089 | 0.106 |
| 40 | 0.030 | 0.037 | 0.051 | 0.058 | 0.067 | 0.075 | 0.084 | 0.102 |
| 50 | 0.026 | 0.032 | 0.047 | 0.055 | 0.063 | 0.072 | 0.082 | 0.101 |
| 75 | 0.019 | 0.026 | 0.042 | 0.051 | 0.061 | 0.070 | 0.080 | 0.100 |
| 100 | 0.016 | 0.023 | 0.041 | 0.050 | 0.060 | 0.070 | 0.080 | 0.100 |

*Example 4–1*

If you take out a $40,000 mortgage on a house, agreeing to pay 6% interest, and repay the loan in 25 years, what is your annual payment? What is the corresponding average monthly payment? What is the total payment over 25 years?

From Table 4–1, the repayment multiplier r is 0.078. Hence the yearly payment is

$$R = 0.078 \times \$40,000 = \$3,120$$

This corresponds to an average monthly payment of $260. Over 25 years you pay $78,000.

This completes our study of fixed costs. We have noted the existence of taxes and insurance as costs, and we have studied one method for calculating the cost of capital investment. We turn now to operation and maintenance charges.

Fuel costs will be the most important operation charge in a fuel-burning plant. In the case of hydroelectric plants, however, fuel costs are neglected. These plants typically have high initial investment costs, and hence high fixed charges, but relatively low operation and maintenance charges. Maintenance is lower for hydroelectric plants than for fuel-burning plants because of the relative simplicity and reliability of the former. Most fuel conversion plants, such as refineries, will have high fixed and operating costs.

Once all of the costs, fixed and non-fixed, of the proposed plant are identified, we can proceed to find the net cost of producing energy. In the case of electric energy we usually express our final answer in mills/KWH. If this figure is equal to or less than the rates we presently charge or anticipate charging, the project is financially feasible.

We conclude this section with a typical example. The figures given are not taken from a specific case but are nonetheless representative of projects of this size.

### Example 4-2

We wish to build a 200 MW hydroelectric plant for a total project cost of $71,000,000. The interest rate is 6%, and the amortization time is to be 50 years. Taxes and insurance are estimated to be $1,000,000 per year. Operation and main-tenance costs will be about $1.60 per kilowatt. It is assumed that the facility will have a plant factor of 40%, which is the ratio of the average load on the plant to the power rating of the plant. Determine the cost of producing energy.

A quick calculation shows that the plant cost per kilowatt is:

$$\frac{71,000,000}{200,000} = \$355$$

Hydroelectric plants typically have plant costs of $250 to $500 per kilowatt. This is high as electric plants go, but is compen-sated by the lower operating costs.

Now we determine the number of KWH produced per year. There are 8760 (24 × 365) hours in a year. The number of KWH per year is the power rating of the plant times the plant factor times 8760.

Energy $= 200{,}000 \times 0.4 \times 8760 = 700{,}000{,}000$ KWH

We find next the cost of borrowing \$71,000,000 at 6% for 50 years. From Table 4–1, the equal payment rate is seen to be 6.3% of the original capital.

$0.063 \times 71{,}000{,}000 = \$4{,}473{,}000$

Total annual fixed costs (cost of money plus taxes and insurance) are

$\$4{,}473{,}000 + 1{,}000{,}000 = \$5{,}473{,}000$

and the resulting cost per KWH is:

$$\frac{5{,}473{,}000}{700{,}000{,}000} = 7.82 \text{ mills/KWH}$$

Operation and maintenance costs are:

$\$1.8 \times 200{,}000 = \$360{,}000/\text{year}$

and the corresponding energy cost is:

$$\frac{360{,}000}{700{,}000{,}000} = 0.514 \text{ mills/KWH}$$

Hence, total energy costs are:

| | |
|---|---|
| Fixed Costs | \$7.82 |
| Operation and Maintenance | 0.51 |
| | 8.33 mills/KWH |

It should be apparent that a higher plant factor would reduce the energy costs. The usual reason for the relatively low plant factor in a hydroelectric plant is the lack of water. In a particularly wet year this factor may rise significantly and cut the cost of producing power. As we shall see in the next chapter, the plant factor is a little less important in reducing the cost of fossil-fuel generated energy because the more energy you produce, the more fuel you need to produce it and the more the fuel costs. (See Figure 4–2.)

**Figure 4–2.** Coal handling facility. This is a 250 MW coal-burning plant in central Missouri. Coal is stockpiled at 1,800 tons per hour by a dual system of 42″-wide belt conveyors. It is delivered to the power plant at a rate of as much as 700 tons per hour. The huge stockpile and the fuel-flow rates indicate the very large quantities of coal which are burned in fossil-fuel power plants. These large quantities of fuel are a major factor in the economic analysis of steam power plants. (Courtesy of Bulk Handling Systems.)

## 4.3 FIXED AND VARIABLE COSTS

In this section we study in more detail the role of fixed and variable costs by considering three very different examples. The first is the hydroelectric plant observed in the previous example. The second concerns the cost of heating a house. The third example treats a small household appliance.

In Example 4–2 we saw how three fixed costs contributed to final energy cost. The cost of energy for that case can be expressed generally as:

$$C_E = \frac{R + T + O}{8760 \, fP} \, (\text{mills/KWH})$$

where R is the annual payment on capital and interest, T stands for taxes and insurance, and O for operation and maintenance, f is the plant factor, and P the power capacity of the plant in KW. For the plant in Example 4–2 the energy cost becomes

$$C_E = \frac{3.33}{f} \, (\text{mills/KWH})$$

The cost of energy is inversely proportional to the plant factor. Thus the more the plant is used, the less the cost of energy. $C_E$ is plotted in Figure 4–3. In this example all costs are assumed fixed and the only energy costs depend on plant factor. When we study fossil-fuel plants, we add a fuel-cost term which is independent of plant factor. Total energy cost for that situation can be expressed as

$$C_E = \frac{F.C.}{8760 \, fP} + F \, (\text{mills/KWH})$$

where F.C. stands for total fixed costs and F represents the cost of fuel. The latter does not depend significantly on plant factor.

For our second example we consider a situation in which capital or fixed costs can be traded off against operating or variable costs.

## Example 4–3

In the spring of 1973 the Pacific Gas and Electric Co. of San Francisco announced a new Energy Conservation Home project.(4) According to a PG&E official, such a home " ... of 1,370 square feet located in San Jose would cost about $140 more to meet Energy Conservation Home requirements, but this home will cost about $20 less to heat each year." Assume that the $140 is added to the mortgage and amortized over 30 years at 7% interest. Compare the added cost of the mortgage

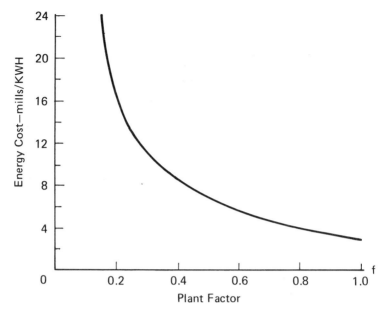

**Figure 4–3.** Effect of Plant Factor on Energy Cost.

payment (fixed capital cost) with the savings in operational costs.

From Table 4–1 we see that the repayment factor r is 0.081. Hence the added mortgage payment is:

0.081 × $140 = $11.34 per year

Thus the homeowner pays an additional $11.34 per year or $0.95 per month to the mortgage company, but saves $20 per year or $1.67 per month on the heating bill.

This is an example of energy conservation that saves money without decreasing one's "standard of living." This concept is discussed again in Chapter 16.

Our final example concerns the cost per hour of operating a small appliance.

## Example 4–4

Determine the cost per hour of operating a circulating fan. (See Table 2–4.) Assume that the fan costs $20. It will be used for 10 years and then junked, and will require no maintenance (a fair assumption for fans). Assume energy costs $0.02/KWH.

The fixed cost or cost of owning the fan per year is $2. Since the fan requires 88 watts, in one hour it uses 0.088 KWH at a cost of $0.00176. Thus the cost of running the fan per hour is:

$$C = \frac{2}{H} + 0.00176 \text{ (dollars/hour)}$$

where H is the number of hours the fan is operated per year.

If the fan is operated 100 hours per year, the cost is $.02176 per hour. If the fan is operated 1,000 hours per year, the cost is $.00376 per hour.

For many devices such as lightbulbs, the analysis above would be quite inappropriate, since the life of a lightbulb is highly dependent on the hours of use. This is much less true of a fan.

## 4.4  THE ECONOMICS OF OTHER ENERGY SYSTEMS

In this chapter we have shown that almost all systems or devices have both fixed and operating costs; generally, both must be considered when making economic decisions. Also, capital costs money to use. Interest rates are a normal and legitimate means of paying for the use of capital. When a plant or a device is built, the capital appears as an organized collection of materials dedicated to the performance of a particular task. The cost of gathering and assembling these materials becomes a part of the work desired. This principle applies to electric razors, nuclear power plants, supertankers, solar panels, and just about everything else.

In the chapters ahead we shall be applying cost principles

repeatedly. We live in a society which is largely dependent upon the operation of the marketplace for individual and group decisions. The operation of the marketplace is not totally free. (There are government regulations and policies that partially control the market.) On one hand there are industrial cartels organized to increase company profits. On the other hand, we have government regulations designed to protect the consumer, or to further some element of national policy.

An extremely interesting and important argument made by a number of energy economists is that energy should be bought and sold in a *free market*. That is, government regulations should be removed from wholesale and retail prices. The principle is that there can exist neither shortages nor surpluses, since seller and buyer must eventually agree on a mutually acceptable price, called the *clearing price*. The argument is summarized quite succinctly by one of its better spokesmen, Edward J. Mitchell (See Additional Reading 3 below): "The shortage of energy now facing the nation is not a problem for public policy—it is a public policy. Shortages can be eliminated very simply: Remove price controls on energy."

Opponents of the free market position argue that the energy industry is cartelized to a significant degree, and government controls are needed to protect the consumer. Proponents argue that this is not so, and that in fact government regulations are almost certainly inefficient, and lead to increased energy costs in the long run. It is not within the scope of this text to present these countering arguments in any detail. The reader interested in energy economics is strongly urged to read Mitchell's monograph, referenced below. For the time being it seems likely that we will continue to see a mix of some market freedom along with some government regulation.

As time goes on we will certainly see shifts in these organizational balances. But regardless of the mix of regulations and market freedom, the price of energy will continue to play a major role in determining the decisions we make in this sector.

As new devices, uses, or systems are proposed, they will have to meet the test of financial feasibility as well as overall economic desirability.


## REFERENCES FOR CHAPTER 4

1. Federal Power Commission, "Hydroelectric Power Evaluation,"U.S. Government Printing Office, 1968.
2. P. Sporn, *Technology, Engineering, and Economics*, MIT Press, 1969.
3. E.L. Grant and W.G. Ireson,*Principles of Engineering Economy*, The Ronald Press Co., New York, Fourth Edition, 1960.
4. *P G and E Progress*, Pacific Gas and Electric Co., San Francisco, Cal., June, 1973.

## ADDITIONAL READING FOR CHAPTER 4

1. Reference 2 above is a short and very readable discussion of economic factors in technical development. It requires no background in economics or mathematics.
2. R. Dorfman and N. Dorfman, Eds., *Economics of the Environment*, W. W. Norton & Co., New York, 1972.

   This book contains selected readings and extensive bibliography on a number of general problems in economics related to the environment.
3. E.J. Mitchell, "U.S. Energy Poliey: A Priner," American Enterprise Institute for Public Policy Research, Washington, D.C., 1974.

   This book is an outstanding presentation of the argument for free markets in the energy sector. It should be read and understood—though not necessarily approved—by every serious student of energy problems.

## PROBLEMS FOR CHAPTER 4

*General Problems*

4.1. Explain why there are undesirable qualities in the maximum and minimum sizes or scales of the following examples;

a) Capacity of a theatre
b) Loudness of a radio
c) Size of a cornflake box
d) Strength of a cable holding up an elevator
e) Width of a fixed-weight triangular cross-section gravity dam
f) The Statue of Liberty

4.2. Suppose you wish to buy a house for $35,000. You pay $5,000 down and borrow the rest from the bank, agreeing to make equal annual payments over 30 years. Find your annual payment for interest rates of 4 percent and 8 percent. Find the total amount of money you will pay back to the bank in 30 years for these two rates. ($1,740, $2,670; $52,200, $86,100)

4.3. Consider Example 4–2. What is the cost of energy production in a wet year in which the plant factor is 60 percent? (5.55 mills/KWH)

4.4. A 500 MW hydroelectric plant will cost $150,000,000. Interest rates are 7 percent and the repayment time is 50 years. Taxes and insurance will be $3,000,000/year. Operation and maintenance costs will be $1.25/KW. Plant factor is 50 percent. Find the cost of energy. (6.58 mills/KWH)

*Advanced Mathematical Problems*

4.5 Show that capital P invested at a rate i compounded annually has a value after n years equal to:

$$S = P(1 + i)^n$$

(Compounding annually means that once each year the value of the accumulated capital is increased by the percentage interest rate.)

4.6. Using the formula of Problem 4.5, find the value of $1,000 invested at 5 percent interest for: 1 year, 5 years, 30 years, 100 years. ($1,050, $1,276, $4,320, $132,000)

4.7. Using the formula of Problem 4.5, find the value of $1,000 invested for 30 years at: 1 percent, 3 percent, 5 percent, 10 percent. ($1,348, $2,428, $4,320, $22,900)

4.8. *Present worth* of some amount of money S available n years in the future is defined as the amount of money which would have to be invested at the present rate of interest to yield S dollars in n years. Present worth is easily found from Problem 4.5, for annual compounding, to be:

$$P = \frac{S}{(1 + i)^n}$$

Find the present worth of $100,000 payable in ten years if that present worth is invested at 6% interest. ($55,900)

4.9. Consider the following example of the applicatiion of the present worth principle introduced in Problem 4.8. You are building a power plant which will eventually house two generation units, although only one is required today. The second one can be built at a cost of $10,000,000 today or $15,000,000 in five years. If the present interest rate is 7% determine whether it is better to put in the generator now or in five years.

*Advanced study Problems*

4.10. Make an extensive analysis of the operating costs and other (indirect) costs of an automobile. *After* you have completed your own analysis, consult "Cost of Operating an Automobile," U.S. Department of Transportation,

April 1972. (U.S. Government Printing Office.) What part of total cost is the initial capital cost?

4.11. Contact a local power company, or other industry, which is building a new plant. Determine the capital cost, the method of financing, the amortization period, and the part which the capital cost plays in final product cost.

# 5

# NEW FUELS FROM OLD SOURCES

*Since 'tis Nature's law to change,*
*Constancy alone is strange.*

John Wilmot, Earl of
Rochester

The dream of the alchemist of the middle ages was to transmute base metals into gold. His work was futile because his premises were wrong. Today, the dream of the seeker of alternate fuels is more realistic. He would change material resources which are difficult or impossible to use as energy sources into fuels which can be used for a wide range of energy needs. He seeks gas and oil and methanol from coal, oil

99

(kerogen) from oil shale, combustibles from waste products, hydrogen from water.

We saw at the end of Chapter 3 that one of the options for filling the gap between existing domestic energy supply and demand is the development of new sources of energy. New fuels from old sources may be an important answer to the problem of the so-called energy gap.

In seeking to develop large-scale conversion systems and plants we start with one major advantage. We know that we can do it. Kerogen was retorted from oil shale in New Brunswick, Canada when Abraham Lincoln was six years old. Gas made from coal lighted the streets of Great Britain in the early nineteenth century, and later fueled much of German industry in the Second World War. Almost all of the conversions we might consider have been with us for decades or centuries.

An obvious question arises. If we know how to effect all of these conversions, why are we uncertain about the future of new fuels made from old sources?

In the past the amounts of fuels converted have been relatively small. The quality of these fuels has sometimes been low. Most of the gas presently made from coal has had a very low energy content, compared with that of natural gas, for example. It has often been possible to neglect environmental effects because of the small scale of the conversion or the need for the fuel. Cost has not always been competitive with that of fuels we have today or with possible future fuels.

But if alternate fuels are to make a significant impact on our energy needs, the rules will change. The scale of plants will be huge; environmental effects will be significant. And costs must be competitive. Other questions must be asked as well. We'll look at some of these in the section to follow. After we have considered the general questions which need answers and the criteria which must be met, we will examine a few of the most promising and representative proposals for converting existing material resources to new fuel resources.

## 5.1 EVALUATING CONVERSION PROCESSES

A general process for fuel generation or conversion is shown in Figure 5–1. When a specific process is to be considered, seven factors must be evaluated:

1) Material resource availability
2) Energy requirements of conversion
3) Air and water pollution
4) Additional environmental effects
5) Availability of water
6) Development time scale
7) Cost of conversion

Some of the major conversion possibilities and considerations above are summarized in Table 5–1.

Our first consideration is material resource availability. It is necessary that an adequate supply of the material which is to be converted into a fuel exist at the conversion site. In the case of coal, for example, this could mean siting the conversion plant in a coal-rich region, such as in parts of the Rocky Mountains. Alternately, it is possible to bring the coal, by train or slurry line perhaps, to a conversion site. In general, there is a complex trade-off between doing the conversion near the material resource and doing it near the point of fuel use.

Next we consider the energy used to carry out the conversion process. There is a common misconception that it would not be "logical" to use more energy in the conversion process than is available in the final fuel resource. This is not necessarily so.

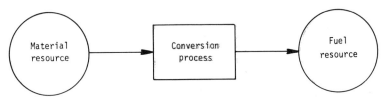

**Figure 5–1.** Converting Old Materials to New Fuels.

Such a conversion might well be logical and desirable, if the output fuel resource is more useful or more valuable than the fuel used in the conversion process. For example, if coal were burned as a fuel in a process that converted coal to methanol, we might accept the loss of the coal fuel energy to get the more versatile methanol output. In practice, however, it will be almost certainly desirable to minimize conversion energy needs to keep down costs, pollution levels, and resource depletion.

Air and water pollution are important considerations in any conversion proposal. For example, it appears at this time that the threat of air pollution is a significant deterrent to the increased use of Rocky Mountain coal. There will probably be costly efforts made to clean up emissions from such plants. These costs represent an internalization of environmental costs. They must, of course, be passed on to the consumer, and they will then affect the competitive position of the fuel in the energy market.

Besides air and water pollution, a number of other environmental factors may be pertinent to a particular process. Strip-mining operations raise concerns about leaching of acid residues and scarring of the land. A large plant in an area could result in excessive noise or in aesthetic pollution. These and other factors could affect the success of new proposals.

Water is necessary in a number of conversion processes, such as oil shale processing and, of course, the electrolysis of water to obtain hydrogen. In the case of oil shale, water tends to be relatively scarce where most of our oil shale is found. Similar conflicts exist for many other conversion proposals.

Development time scale is important if a fuel is needed quickly, and because it is expensive to tie up capital for long periods before a fuel product becomes available.

Finally, we come to the cost of conversion, or the final cost of the fuel resource. In the end, the new fuel must be competitive in cost with the old fuels for which it is a potential substitute. In an ideal market, with full internalization of all costs to society, this final consideration would subsume all of the others. In practice, however, cost continues to be one of a number of considerations.

We turn next to applications of the considerations above by looking at a number of examples of proposed conversion schemes.

## 5.2 FUEL RESOURCES FROM COAL

We saw in Chapter 3 that the reserves of coal in the United States are very large, offering an abundant source of fossil fuel energy for perhaps hundreds of years to come. However, coal is not always a convenient fuel to use. It is often more difficult to transport and burn than gas or petroleum. Also, it does not burn as cleanly. Hence it is not surprising that much attention is being focused on a number of processes for obtaining either gas or oil from coal. (See Figure 5–2.)

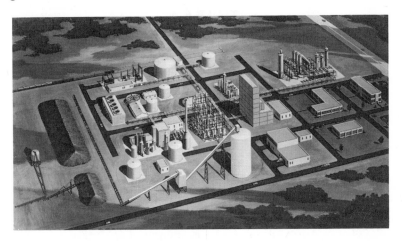

**Figure 5–2.** New fuels from coal. On January 21, 1975, the Office of Coal Research awarded a $237,222,300 contract to the Coalcon Company to build and operate the plant shown above. Outputs of the plant will be 3,900 barrels per day of liquid products and 22 million cubic feet per day of pipeline-quality gas. The demonstration plant may be the forerunner of a new breed of fuel-producing plants. (Courtesy of the Office of Coal Research.)

Some of the major fuel resources which can be obtained from coal are given in Table 5–1. Low-BTU fuel gas contains about 250–400 BTU per cubic foot (CF). For comparison, natural gas contains about 1,030 BTU/CF. Low-BTU gas is too expensive to transport by pipeline, and could not be mixed, in pipelines, with natural gas without significant energy dilution. However, this type of gas is fairly inexpensive, and it can be obtained from existing technology. One attractive prospect is to burn the gas in a *combined-cycle* electric energy generation plant. In the first part of the plant the gas is burned and then passed through a gas-turbine electric generator. The exhaust gases are then used to create steam for a second electric generation step. The efficiency of such a two-cycle plant may be as high as 50% to 60% compared with 40% for modern fossil fuel plants. Low-BTU gas can be produced by burning coal in the presence of steam and air or oxygen at high pressure.

### TABLE 5–1

### Fuel Resources Available from Coal

Low - BTU fuel gas
High - BTU pipeline gas
Low - sulfur fuel oil
Solvent - refined coal
Methanol

Unlike low-BTU gas, high-BTU gas has not been produced commercially in significant amounts. One approach to producing high-BTU gas (containing 950–1,050 BTU/CF) is to pass low-BTU gas through a step called *methanation*. In this step the concentration of methane is increased. (Methane is the major constituent of natural gas.) High-BTU gas contains about as much energy as natural gas, and it can be combined with natural gas in existing pipelines for present and future gas customers. The Office of Coal Research of the Department of the Interior has under study four separate processes for converting coal to high-BTU gas. Other studies or pilot projects are being carried out by private industry.

Low-sulfur fuel oil can be produced by a process called *liquefaction*. A small plant producing crude oil, medium-BTU gas (500 BTU), and a residual char has been operating for several years at Princeton, New Jersey. Rising oil import costs have led a number of oil companies to study liquefaction seriously. Solvent-refined coal is a heavy organic material which melts at about 350° F. It has a low percentage of ash and sulfur and a high energy content. A pilot plant is under development by the Office of Coal Research at Fort Lewis, Washington.

Methanol (wood alcohol) is a liquid which can be obtained from a wide range of sources including coal, natural gas, and organic wastes. We will return to this fuel in Section 5–4.

We turn next to an evaluation of coal conversion in light of the factors suggested for consideration in Section 5–1. We start by presenting a possible Regional Energy Resource Development Plant as projected by the Office of Coal Research.(1) The projected resource needs and plant products are shown in Figure 5–3. If we compare resource needs and product production amounts to 1974 levels, we find that such a plant would require about 5% of our coal production, and it would produce about 1.2% of our coal demand in an ashless low sulfur form, 0.5% of our gas needs, 0.5% of our oil demand, and 0.2% of our power capacity. The hypothetical plant promises important increases in fuel resources. Let us consider the seven specific factors given in Section 5–1.

**1. Material resource availability.** The required 28 million tons of coal per year are certainly available in many parts of the United States, including the Appalachians, the midwestern coal fields, the Rockies, and perhaps some other areas.

**2. Energy requirements of the conversion process.** Energy needs of this plant are not projected. However, a similar multi-product refinery is expected to produce about 3 BTU of fuel resources for every 4 BTU of material resources put into the

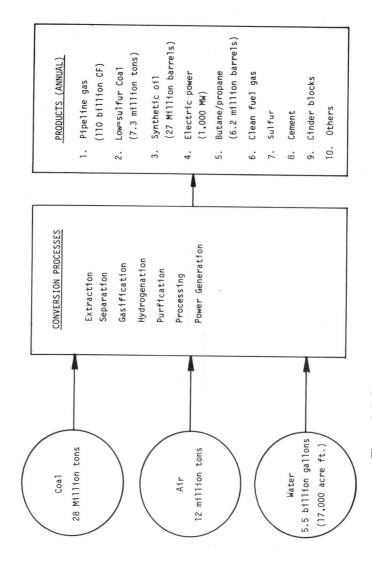

**Figure 5–3.** Projected Regional Energy Resource Development Plant.

plant. This represents an efficiency of 75%. This would probably represent an acceptable level of process energy needs. Actual energy needs will not be known until plants are designed and developed.

**3. Air and water pollution.** These levels have not been evaluated by the Office of Coal Research. It should be noted, however, that the produced fuels tend to be cleaner or less-polluting than the fuels they replace. It is very likely that any processes or plants developed will be required to produce only low levels of pollution. This will mean added process-energy use and increased fuel costs.

**4. Additional environmental effects.** There will certainly be environmental effects related to the coal mining operation, whether it is strip mining or deep mining. The aesthetics of coal mines and processing plants are negative factors. Whether they are outweighted by the value of the fuel products is yet to be determined. One of the advantages of the rather long development times expected is that we will have time to consider positive and negative factors at a number of stages in the development process.

**5. Availability of water.** The water demand of this plant is not a serious problem in the East or Midwest. In the Rocky Mountain region, water is much less abundant. One recent study, however, suggests that water should not be a problem, even in the Rockies, before 1985.(2) After that we will again need to make some important decisions about our energy needs and competing considerations.

**6. Development time scale.** According to the Office of Coal Research, about 12–15 years are required to go from initial research through pilot and demonstration plant phases to the engineering and cost data which must precede commercial plant development. This means that it will probably be 1990 before a major regional plant could contribute significantly to U.S. energy needs. In the meantime, the Office of Coal Research is studying some existing plants, and funding development of a number of new pilot plants or processes. A wide range of coal technology concepts will be tested in the period from 1975 to 1980.

**7. Cost of conversion process.** The Office of Coal Research presently estimates prices of about $1.10 per 1,000 cubic feet of synthetic gas, and about $4.50–6.00 per barrel for liquid fuels. These prices will no doubt increase with inflation, but it seems likely that they will still be competitive in the years ahead. (Compare with Table 3–9.)

In conclusion, the example and evaluation above should not be considered as the only likely plant to be developed, but rather as an example which does present some speculative data for consideration and study. We cannot say what form coal conversion is likely to take on a large scale. It does seem likely, however, that future plants will have some of the features discussed above, and will require an evaluation similar to the above.

## 5.3  SHALE OIL

Our second example of a potential major fuel resource is shale oil. In this case the material resource is oil shale, a fine-grained sedimentary rock. One ton of oil shale contains from 10 to 100 gallons of the waxy organic material kerogen. When oil shale is processed, a wide variety of petroleum products is obtained.

A simplified block diagram of an oil shale plant is shown in Figure 5–4.(3) After the oil shale is mined, crushed and screened, it is fed to a retort or reactor. Here it is heated to about 1,300° F in a hydrogen atmosphere. The output of the

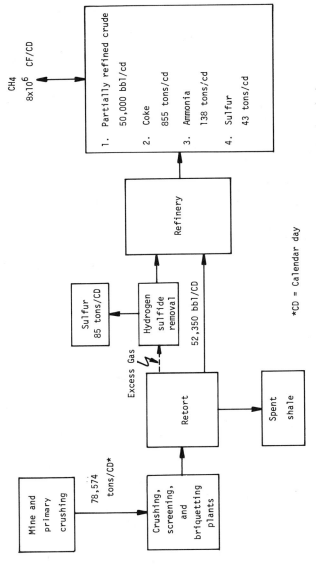

**Figure 5-4.** Shale Oil Processing Plant (50,000 barrels per calendar day).

109

retort is unrefined crude and excess gas, which is used in the refinery after hydrogen sulfide is removed. The crude then goes to a fairly conventional refinery stage where it is partially refined.

We obtain a very tentative evaluation of the proposal by considering the seven factors from Section 5–1.

Oil shale is a very abundant resource. It has been estimated that oil shale equivalent to more than 2,000 billion barrels of oil exists in three Rocky Mountain states, Colorado, Utah, and Wyoming.(4) This quantity is much greater than all of the proved reserves of oil in the world. However, that comparison is probably not too valuable, since only a fairly small fraction of this oil can be recovered economically. Nonetheless, oil shale could probably supply much of our oil needs for a few decades.

The energy requirements of the conversion process are not yet known accurately. However, it is anticipated that an acceptable efficiency will evolve for commercial plants.

Water pollution from the leaching of matter from mine tailings and from the spent shale is an important factor. It will be necessary to recover mined areas and to keep rain from spent shale. This is an added, but no doubt necessary, expense if shale oil is to be recovered at an acceptable level of environmental damage.

Perhaps the most serious environmental problem is raised by the volume of spent shale, which exceeds the volume of the original mined shale by as much as 30%. Hence, while most of the spent shale can be returned to the mine, a significant amount must be deposited elsewhere. Likely deposit areas are nearby canyons or gulches. These areas would then have to be compacted, covered, and revegetated. This entire process is likely to result in major environmental opposition to oil shale development.

Oil-shale processing requires large amounts of water. Twenty plants producing 1,000,000 barrels of crude per day would require about 170,000 acre-feet of water each year.(2) This is a large amount of water in the arid states where oil shale is found.

It would probably take at least 15 years to bring on-line an important amount of shale oil. Hence, it cannot be considered in any sense as a short-term solution. (See Figure 5-5.)

The cost of shale oil production has been recently estimated as $5.15 per barrel for a 100,000 barrel per day plant.(3) This price is competitive with crude oil today (1975).

In conclusion, oil shale is a very abundant material resource. If it is to be converted to crude oil in large amounts, we will have to solve some very important environmental and technological problems.

## 5.4 SOME OTHER FUELS

In the previous two sections we have considered two major material resources and some new fuels which can be obtained from them. In this section we look at a number of other fuels in less depth than in our previous examples. It would be impossible to evaluate in detail all of the possible new fuels. We shall be content to mention some of the most promising or interesting prospects.

Methanol (wood alcohol) has been known for over a century and has been used as a fuel for many years. It has a number of important potential applications, including fuel for automobiles, for gas turbine power plants, and for steam power plants. Its use as a partial or total substitute for automobile gasoline has been questioned. More analysis will be necessary before this issue is resolved. Its use in power plants is less controversial. Methanol can be obtained from natural gas or coal or from waste products. Since natural gas is a scarce resource, it is not likely that it would be used as a source of methanol. Coal is a much more likely source.

Organic wastes from agriculture, logging, and humans and animals are a particularly interesting source for methanol since waste products must be disposed of and are a renewable resource. (Organic wastes could also be used to produce oil or

**Figure 5–5.** Rocky Mountain oil. Many hundred of billions of barrels of oil are locked within shale deposits in the western Rockies, primarily in Wyoming and Colorado. The energy potential is great, but so are the problems—primarily environmental and economic. The small retort shown here produces 50 barrels of oil from 66,000 tons of shale each day. We do not as yet know if experimental plants such as the one shown will provide acceptable answers to the questions raised about shale oil. (Courtesy of United Press International.)

gas, or burned directly to generate electric power.) It has been estimated that more than one billion tons of wastes will be produced in the United States in 1980, with the potential to yield more than one billion barrels of oil, or 10 TCF of gas.(5)

In summary, methanol may be a very attractive source of energy in the years ahead, but a number of important problems must be solved first.

Tar sands are a blend of clay, sand, and heavy oil. Important deposits are found in 14 states, in Canada, and in six other countries. The Athabasca tar sands in North Alberta, Canada represent one of the largest potential hydrocarbon resources in the world. These fields contain an estimated 900 billion barrels of crude bitumen from which about 250 billion barrels of synthetic oil might be obtained. Processing tar sands involves strip mining the sands, hot water extraction to obtain the bitumen, coking to produce distillate oils, and hydrogenation to upgrade the distillate oils to commercial quality synthetic crude oil. One plant, producing 45,000 barrels per day, was completed in 1968 in Alberta. A second plant, scheduled to produce 100,000 barrels by 1979, is being built by Syncrude Canada, Ltd. The first plant lost money in its early years of operation. However, the present high price for crude oil should make this approach much more financially attractive. The major environmental concerns center on land reclamation and disposal of process wastes.

Hydrogen has been widely discussed as an alternate fuel. It can be obtained in a number of ways, including the electrolysis of water. Advantages of hydrogen are that it does not require a fossil material resource, it burns cleanly, and it is fairly easily transported. Disadvantages are that it would be somewhat dangerous to handle; also, electrolysis would require electric energy. It has been argued that if the electric energy is available, it should be transmitted and used in that form, rather than used to create a secondary source of energy. Still, there may exist some situations in which it is best to produce hydrogen. Any specific proposal will have to be shown to use the available energy and material resources in the best possible way, compared with other approaches. This may turn out to be a very significant hurdle for hydrogen energy systems.

In conclusion, we ask whether any one of the approaches discussed in this chapter is clearly superior to the others. It is this author's opinion that no single approach stands out, and that much more study needs to be dedicated to a wide variety of processes. And this is in fact what is happening. A number of pilot plants are being built or studied for coal conversion; treatment of oil shale and tar sands; methanol production; and waste-matter conversion. From these efforts there will probably emerge in time some mix of alternate fuels for energy purposes.

## REFERENCES FOR CHAPTER 5

1. "Clean Energy from Coal Technology," Office of Coal Research, United States Department of the Interior, United States Government Printing Office, Washington, D.C., 1973.
2. C.A. Anderson, et. al., "An Assessment of the U.S. Energy Options for Project Independence," Lawrence Livermore Laboratory for the U.S. Atomic Energy Commission, National Technical Information Service, September 1, 1974.
3. S. Katell and P. Wellman, "An Economic Analysis of Oil Shale Operations Featuring Gas Combustion Retorting," Technical Progress Report 81, Bureau of Mines Oil Shale Program, U.S. Department of the Interior, Washington, D.C., September, 1974.
4. "Shale Oil," in *Minerals, Facts and Problems—1974 Edition*, U.S. Department of the Interior, Washington, D.C., 1970.
5. L. Anderson, "Energy Potential from Organic Wastes: A Review of the Quantities and Sources," Information Circular 8549, Bureau of Mines, U.S. Department of the Interior, U.S. Government Printing Office, Washington, D.C., 1972.

## PROBLEMS FOR CHAPTER 5

*General Problems*

5.1. Explain why an alternate fuel isn't necessarily a viable major source of energy even though we know how to obtain it from a material resource.

5.2. From an environmental viewpoint give at least one advantage and one disadvantage of the Energy Resource Development Plant discussed in Section 5.2.

5.3. If synthetic crude oil can be produced for $6.00 per barrel, will it compete with natural crude? Explain.

5.4. Write a short history on the production and use of methanol in the United States. You will need to consult other references.

*Advanced Study Problems*

5.5. Use the seven factors introduced in Section 5.1 to analyze proposals for processing and using hydrogen as a fuel. You will need to consult additional references.

5.6. Make a detailed study of the production of alternative fuels from coal. Include a discussion of the types of coal available, regions of the country where they are found, types of fuels which can be produced, and the status of pilot plants which study these processes.

# 6

# THE INTERNATIONAL
# ENERGY MARKET

*Then all those virgins arose and trimmed
their lamps. And the foolish said to the
wise, "Give us some of your oil, for our
lamps are going out."*

Matthew 25:7,8

In the early afternoon of October 6, 1973, Egyptian forces suddenly left their bases on the west bank of the Suez Canal, quickly moved across the Canal and established a beachhead on the Sinai Peninsula. Simultaneously the Syrian army attacked and captured much of the Golan Heights. The fourth Arab-Israeli war had begun. As the battle raged, diplomats at the United Nations fought a bloodless battle of the cease-fire resolutions, passed by the Security Council on October 22, 23, and 25. A cease-fire was signed by Arab and Israeli commanders on November 11.

Our immediate interest here is in a series of events during and after that war. On Wednesday, October 18, with the battle turning against the Arabs, five Arab oil-producing nations turned to the ultimate weapon—oil. Saudi Arabia, Iraq, Qatar, Abu Dhabi, and Kuwait agreed among themselves to decrease oil production by 5%. Further cuts of 5% each month were to follow until Israel withdrew from occupied territories, and certain concessions were made to the Palestinians. All oil shipments to the United States, the Netherlands, and Canada were embargoed. In Europe and North America, the winter of 1974 was cold and travel-light. By the time the embargo had ended in March of 1974, the price of crude oil had risen from about $3.50 in 1973 to about $10.00. Gasoline in 1974 cost $0.55 to $0.60 instead of the $0.35 to $0.40 of 1973.

To the millions of Americans who shivered in long gasoline lines in the winter of 1974, the fourth Arab-Israeli war seemed to have been the cause of the much touted energy crisis. In fact it was not the cause, but only the immediate provocation of an inevitable economic confrontation. The long-term confrontation had almost nothing to do with Israel, and would not change significantly if Israel had ceased to exist.

To trace the origin of the real oil war, we must consider in some detail the fundamentals of international energy markets. We start with a study of what is exported and imported (this isn't limited to oil). Then we turn to a short survey of the middle-eastern oil market. This raises the question of how the oil exporting countries view their situation. With that perspective, we turn to the question of the economies of the international energy market today. Finally, we consider the United States response to this market. One response is energy self-sufficiency. The international market and self-sufficiency are inexorably tied to each other. We end the chapter with some comments on this extraordinarily complex and important relationship.

## 6.1  EXPORTING AND IMPORTING ENERGY RESOURCES

Many goods flow in the international marketplace. A country exports goods when it has a surplus at a price another country is willing to pay. Sometimes countries use import or export tariffs or embargoes to control the flow of goods. Energy and energy resources are among the goods that flow. This flow constitutes the international energy market.

Energy can cross international boundaries in many forms. Electric energy flows back and forth between the United States and Canada, depending on the immediate needs of each country. Electric energy also flows among some European countries. It does not, however, flow across the oceans because of the losses inherent in long power transmission cables.

Natural gas is imported in major quantities by pipeline, into the United States from Canada. It cannot be shipped economically in gaseous form across the oceans. It is possible, however, to cool natural gas to the extremely low temperatures at which it has a liquid form. Liquified natural gas (LNG) can be shipped in specially built insulated ships for very long distances. At the present time it is not clear whether large amounts of LNG will be imported at a price competitive with that of natural gas.

Coal is exported by the United States, primarily to Japan, where it is used for steel production. The importing and exporting of coal by the United States does not significantly affect the availability of coal, since coal is so abundant in this country.

This brings us finally to petroleum or oil. Very large amounts of energy resources flow across international boundaries as petroleum or petroleum products. Today oil is the most important and controversial commodity in the international energy market. (See Figure 6–1.) Table 6–1 clearly shows the tremendous importance of oil imports to the United States, Western Europe and Japan.(1)

**Figure 6–1.** Arab oil. Beneath the white sands of Saudi Arabia are much of the world's known oil reserves. But political and economic problems may drive consumers to seek alternatives to Mid-East oil. Today these resources are still critical to the smooth operation of the industrialized world. (Courtesy of the Exxon Corporation.)

## TABLE 6–1

## Petroleum Use and Dependence in Major Consuming Areas (1973)

|  | Petroleum Consumption (million barrels per day) | Petroleum as Percent of Total Energy | Percent of Petroleum Dependent on Imports | Percent of All Energy Dependent on Imports |
|---|---|---|---|---|
| United States | 16.8 | 47% | 36% | 17% |
| Western Europe | 15.1 | 64% | 97% | 62% |
| Japan | 5.4 | 80% | 100% | 80% |

It is evident from Table 6–1 that Western Europe and Japan are highly dependent on imported oil, much of it from Arab nations, for their economic and industrial survival. It is certainly understandable that these nations chose to support the Arabs in the most recent Arab-Israeli war. The United States, on the other hand, is far less dependent on Arab oil. While energy self-sufficiency, or independence from imports, may be credible for the United States, it is hard to see how it could possibly come about in Western Europe or Japan sooner than many decades from now. The percent of United States dependence on Arab oil for all energy purposes increased steadily until the embargo. Today the growth is uncertain. Supplies of Arab oil depend on the political stability of the Middle East. In the meantime, the United States grapples with the critical question of whether it should pursue an all-out policy of energy independence. We shall return to this question in the last section of this chapter.

One of the implications of the growing amounts of petroleum imports is the need for larger tankers. (See Figure 6–2.) These new ships, often called *supertankers*, provide two major advantages. First, they reduce the cost of transporting oil very significantly because of the economy of scale effect. Savings of up to 50% are possible for very large tankers operating over long routes. Second, supertankers reduce the number of ships required to transport a given amount of oil. This reduces congestion and decreases the number of trained crews required.

Supertankers have at least three major drawbacks. First, they have very deep drafts, up to 90 feet for a 400,000 deadweight ton ship, compared with about 40 feet for a typical 50,000 ton ship, common in today's fleets. The largest tanker in service today is about 500,000 tons, nearly ten times the weight of a

**Figure 6–2.** A supertanker. Supertankers such as *Esso Scotia* are carrying an increasing part of the crude oil that moves between countries. At 250,000 tons, *Scotia* is 100 feet longer and 50 feet wider than the largest passenger liners built; crew members ride bicycles on her deck. Very large oil tankers offer major savings in economics of scale of transportation; such savings are imperative when we are importing quantities of petroleum. *Esso Scotia* carries almost two million barrels of oil. This is still only enough to meet U.S. petroleum demand for about three hours. No port in the United States can handle such large ships. Major new imports would require construction of many additional off-loading facilities. A tanker of conventional size, *Esso York*, is shown alongside *Scotia* taking on a load of oil for transshipment to a shore facility. The cargo tanks of oil-carrying vessels must be flushed clean from time to time. The reader may wish to speculate about what happens to the flushing water and the residual sludge, most of which is poisonous. (Courtesy of the Exxon Corporation.)

World War II battleship. Ships up to 750,000 tons are on the drawing boards. No port in the United States can presently accept a ship larger than about 125,000 tons. No port on the East Coast or Gulf Coast can be deepened sufficiently to permit very large supertankers. One alternative is off-shore terminals with oil lines or smaller tankers used for delivery to port. Such terminals have been strongly opposed on environmental grounds.

A second drawback of supertankers is their relatively poor maneuverability. They can be stopped or turned only over very long distances. This provides new navigation problems in narrow or restricted waterways.

Finally, supertankers, of course, have a superpotential for oil spills should they be involved in an accident or run aground. Nonetheless, these ships are under development, and major safety precautions should be taken for their operation.

## 6.2  THE OIL PRODUCING COUNTRIES

Table 6.2 shows the major sources of oil production and the proved reserves for 1973.(2) Recall from Chapter 3 that proved reserves are those reserves which are known to exist and be recoverable under existing economic conditions. The total oil in the ground is much greater than the proved reserves.

From Tables 6.1 and 6.2, we see that the United States produced 10.7 million barrels per day in 1973, but consumed 17.3 million barrels per day. The result is that the United States must look to other oil-rich nations for oil imports. The major oil-exporting nations in the world, with the exception of Canada, belong to an international cartel called the Organization of Petroleum Exporting Countries (OPEC). Major members of OPEC are indicated by asterisks in Table 6–2. The primary goals of OPEC are to increase revenues, (from oil exports) to member nations, and to gain control over exploration and production from international oil companies.

Table 6–3 gives the sources of United States crude oil imports for 1972 and 1973.(3) From 1972 to 1973, U.S. crude oil imports jumped from 2,216,220 barrels per day to 3,243,820. As Table 6–3 indicates, most of the increase came from OPEC countries, primarily from Saudi Arabia and Nigeria. Canada's total exports of crude oil to the United States increased by about 150,000 barrels per day from 1972 to 1973. But her percentage of the export market to the U.S. declined by more

## TABLE 6–2
### World Oil Production and Reserves (1973)

|  | Production (million barrels per day) | Proved Reserves (billion barrels) |
|---|---|---|
| Western Hemisphere | | |
| United States | 10.7 | 34.6 |
| Venezuela* | 3.4 | 14.2 |
| Canada | 1.7 | 9.7 |
| Others | 1.8 | 17.6 |
| Western Europe | 0.4 | 15.9 |
| Middle East | | |
| Saudi Arabia* | 7.7 | 140.8 |
| Iran* | 5.9 | 60.2 |
| Kuwait* | 3.1 | 72.7 |
| Iraq* | 2.0 | 31.2 |
| Others | 2.7 | 45.4 |
| Africa | | |
| Lybia* | 2.2 | 25.6 |
| Nigeria* | 2.0 | 19.9 |
| Algeria* | 1.0 | 7.4 |
| Others | 0.6 | 14.7 |
| Asia-Pacific | | |
| Indonesia* | 1.3 | 10.8 |
| Others | 0.9 | 5.1 |
| Communist Countries | | |
| U.S.S.R. | 8.4 | 34.6 |
| China | 1.0 | 7.4 |
| Others | 0.4 | |

* Members of O.P.E.C.

## TABLE 6–3

### United States Crude Oil Import Sources by Percent of Total Crude Oil Imports

|  | 1973 | 1972 | Percent Change |
|---|---|---|---|
| OPEC Arab Countries |  |  |  |
| Saudi Arabia | 14.23 | 7.84 | 6.39 |
| Libya | 4.10 | 4.94 | (0.84) |
| Algeria | 3.68 | 3.91 | (0.23) |
| United Arab Emirates | 2.18 | 3.31 | (1.13) |
| Kuwait | 1.28 | 1.63 | (0.35) |
| Qatar | 0.22 | 0.16 | 0.06 |
| Iraq | 0.13 | 0.16 | (0.03) |
| OPEC Non-Arab Countries |  |  |  |
| Nigeria | 13.83 | 10.96 | 2.86 |
| Venezuela | 10.62 | 11.50 | (0.88) |
| Iran | 6.67 | 6.13 | 0.54 |
| Indonesia | 6.17 | 7.35 | (1.18) |
| Ecuador | 1.46 | 0.66 | 0.80 |
| Non-OPEC Countries |  |  |  |
| Canada | 30.86 | 38.52 | (7.66) |
| Other | 4.56 | 2.93 | 1.63 |

than 7%. Total imports from Canada are expected to decrease in the next ten years.

Taken together, Tables 6–2 and 6–3 tell a very important story. The majority of U.S. imports is shifting from near neighbors, whose reserves are not great, to more distant oil-rich nations, particularly in Africa and the Middle East. This shift has serious economic implications because of OPEC control of export prices; political implications because of the unsettled politics of the Middle East; and environmental implications because of the need to ship oil over thousands of miles.

## 6.3   PETRO DOLLARS IN THE WORLD ECONOMY

In 1972 the 13 OPEC countries earned about $14 billion from oil exports. By 1974 oil income to OPEC had skyrocketed to about \$112 billion, partially because of rising export levels, but mainly because of a huge increase in oil price, from about \$2 to more than \$10 per barrel. Most of the new price is in fees or tariffs to the producing countries. Only a very small fraction is production costs. This means that there is a great deal of latitude over which the OPEC cartel might set prices. At the present time (early 1975) the cartel appears to have the solidarity and strength to continue to demand high prices for oil.

It is sometimes believed that OPEC nations could charge *any* price for oil. Actually that is not true. A sufficiently high price would not be acceptable to importing nations, and oil would not be traded. What the OPEC nations learned in 1974 is that they could charge over \$10 per barrel without losing many sales. Nobody knows how much higher a price the market could stand. It is, however, evident that the \$10 price is putting a severe strain on many world economies. It is not in the interest of OPEC nations to raise prices to so high a level that other economies fail. First, that would eliminate the market which OPEC needs to continue to earn oil dollars. Second, OPEC countries depend on the products of industrialized nations for their own industrial growth. A healthy world economy is necessary to sustain growth in the economy of OPEC nations.

Dollars that flow into OPEC nations to pay for oil are sometimes called *petro dollars* or *recycled dollars*. Petro dollars are recycled in the sense that they must be spent or invested in the industrialized nations from which they have come if they are to be of value. Dollars stored in a Saudi Arabian bank are of little value. Dollars spent in Germany, or Japan, or England, or the United States can bring needed goods and industry to OPEC nations. Dollars invested bring a return which can be used for later purchases. Hence, petro dollars tend to be recycled back to the industrial nations to support their economies and to provide needed capital.

Unfortunately, the recycling of dollars is far from complete or perfect. In 1974 about \$65 billion dollars earned by OPEC countries was not spent or invested. Money which was spent did not go back to industrialized nations in proportion to their oil payments. Money which was invested tended to be placed in short-term low risk investments. These investments or deposits, particularly if they are large, can be very precarious for a borrowing-lending institution, which must maintain a balance between money borrowed and money lent. The effect of petro dollars is not, at least in theory, to upset the world economy totally. But they have had the short-term effect of seriously changing the *balance* in the world economy, of removing billions of dollars from the capital market, and of changing the balance of trade of the various industrialized nations.

At this point we must ask what can or should be done to move toward stability in the economies of the nations of the world. One approach is to attempt to break the OPEC cartel by a boycott, or by trying to make special arrangements with individual OPEC nations. This does not seem too likely at this time. The industrial nations need oil more than OPEC needs money, and OPEC nations have little incentive to break the cartel which has brought them great wealth in a short time. A second approach to economic stability is to establish a system by which the more affluent nations would provide assistance to weaker countries in the form of loans if a country's economy was seriously threatened.

What is the future of petro dollars and the world economy? There is no way to know. We are dealing with an extremely complex world economy which has suddenly experienced an extraordinary shift in the directions of the flow of money. It will take the system many years to adjust to this new set of conditions. And the conditions will change. It is not clear how an institution, or a nation, or a world organization should act. There certainly is no unique best solution. There are instead many options having many different outcomes, some good and some bad.

In the years ahead, we shall have to probe our way cautiously through the maze of problems, trying always to select those approaches which seem to lead to the most good and the least bad.

## 6.4  ENERGY SELF-SUFFICIENCY

The precarious political situation in the Middle East and the rapid increase in the cost of imported petroleum have led the United States to seriously consider ways to decrease or eliminate our dependence on foreign oil. In April, 1973, the President of the United States sounded a call for *Project Independence—1980*. The concept was to make the United States energy self-sufficient by 1980. That is, all energy consumed was to be produced domestically. The concept was debated widely, with a growing consensus that there was no way that the United States could be self-sufficient by 1980 without a massive enforced conservation program. Furthermore, it was argued that self-sufficiency would result in much high prices than would a mix of foreign and domestic energy sources.(4) In short, it would constitute a very expensive insurance policy designed to protect us from the uncertainties of oil disruptions. We would pay high premiums for the knowledge that our gas tanks would always be full.

Today the concept of total energy self-sufficiency seems to have been abandoned for economic and perhaps political reasons. But the concept of energy independence is still very much with us—with a new definition. One definition of independence is a "situation in which the United States does import to meet some of its energy requirements, but only up to a point of 'acceptable' political and economic vulnerability."(5) The question of what is acceptable has yet to be resolved, and will be central to the determination of United States energy policy.

Following the logic of the last section in Chapter 3, energy independence can be approached by energy conservation (Chapter 16), or by extended development of conventional energy sources (Chapter 3), or by development of alternate fuel sources (Chapter 5). The argument over independence largely centers about the cost of domestic developments compared with the cost of international oil. The Federal Energy Administration's Project Independence Report is essentially developed around two possible future oil prices, $7 and $11 per barrel.(5) If the future price of oil is close to $11, the demand will be lower than if the price is near $7. Also, the higher-priced oil will tend to encourage the development of alternative domestic fuels which might not be economically competitive at the $7 level. Hence, high priced oil will tend to reduce demand, increase domestic production, and thereby narrow the gap which must be filled by imports. While this narrowed gap might be conceived as a good, it will also be quite costly for the consumer. The message is clear. Whether imports are cut by government fiat or by the normal action of the marketplace, relative independence from foreign energy sources will be expensive.

From an environmental viewpoint, energy independence tends to have the *advantage* of limiting oil shipments, but the *disadvantage* of additional pollution resulting from the accelerated development of alternate fuels in this country.

From a global viewpoint, energy independence would tend to isolate the United States from other industrialized nations.

It seems extremely likely that in the short to middle term (up to 15 years), the United States will continue to be a major participant in the international energy market. In the longer term, it is this writer's opinion that the United States will remain in this market for many decades to come.

## REFERENCES FOR CHAPTER 6

1. "BP Statistical Review of the World Oil Industry—1973," The British Petroleum Co., Ltd., London, 1973.
2. "International Economic Report of the President," U.S. Government Printing Office, Washington, D.C., February, 1974.

3. "The PIMS U.S.-OPEC Petroleum Report, 1973," Federal Energy Administration, Washington, D.C., July 1, 1974.
4. M.A. Adelman *et. al.*, "Energy Self-Sufficiency: An Economic Evaluation," *Technology Review*, May, 1974, pp. 23–58.
5. "Project Independence Report," Federal Energy Administration, U.S. Government Printing Office, Washington, D.C. November, 1974.

## ADDITIONAL READING FOR CHAPTER 6

1. "Project Independence Report," Federal Energy Administration, U.S. Government Printing Office, Washington, D.C., November, 1974, 775 pp.

   This is a rather detailed government report on the prospects for achieving energy independence, and the costs associated with this activity. It is not particularly light reading but it does contain a wealth of data for the student who wishes to pursue this subject in detail.

2. M. Adelman *et. al.*, "Energy Self-Sufficiency: An Economic Evaluation," *Technology Review*, May, 1974, pp. 23–58.

   This is a brief, interesting economic analysis of energy self-sufficiency. It is quite readable, and it presents the salient problems rather clearly.

3. "Energy Prospects to 1985, Volumes I and II," Organization for Economic Cooperation and Development, Paris, 1974.

   This is an excellent general review of the international energy market, stressing particularly the problems facing OECO countries.

4. N. Mostert, *Supership*, Alfred Knopf, New York, 1974.

   This is a fascinating and illuminating book on supertankers and life at sea on these big ships. It almost certainly has flaws, but the basic argument about superships on the high seas should be understood. The book has been criticized by the petroleum industry. (See, for example, "Very Large Crude Carriers: The Fiction and the Fact," Public Affairs

Briefing, Standard Oil Co. of California, San Francisco, California, January, 1975.)

## PROBLEMS FOR CHAPTER 6

6.1. Read the cover story in *Time* magazine for January 6, 1975. Explain why *Time* believed King Faisal was the Man of the Year in 1975.

6.2. How many barrels of oil were imported daily into the United States, Western Europe, and Japan in 1973?

6.3. What is the ratio of Saudi Arabia's proved reserves to her annual production? Repeat for Canada. What conclusions might you draw from your results?

6.4. How many barrels of crude oil did the United States import from Saudi Arabia in 1973?

6.5. What is a *cartel?* How does it work? What situations must prevail for it to maintain its strength?

6.6. Explain why there are lower and upper limits to the price at which oil will be traded.

6.7. Read at least one recent article on petro dollars, and summarize its major points.

6.8. What is the difference between energy self-sufficiency and energy independence?

6.9. What is *Aramco?* What is its origin, and likely future?

6.10. Explain why attempts to reach energy independence are helped by high international oil prices.

## ADVANCED STUDY PROBLEMS

6.11. Read *Supership.* (Additional Reading 4) and three reviews of the book. At least one should be critical. Indicate which parts of the book are in controversy. Try to resolve the controversy for yourself by looking at additional references.

6.12. Write a history of OPEC. Explain how, when and why it was formed, and what its future prospects may be.

6.13. Read B. Brodie, "American Security and Foreign Oil," *Foreign Policy Reports*, Volume XXIII, Number 24, March 1, 1948. Explain which aspects of the international oil market have changed since 1948 and which are the same.

6.14. Read pages 17–62 in the Project Independence Report (Additional Reading 1). Summarize the major points and conclusions. Note how various data differ for $7 and $11 oil, and explain these differences.

# 7

# HYDROELECTRIC ENERGY

*What, man! more water glideth by the mill
than wots the miller of . . . .*

William Shakespeare

With this chapter we begin a study of the generation of electric energy. The next seven chapters are partially or completely concerned with electric power plants. There are two important reasons for this emphasis on electric energy. First, electric energy is the fastest-growing major user of primary energy sources. About 25% of all primary energy was used to generate electric energy in 1973. This use has been growing for many decades at about 7% per year, whereas total energy growth has been only about 4%. (Growth rates decreased very significangtly in 1974 with the shortage of a number of fuels, increased prices, and an economic recession. It is not clear at this writing whether growth rates will tend to return in time to their historical average levels.) The rapid growth of demand for electric energy has resulted in a wide range of problems facing the industry and the public in the years ahead. The second reason for concentrating on electric energy is that its problems are representative of many other problems having technical, political, social, legal, and environmental dimensions.

By the end of 1973 the electric power capacity in the United States was almost 440,000 MW. Table 7–1 shows how this capacity was generated.(1) The table also shows the projected additions to capacity in the indicated types of generation.(2) These projections represent plants under construction or expected to be constructed by 1983. These figures should not be viewed as predictions of the future, but rather as today's best guesses about areas of growth. It is likely that electric capacity will grow much as indicated in this short period, barring any major unexpected growth enhancing or inhibiting factors.

We will be considering each of these types of generation in the chapters ahead. We begin in this chapter with a study of hydroelectric power.

## TABLE 7–1
### United States Electric Power Capacity

| Type of Generation | Existing Capacity December 31, 1973(1) | Projected Additions 1974-1983(2) | Chapter in This Text |
|---|---|---|---|
| Fossil steam | 318,357 MW | 194,077 MW | 8 |
| Hydro | 53,667 | 12,671 | 7 |
| Gas turbines | 32,877 | 8,975 | 13 |
| Nuclear fission | 21,070 | 190,010 | 9 |
| Pumped storage | 7,613 | 13,251 | 7 |
| Internal combustion | 4,908 | 82 | 13 |
| Geothermal | 300 | 1,172 | 10 |
| Combined cycle | | 11,354 | 13 |
| Totals | 438,792 | 431,592 | |

## 7.1  HARNESSING THE RAIN CYCLE

Mankind has used the energy of falling water for scores if not hundreds of centuries. Rivers were harnessed long before history first recorded the event, to grind wheat and other grains into a source of food. About a hundred years ago people began to use water to drive hydraulic turbines and to generate electric energy.

Hydroelectric power has a number of advantages which make it very desirable in some situations. Among the advantages are the following:

1) Costs of operation and maintenance are low, relative to most other types of generation.

2) Generating plants have a long life.

3) Unscheduled breakdowns are relatively infrequent and short in duration, because the equipment is relatively simple.

4) Hydroelectric turbine-generators can be started and put on-line very rapidly.

5) Hydroelectric facilities have a relatively small impact on the environment in some cases.

Just how does the water cycle operate to provide man with energy from water? Strangely enough, it all starts with a thermonuclear explosion on the sun, some 93 million miles away. Energy is radiated from the sun into space. Some of it reaches the earth. The atmosphere is warmed and water evaporates from the ocean. A small low pressure cell develops far out in the Pacific Ocean. A storm is born; it grows as it moves. It accumulates great quantities of moisture by the time it reaches the Pacific Coast of the United States. The water cycle has begun. The rain and snow which are to fall are nature's gift to man to use as he will.

The water cycle is one of the most important phenomena in nature. It goes on continuously and it is a critical element of man's life on earth.

The major steps in the water cycle are shown in Figure 7–1. The primary source of energy is the sun, which starts the cycle by heating the ocean. The heated water partially evaporates; that is, it releases some water vapor to the air. (We shall restrict our discussion of the water cycle to the ocean as a source of water vapor. Actually, water evaporates from land, vegetation and even animals, and this can be significant in some regions. However, the oceans are the major source of water vapor.) The water vapor released from the ocean is lighter than air and rises. It is moved as it rises by winds, whose energy also originates from the sun. We are interested here in water vapor, which is caused to drift over land masses, as suggested by the picture. This water vapor may form clouds. If there is sufficient water vapor available, and, if other necessary meteorological conditions are met, the water vapor condenses and falls as rain or snow. A particularly marked effect occurs if the clouds are blown against a range of hills or mountains. In this case the clouds are forced to rise and the resulting cooling increases the amount of precipitation. As the cloud passes over the mountain it tends to fall again, warm up and actually absorb moisture from the air and ground rather than produce precipitation. Hence the windward sides of mountain ranges tend to get much more rain than the opposite sides. This is the so-called rain shadow effect; it is found in many parts of the world.

Water which falls as rain or snow either evaporates again, enters the ground to irrigate vegetation, or flows in streams into lakes and eventually back to the ocean. This completes the water cycle. It is this flowing water, at some elevation higher than the ocean, which can be harnessed to produce hydro-electric power. Let us see how the water cycle provides us with this great source of energy.

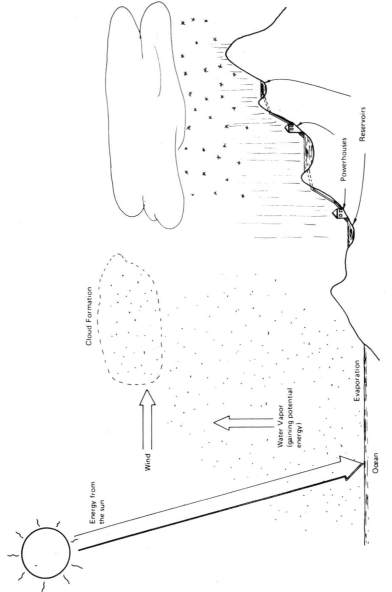

**Figure 7–1.** The Water Cycle and Hydroelectric Power.

Energy from the sun

Cloud Formation

Wind

Water Vapor (gaining potential energy)

Evaporation

Ocean

Reservoirs

Powerhouses

137

## 7.2 THE POTENTIAL ENERGY OF WATER

The potential energy (P.E.) of a body is its capacity to do work by virtue of its position. Water at some elevation greater than a reference plane (such as the ocean) has a capacity to do work because of the earth's gravitational force, which will cause the water to fall when it is released. Consider the diagram in Figure 7–2.

In Figure 7–2a an object with weight W is at a height H above a reference plane. If the object is pushed over the edge, it will fall to the reference plane and in so doing change its potential energy into kinetic energy, which is energy of motion. (Every moving body has kinetic energy.) A little of this energy will heat up the air, but most of it will be converted into heating the object and the reference plane when the object strikes the plane. Now let us put a bottle on the plane. Will the object break the bottle? We are really asking whether the object has enough *energy* to break the bottle when it reaches it. Intuitively we sense that the answer is yes if, for a constant height, the weight of the object is great enough; or, for a constant weight, the height is great enough. And it turns out that the gravitational potential energy of an object is defined as the product of its weight and its height.

$$\text{P.E.} = WH \qquad\qquad\qquad (7\text{--}1)$$

If the weight W is expressed in pounds, and the height H is in feet, the units of P.E. are foot-pounds (ft.-lbs.). (In a hydroelectric project, H is usually called *head*.)

*Example 7–1*

a) What is the potential energy of 100 lbs. of water 500 ft. above the ground? b) How many lbs. of water would have to be placed 25 ft. above the ground to obtain the same P.E.?

a) P.E. $= 100 \times 500 = 5 \times 10^4$ ft.-lbs.

b) $W = \dfrac{\text{P.E.}}{H} = \dfrac{5 \times 10^4}{25} = 2 \times 10^3$ lbs. = 1 ton

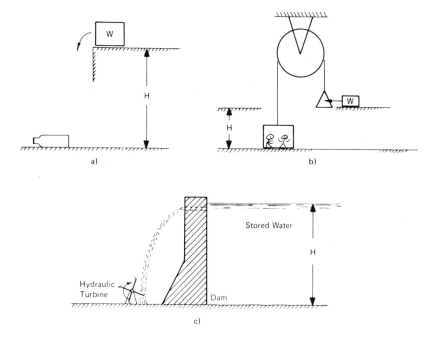

**Figure 7–2.** Using Potential Energy to Do Work.

Clearly, if the height of the water decreases, we will need more water to obtain the same energy.

If you wish to do more work, you must increase either the weight or the height of the weight above a reference. We will see that in the case of hydroelectric power, either of the two factors may be strongly emphasized.

As an example, Figure 7–2b suggests a simple way in which potential energy can be used to do work. An elevator rests on some plane. One way to raise the elevator is to move a weight W (heavier than the loaded elevator) into a platform attached to the elevator by a rope through a pulley, as shown. The weight will move down and the elevator will move up. As always, energy is conserved. The potential energy of the weight W is changed into potential energy of the elevator and its load in its raised position, losses in the pulley system, in air resistance, and in the braking system required to slow and stop the moving bodies at the new steady-state position. (A system is said to be in "steady-state" whenever some particular variables of interest, such as position of the weight W and the elevator in this case, cease to change.)

Finally, in Figure 7–2c we come to the example of basic interest. An obstruction or dam impedes the flow of rainwater toward the ocean, storing it in a reservoir. Water is then released from a height H and allowed to fall on a water-wheel, or hydraulic turbine, which turns on its shaft. The shaft is coupled to an electric generator. When the generator turns, voltage is produced, and the generator can supply electric energy to a load.

## 7.3  HYDROELECTRIC POWER

Man is usually concerned not only with capacity to do work but also with the rate at which work is done. As an example, let us return to Figure 7–2b. The occupants of the elevator want to reach the new level, representing a change in height H, but they also want this change to take place fairly rapidly. They probably would not be happy to have a very slow rate of ascent. The *time rate* at which work is done, or energy is expended, is of great interest. This is true in most situations.

The time rate of doing work is called *power*. One measure of power is foot-pounds per second. If we look at Figure 7–2c again, it is evident that the power depends not only on the weight W of the water released and the height H from which it is released, but also on the *rate* at which it is released. With the definition above we can easily determine the power of our hydroelectric plant. Assume that some weight of water W falls the distance H in the time T. Then the power is:

$$P_w = \frac{\Delta P.E.}{T} = \frac{HW}{T} \tag{7–2}$$

where $\Delta P.E.$ stands for the change in potential energy as the weight W falls a distance H.

The weight of water can be expressed as the weight density w (pounds per cubic feet) times the volume of water V (cubic feet).

$$P_w = \frac{HwV}{T} = Hw\frac{V}{T} = HwQ \text{ (foot-pounds per second)}$$

(7–3)

where $Q = V/T$ is the volumetric rate at which water flows out of the reservoir, expressed in cubic feet per second (cfs). Power as defined in Equation 7–3 is sometimes called water power, as it is the total power the falling water contributes to the system. However, a certain amount of this power is lost due to friction in the pipes (penstocks) which carry the water, incomplete transfer of all of the water's energy to the hydraulic turbine blades, and other factors. To account for these losses we multiply $P_w$ in Equation 7–3 by $e_t$, a number less than 1, called the *turbine efficiency*, to obtain the turbine power. That is:

(turbine power) = (water power) $\times$ $e_t$

The turbine efficiency is a complex function of the type of turbine used, the head, the percentage of the maximum power being generated, and other factors. It is usually in the range of 80–95 per cent, with a common value in the mid-eighties.

Ordinarily we express the turbine power in horsepower, rather than foot pounds per second. Since 550 foot pounds per second equals one horsepower and water weighs 62.4 pounds per cubic foot, turbine power becomes:

$$P_t = \frac{e_t HQ \times 62.4}{550}$$

$$= \frac{e_t HQ}{8.8} \text{(hp)}$$

(7–4)

### Example 7–2

Hydraulic turbines at the San Luis Pumping-Generating plant in central California have a water flow rate of 2,130 cfs when the head is 327 ft. The efficiency for these conditions is about 92%. Find the turbine horsepower.

$$P_t = \frac{0.92 \times 327 \times 2,130}{8.8} = 73,000 \text{ hp}$$

The shaft of the turbine is connected to a generator. Since the generator has some losses also, the electric power out of the generator is obtained by multiplying the turbine power by another number less than 1, called $e_g$, the generator efficiency.

$$\begin{aligned}
\text{(generator power)} &= \text{(turbine power)} \times e_g \\
&= \text{(water power)} \times e_t \times e_g \\
&= \text{(water power)} \times e
\end{aligned}$$

where $e = e_t e_g$ is the overall efficiency of the water penstock-turbine-generator system. Note that the overall efficiency is the product of the two efficiencies of operations which are in "series" or "cascade." These terms indicate that the operations or processes occur sequentially, with the second operation using the output of the first operation. It is always true that when operations occur in this cascade form, the total efficiency is the product of the efficiencies of all the cascaded operations.

The generator power, which is electric power, is expressed in kilowatts (KW). There are 0.746 kilowatts in one horsepower. Using this relation, the new expression for total efficiency, and Equation 7–4, we obtain, for generator power:

$$P_g = \frac{eHQ}{11.8} \text{ (KW)} \tag{7–5}$$

The efficiency of a modern high-power electric generator is very high, perhaps near 98 per cent. Hence, e is nearly equal to $e_t$; it has an approximate range of 80 to 95 per cent.

The points made in this section are summarized in Figure 7–3.

### Example 7–3

We have a reservoir which can store up to $4.35 \times 10^9$ cu. ft. of water (100,000 acre-ft.). The head is 300 ft. How long will we

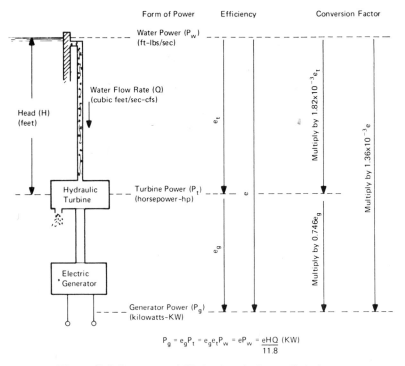

Figure 7–3. Summary of Hydroelectric Power Relations.

be able to generate 500,000 KW before we empty the reservoir? Assume that the head does not change. Total efficiency is 85 per cent.

$$Q = \frac{P_g \times 11.8}{eH}$$

$$= \frac{5 \times 10^5 \times 11.8}{0.85 \times 300}$$

$$= 23{,}100 \text{ cfs}$$

$$\text{Time} = \frac{V}{Q} = \frac{4.35 \times 10^9}{2.31 \times 10^4} = 1.98 \times 10^5 \text{ sec.} = 2.29 \text{ days}$$

## 7.4  TYPES OF HYDROELECTRIC POWER FACILITIES

The simple sketch of Figure 7–2c shows all of the basic elements of a hydroelectric power facility. Likewise, Equation 7–5 gives the power relation common to all such facilities. However, there are a great many different forms which these facilities may take. It is the objective of this section to explore some ways of generating electricity from water power.

One of the simplest and probably earliest examples of man's harnessing of water power was the use of flowing water in a river to drive some sort of paddlewheel. Such a scheme can be adequate for pumping water, grinding flour, and performing certain other tasks. In theory it can be used to generate electric energy. However, variability in stream flow will lead to variations in the electric generator voltage and frequency. One of the purposes of a dam is to smooth out such variations by storing water and releasing it at a controlled rate. (See Figure 2–4.)

We can classify hydroelectric facilities in terms of their capacity to store water. Another way to state the same principle is to give the length of time over which facilities can smooth out variations in stream flow. One class of project is the "run-of-river" project. Essentially, it uses water as it arrives at the facility. Its reservoir usually has limited storage—for perhaps daily or weekly stream flow regulation. An example of this type of project is the Bonneville facility on the lower Columbia River in the Pacific Northwest. It is significant that Bonneville is on the lower part of the river, which benefits greatly from the flow regulation provided by upstream storage dams, including Grand Coulee Dam.

"Storage" projects, a second class of facility, provide water storage for longer periods of time, usually between annual rainfall seasons, although some are built to accommodate more stored water in case of dry years. Examples of the latter are Hungry Horse in Montana, Glen Canyon in Arizona, and some of the projects on the Missouri River. Examples of projects

**Figure 7–4.** Morrow Point Dam, Colorado. Buried deep within the earth, these two units deliver 60 MW of electric power each. The large cylinders enclose the electric generators. Below the floor surface are the hydraulic turbines, connected to the generators by large shafts. Morrow Point Dam cost $60 million to build. (Courtesy of the Bureau of Reclamation, U.S. Department of the Interior.)

operating on an annual cycle of storage and use are Grand Coulee on the Columbia River and Fontana in the Tennessee River Basin.

It should not be assumed that the reservoir of a storage project will necessarily hold enough water for continuous operation of all turbines. It is very common that a reservoir will have less water than required for continuous operation; see Problem 7.5. These plants are often used for peaking—that is, for providing power only during peak demand periods, such as during the early evening hours. It is usually quite a challenging task to use just the right amount of water from a reservoir. We wish to use as much hydroelectric power as we can since the "fuel" (water) is free, but we want to save water for peak demand periods. Decisions on when to use water involve expected weather conditions, power demands, other fuel prices, size of the mountain snow-pack, and many other factors.

Storage projects can be of two types. In the first type the power plant (with the turbine-generator) is inside, or at the base of, the dam which stores the water. Bonneville Dam, which is an example of this form, has eight large generators rated at 54 MW under a 59 ft. head and two smaller generators rated at 43.2 MW under a 49 ft. head. The turbines are of the Kaplan type with adjustable blades. Hydraulic turbines have different forms, depending on the head and the water flow, to maximize the efficiency. Bonneville's turbines rotate at 75 rpm and discharge water at a rate of 13,300 cfs.

In the second type of storage project, the storage reservoir and the power plant are separate. Water is delivered to the power plant through tunnels or pipes, called penstocks, from the reservoir. The Big Creek #1 facility of the Southern California Edison Company, in the Sierra Nevada, is an example of this type of project. The essential elements of this project, which was built in 1912, are sketched in Figure 7–5. A suitable valley or "bowl" was located in the High Sierras. Three dams were built to hold the water, forming Huntington Lake, which stores a maximum of 89,166 acre-ft. (an acre-ft. is an acre of water one foot deep). A tunnel and penstocks were built to deliver water stored in Huntington Lake to Powerhouse #1, located near the 5,000 foot elevation. This powerhouse uses a Pelton turbine. This type of turbine, called an impulse turbine, is often used in plants with high heads. The outlet of the penstock is essentially a nozzle which directs a stream of water at buckets attached to the wheel. The buckets are shaped to make maximum use of the power in the water. When the water falls from the bucket it has transferred almost all of its kinetic energy to the rotating wheel through the force exerted on the bucket. The total power generated by the Big Creek Powerhouse #1 is approximately 81,000 KW.

The water flowing out of Powerhouse #1 is stored briefly in a small reservoir before flowing down a second tunnel-penstock complex to Powerhouse #2, about 2,000 feet lower in elevation. This same water is used four more times to generate electric power before it approaches sea level. The cumulative head is close to 6,200 feet. The result is that more energy per cubic foot of water is generated at Southern California Edison's Big Creek project than at any other hydroelectric project in the world.

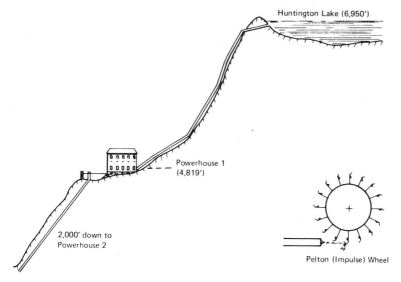

**Figure 7–5.** Big Creek Number 1, a High-Head Hydroelectric Project.

The company calls this "the hardest working water in the world."

## Example 7–4

Suppose that Big Creek Powerhouse #1 were run on a peaking basis for six hours a day during all of July. There are two more lakes above Huntington whose water is used to keep Huntington Lake's level nearly constant during the vacation season, but for the sake of this example do not consider them. At the rate of use given above, what percentage of Huntington Lake's storage would be used? Assume a total efficiency e = 80%. Solve Equation 7–5 for Q. One acre-ft. equals 43,560 cu. ft.

$$Q = \frac{11.8 \, P_g}{eH}$$

$$= \frac{11.8 \times 81,000}{0.8 \times 2,131}$$

$$= 561 \text{ cfs.}$$

The total volume of water released is:

$$
\begin{aligned}
V &= Q \times \text{Time} \\
&= 561 \times 3,600 \times 6 \times 31 \\
&= 375,000,000 \text{ cu. ft.} \\
&= 375,000,000/43,560 = 8,610 \text{ acre-ft.}
\end{aligned}
$$

The percentage of Huntington Lake's storage which is used is:

$$8,610/89,166 = 9.67\%$$

## 7.5  PUMPED-STORAGE PROJECTS

We come now to a very interesting variation of the hydro-electric project, the pumped-storage project. It is a hydroelec-tric facility to the extent that it uses water stored in reservoirs to generate electricity with conventional hydraulic turbines. The variation comes from the fact that it does not use the rain cycle to develop the water head. Instead it uses energy generated by some other source to pump the water "uphill" into a reservoir where it can be stored for later use. The basic scheme is illustrated in Figure 7–6.

Recall that the demand for electric energy changes throughout the day (Figure 2–4). Some pumped-storage projects are used to smooth these daily variations (a few have been designed to smooth longer variations). The thermal plant (atomic or fossil-fueled) in the upper left corner of Figure 7–6 supplies power to the city at a nearly constant rate. It is generally not economically desirable to shut down such plants partially or totally for short periods each day. During the late night hours the power needs of most areas decrease significantly, and the thermal plant has excess power available which is used to pump water uphill from the lower reservoir to the upper reservoir of the pumped-storage facility. On the following day, at the time of peak customer demand, water in the upper reservoir is released to generate the power demand which exceeds the

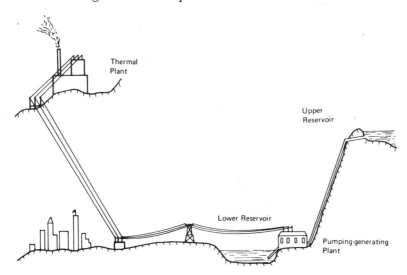

**Figure 7–6.** Pumped-Storage System.

capacity of the thermal plant. Usually the same unit is used to pump water uphill and to generate electricity when the water falls back downhill.

The efficiency of a pumped-storage plant is the product of the efficiencies of the pumping stage and the generating stage. As a rule of thumb, a pumped-storage facility requires 3 KWH of pumping energy for every 2 KWH of generated energy (equivalent to an overall efficiency of 67 per cent). While these losses may be acceptable economically, it is possible that the resulting negative environmental effects will be more than can be accepted. These points will be discussed later.

A number of pumped-storage projects exist now in the United States, including, for example, Taum Sauk (400 MW) in Missouri, Northfield Mountain (1,000 MW) in Massachusetts, and Kittatinny Mountain (330 MW), adjacent to the Delaware River. At the end of 1973 the total capacity of pumped storage was nearly 8,000 MW. This is expected to increase quite signifigantly in the next ten to fifteen years, as we shall see in Section 7.9.

## 7.6 MULTI-PURPOSE HYDROELECTRIC PROJECTS

Many electric energy generating plants are a part of multi-use or multi-purpose projects. There is increasing interest in multi-purpose developments to justify the use of diminishing resources, and to accomplish more than one objective. Hydroelectric plants have often been involved in such projects, and there is every evidence that this practice will continue.

Objectives which may be combined with a hydroelectric plant include:

1) Flood control
2) Irrigation
3) Recreation
4) Public water supply
5) Navigation

When multi-purpose projects are developed it is necessary that the needs of each area be given adequate attention, and the final design must be an acceptable compromise in light of all of the objectives. This is often a difficult task because needs commonly are in conflict, and it is difficult to put an equitable measure of value on objectives in different fields. As an example, a project may be designed for both pumped-storage power generation and water recreation (swimming, boating and fishing). It might be desirable from the power generation standpoint to have a large daily drawdown of the reservoir. (Drawdown is the decrease in water level as water is released to flow through the turbines.) But the large drawdown would very possibly decrease or eliminate the value of the reservoir as a recreational facility. Hence, a compromise must be effected in the project design to permit a drawdown acceptable to both needs.

For specific examples of multi-purpose hydroelectric projects we refer to some of the examples discussed earlier in this chapter.

A project with a wide range of uses or related activities is the Big Creek facility of the Southern California Edison Company discussed above. See Figure 7–5 for a portion of the project. Besides providing for generation of 690 MW, Big Creek also uses its storage dams and associated reservoirs to aid in flood control and to provide irrigation for the San Joaquin Valley. Huntington Lake and Shaver Lake, which are reservoirs for the project, are major mountain recreation centers. The Company maintains an excellent camping facility (with *electric* stoves) on Shaver Lake, as well as a small fish hatchery to help stock the lakes, and a tree farm.

An additional interesting feature of the Big Creek facility is the use of a ground-based cloud-seeding program intended to increase precipitation. Twelve cloud-seeding generators are located at various ground points in the Sierra Nevada and its foothills (six are quite remote and are fully automatic). The generators burn Propane gas with a Silver Iodide-Acetone mixture producing Silver Iodide particles which rise through moisture-laden clouds. The particles act as water-attracting nuclei. If sufficient moisture is attracted by the nucleus, its weight will eventually cause it to precipitate. Results of the program are difficult to evaluate, but the company feels that the possible very significant increase in stored water justifies the rather small expense involved. Essentially unanswered are questions concerning the side effects of the release of Silver Iodide into the atmosphere, and the loss of potential rainfall for individuals further along the "cloudpath."

This example raises again the point mentioned earlier about the difficulty of comparing certain values or objectives. Some costs are fairly easy to obtain. As we shall see shortly, we can determine the cost of electric power generated by a project like Big Creek, and we can compare it with alternative generation schemes. We may be able to obtain a dollar value for irrigation water and perhaps even for flood control. But how shall we measure the value of a swim in a mountain lake, or sunset from a rowboat, or the value of the wilderness we have lost by putting in the project? We have no answers today, but we may have to find answers in the years ahead as the competition for natural resources continues to grow. In the past, power projects have been developed largely in light of criteria which were easily expressed in economic terms. Recreational facilities were often added after the project had met its primary economic objectives. In the future, as man's demand for recreational facilities increases, these needs may play a more significant role in the setting of project criteria.

A second example of a multi-purpose project is the Castaic Pumped-Storage Project. This project uses water being pumped from Northern California to Southern California as part of the California Water Plan. (See Figure 7-7.)

Other examples of multi-purpose water projects include the Columbia Basin Project in Washington State, the Tennessee Valley Project, and the Missouri River Basin Project.

Now we turn our attention to the environmental considerations associated with hydroelectric facilities. Rather than speak in generalities, we consider a single major river; we see through its developments some of the effects which hydro projects can have on river systems. Our subject is the Columbia River in the Pacific Northwest.

**Figure 7–7.** San Luis Dam and Power Plant, California State Water Project. The San Luis facility is part of a huge multipurpose project in California providing public water supply, irrigation, power production, flood control, and recreation. Water is impounded in relatively wet Northern California and transported by canal to Southern California. It is used on farms between the two. At San Luis, over two million acre-feet of water are stored 300 feet above the power station. The plant, shown in the center of this photograph, is used for pump-storage generation. It has a capacity of 424 MW. (Courtesy of Bureau of Reclamation, U.S. Department of the Interior.)

## 7.7 THE COLUMBIA RIVER

The headwaters of the Columbia River lie far up in the Canadian wilderness in a valley flanked on the east by the Rocky Mountains and on the west by the Selkirks. The great winter storms that sweep in from the Gulf of Alaska across Washington State and British Columbia provide ample moisture for the snows of winter that become the raging waters of spring.

The river flows north for more than 200 miles before it flanks the barrier presented by the Selkirks. It then turns south and with only a jog or two along the way flows down into the United States and on to the Oregon border, where it suddenly turns west and surges 300 miles to the Pacific Ocean at Astoria.

Before the dam-builders arrived, the Columbia had a powerful flow, sometimes churning, sometimes falling, sometimes placid. It knew great annual salmon runs, and the Indians came to fish at Celilo Falls and Kettle Falls. It had a life that matched the wild country it traversed. But its life, its power, and its flow were the very qualities which made it a river to be harnessed. The Columbia does not fall a great amount in short distances, but it does carry much water to the sea. Its head (H) is small, but its flow rate (Q) is large.

The first major obstacle to the flow of the Columbia was the Rock Island Dam, begun in 1931, near Wenatchee, Washington. Two years later, the Federal Government began construction of Bonneville Dam, the first of a series of major federal dams on the river. Although Bonneville is not one of the more powerful plants, it is important because it represents the emergence of the Federal Government in the building of Columbia River dams and the establishment of the Bonneville Power Administration, or BPA. The BPA has become the major transmitter and controller of power in the Pacific Northwest.

In 1941 the Bureau of Reclamation began construction of what became the largest power plant in the world at the time of its completion, Grand Coulee Dam. Today the combined capacity of the plant is over 2,000 MW. In the late 1960's construction began on a new addition which, if fully authorized, will have a final capacity in 1990 of almost 10,000 MW. This represents about three percent of the total capacity in the United States in 1970.

Between Bonneville Dam, closest to the Pacific, and Grand

**Figure 7–8.** Grand Coulee Dam on the Columbia River. Grand Coulee Dam, "The mightiest thing every built by a man," was once the largest electric-power generating plant in the world, turning out over 2,000 MW. Grand Coulee has since been eclipsed in size many times. In 1967, engineers blasted away the right 200 feet of the dam and began construction of a new power plant, shown on the left. Initial units should go into operation in 1975. If plans are completely authorized by Congress, they will lead to a plant with a total capacity of nearly 10,000 MW by 1990. (Courtesy of Bureau of Reclamation, U.S. Department of the Interior.)

Coulee, which is the furthest dam upstream which produces power, lie nine other major dams. The period that saw the growth of this system was one of economic optimism, characterized by a belief in the intrinsic value of growth. The spirit of enthusiasm was caught by the great American folk singer and writer Woody Guthrie, who, working in a federally-funded project, wrote 26 songs about the Grand Coulee Dam. Perhaps the best-known of Guthrie's songs on this subject is "Roll On, Columbia," quoted below.

> Green Douglas firs where the water cut through.*
> Down her wild mountains and canyons she flew.
> Canadian Northwest to the ocean so blue,
> Roll on, Columbia, roll on!
>   Roll on, Columbia, roll on.
>   Roll on, Columbia, roll on.
>   Your power is turning our darkness to dawn,
>   So, roll on, Columbia, roll on!
> And on up the river is Grand Coulee Dam,
> The mightiest thing ever built by a man,
> To run the great factories and water the land,
> It's roll on, Columbia, roll on. . . .

The factories were run, the land was watered, floods were tamed, the darkness became dawn. But a price had to be paid. The once-mighty river became a series of long, narrow lakes, formed behind dams. Valleys were flooded and towns lost forever. The salmon runs were cut by nearly 50 percent despite elaborate fish ladders designed to let the fish climb every dam up to the insurmountable Grand Coulee—the end of the line.

For uncounted centuries before the white man came to the Pacific Northwest, Indians had fished the river, particularly at Celilo Falls, where the rocks jutted out into the churning, falling water. The Indians built crude rickety platforms over

* ROLL ON, COLUMBIA. Words by Woody Guthrie. Music based on "Goodnight Irene" by Huddie Ledbetter and Alan Lomax. TRO—© Copyright 1957 & 1963 LUDLOW MUSIC, INC., New York, N. Y. Used by permission.

the water and speared the salmon as they swam upstream. It was one of the most extraordinary and unique features of the area. It belonged to the Indians, and their rights were later ensured by treaty.[†] As the waters slowly rose behind the Dalles Dam, the second dam upstream from the ocean, Celilo Falls was lost to Americans, red and white alike. Today, by the edge of a quiet lake where Celilo once was, stands a small brass commemorative plaque.

## 7.8 DISADVANTAGES OF HYDROELECTRIC POWER GENERATION

Hydroelectric power is usually inexpensive and can often be combined with other desirable objectives, as outlined in Section 7.6. But its costs to the environment are not small, and they will no doubt demand accounting in our decisions for the future. In brief summary, some of the major disadvantages to the environment are listed below.

1) Hydroelectric reservoirs flood regions which may have more desirable uses.

2) Fish migration is restricted.

3) Fish health is affected by changes in water temperatures, and by inadvertent insertion of excess nitrogen into the water at spillways.(3)

4) Available water and water temperatures may be affected by evaporation from reservoirs and water-release practices.

5) Reservoirs alter stream silt-flow patterns and may eventually fill up with silt themselves and thereby become useless as reservoirs.

† The reader may wish to read a fictional account of the negotiations for Celilo Falls between white and red men in Ken Kesey's ONE FLEW OVER THE CUCKOO'S NEST.

## 7.9  CONCLUSIONS

Many more hydroelectric power plants will be built in the years ahead. There are many potential sites.(4) The rate of growth, however, will be much less than that of thermal plants. The result is that hydro will represent an ever-smaller percentage of total capacity as time passes. The slowing of hydro growth rate is primarily caused by the decreasing number of acceptable sites and also by increasing environmental pressures against the building of new dams. One area which will probably see increasing development interest is pumped storage.

One recent projection of hydroelectric growth to 1990 is shown in Table 7–2.(5) Note that this is not a prediction, but a *projection*, or guess, about probable development. As Table 7–2 suggests, hydroelectric power will probably provide some valuable additions to electric capacity, but cannot be expected in any sense to be a panacea. We shall have to look to other types of generation if electric generation capacity is to grow as rapidly as it has in the past.

### TABLE 7–2
### Projected Growth of Hydroelectric Capacity

|  | Conventional Hydroelectric | Pumped Storage |
|---|---|---|
| Installed capacity (end of 1970) | 52,000 MW | 4,000 MW |
| Projected additions (1970-1980) | 16,000 | 23,000 |
| Projected additions (1980-1990) | 14,000 | 44,000 |
| Projected total (end of 1990) | 82,000 | 71,000 |

## REFERENCES FOR CHAPTER 7

1. "News Release No. 20426," Federal Power Commission, Washington, D.C., June 24, 1974.
2. "Hydroelectric Generating Facilities Report," Federal Energy Administration, Washington, D.C., September, 1974.
3. "Nitrogen Supersaturation Problem," Corps of Engineers, U.S. Army, North Pacific Division, Portland, Oregon, June 24, 1971.
4. "Hydroelectric Power Evaluation," Federal Power Commission, U.S. Government Printing Office, 1968.
5. "Hydroelectric Generating Facilities Report," Federal Energy Administration, Washington, D.C., September, 1974.

## ADDITIONAL READING FOR CHAPTER 7

1. D.H. Redinger, *The Story of Big Creek*, Angelos Press, Los Angeles, California, 1949.

   This is the story of the building of the Big Creek Project mentioned in this chapter. It was written by an engineer who helped build the necessary railways and water tunnels over 60 years ago. It is a fascinating historical summary of a great engineering feat which should be interesting to engineer and non-engineer alike.

2. J. McPhee, *Encounters with the Archdruid*, Farrar, Straus and Giroux, New York, 1971.

   This is a trilogy of separate encounters between David Brower, former Director of the Sierra Club and the "Archdruid" of the title, and three "developers." The first and last encounters make the best reading. The last takes place on a raft floating down the Colorado River. The encounter is with an engineer who helped build the huge Glen Canyon Dam on the Colorado. The dialogue is a superb debate over energy needs and wilderness preservation.

3. O. Bullard, *Crisis on the Columbia*, The Touchstone Press, Portland, Oregon, 1968.

   This book discusses the history of the development of the Columbia River, emphasizing the resulting environmental problems. It is highly readable and graphic.

4. J.J. Doland, *Hydro Power Engineering*, Ronald Press, New York, 1954.

   For the reader interested in more complete engineering details on hydro power, this is a good though somewhat dated survey of engineering methods and practices.

## PROBLEMS FOR CHAPTER 7

*General Problems*

7.1.  If 0.1″ of rain falls on a square mile of ground, what is the number of cubic feet of water which has fallen? What is the weight of this water? What is the potential energy with respect to the ocean if the ground is at an elevation of 1,000 feet? (232,000 cu. ft.; 14,470,000 lbs.; 14,470,000,000 ft.-lbs.)

7.2.  If the efficiency of a hydraulic turbine is 90% and an electric generator connected to it has an efficiency of 95%, what is the overall efficiency of the system?

7.3  The Bureau of Reclamation is presently building a huge new third hydroelectric power plant at Grand Coulee Dam in Washington State. Initial Congressional authorization permits six turbine-generator units, with the first three scheduled for completion by 1976. Each turbine will have a nameplate rating of 820,000 horsepower, with a 285-foot head. The penstocks will have a diameter of 40 feet; they will discharge 30,000 cubic feet per second to produce the power specified. What is the turbine efficiency? (85%)

7.4  Consider the data of Problem 7.3 above. Assuming a

generator efficiency of 98%, what is the electric power generated by each unit? (600,000 KW)

7.5. Consider the data of Problem 7.3 above. Lake Roosevelt, the reservoir behind Grand Coulee Dam, has a total capacity of 9,562,000 acre-ft. If one draws down 20% of this capacity, how long can a single unit be run? Why will the answer be approximate? (32 days)

7.6. Consider the data of Problem 7.5 above. If all six 600,000 KW units work at once, and we permit a draw down of Lake Roosevelt of 20%, how long can we run the units? What does this imply about the use of the plant for base or peak loads?

### Advanced Mathematical Problems

7.7. Assume that you wish to store a certain fixed amount of gravitational potential energy. Clearly, different combinations of W and H can be used, with the condition that the product must equal the desired value of P.E. Plot a curve of W vs. H for a fixed P.E. of 100 ft.-lbs. Repeat for P.E. equal to 200, 300, 400, and 500. The result is a "family" of curves, each of which is identified by a "parameter," its P.E. What is the shape of these curves?

7.8. Consider the problems stated in 7.7. Assume that the cost of building the reservoir is $C = 2H^{3/2}$. Write an equation for the cost as a function of P.E. and W. If W must lie between 20 and 50 feet, what is the minimum possible cost of the project?

7.9. For the system of Problem 7.7, assume the cost is $C = 2H^{3/2} + W$. If P.E. is to be 200 ft.-lbs., what is the minimum possible cost of the project, and what are the corresponding values of H, W, and C? (H = 5.36; W = 37.3; C = 62.1)

### Advanced Study Problems

7.10. Read Part 3 of *Encounters with the Archdruid* (see Additional Readings above). Indicate the strongest arguments of

Brower and Dominy. Show how these arguments relate to particular needs or desires of people. In your opinion, who wins the "debate"?

7.11. Identify a fairly complex multi-purpose water project. Indicate who benefits from the project, and how they benefit in your region. Attempt to place a quantitative (perhaps a dollar) value on the good accruing to each person or group.

7.12. Read a history of the Tennessee Valley Authority (TVA), or the Bonneville Power Administration (BPA). Indicate why the Federal Government entered into the projects, and what advantages and disadvantages have resulted.

# 8

# FOSSIL-FUEL STEAM ELECTRIC POWER PLANTS

*We bear the burden and the heat*
*Of the long day, and wish 'twere done.*
*Not till the hours of light return,*
*All we have built do we discern.*

Matthew Arnold

As Table 7–1 indicates, 318,357 MW or 72.5% of all electric capacity in 1973 came from steam power plants fired by fossil fuels. This source of electric energy will continue to be of major importance in the United States for many decades to come.

Table 8–1 indicates how much of each of the fossil fuels was used for electric energy generation in 1973. (1,2) These figures include gas turbines (Chapter 13) as well as steam electric power plants.

The use of coal for electric energy generation is increasing. The use of natural gas is decreasing. In recent years the use of oil has been rising. However, future trends in the use of oil to generate electricity are very difficult to predict because of the rapid increase in the price of oil, and the uncertainty of its availability.

Man has used fossil fuels for at least 10,000 years to produce fire, first for light, warmth, and cooking and later for the first steps toward technology. The development of the practical steam engine about 250 years ago began a new era of using nature's fossil-fuel resources to help do man's work.

A steam power plant burns fuel to turn the shaft of an electric generator. Our first goal is to describe how this task is accomplished. With a simple explanation as a starting point, we proceed to explain certain refinements which can make the system efficient and practical. This leads us to a brief look at the thermodynamic limitations of thermal processes. Then we turn to the process of combustion, with particular attention to troublesome and undesired byproducts. These discussions lead quite naturally to a consideration of the environmental problems relating to fossil-fuel plants. We conclude with a discussion of the economics of such plants.

## TABLE 8–1

### Use of Fossil Fuels for Electric Energy Generation 1973

|  | Coal | Natural Gas | Oil |
|---|---|---|---|
| Total fuel use for all purposes (1) | 570 tons | 22,850 TCF | 6,295 million barrels |
| Fuel use for electric energy generation (2) | 388 | 3,605 | 557 |
| Percent of fuel used for electric energy generation | 68% | 16% | 9% |
| Percent of all electric energy generated by fuel (2) | 46% | 18% | 17% |

A point of clarification is in order. This chapter is particularly concerned with fossil-fuel plants. Steam power plants include not only fossil-fuel plants, but also nuclear plants and geothermal plants. In this chapter we discuss first those features of steam power plants common to all of the above, and then concentrate our discussion on fossil-fuel plant considerations. In Chapter 9 we take up the peculiarities of atomic steam power plants, and in Chapter 10 we deal with geothermal steam power plants.

## 8.1 A BASIC STEAM POWER GENERATION SYSTEM

Two very primitive devices serve as examples of how steam power can be harnessed to do mechanical work. The first device, invented about 2,000 years ago by Hero of Alexandria, is sketched in Figure 8-1a. The fire heats the water to boiling. Additional heat produces steam, which travels up one of the arms into the sphere, which is free to rotate. The sphere has two

**Figure 8–1a.** Hero's Aelopile (First Century A.D.).

jets pointing in opposite directions through which the steam is allowed to flow. (A jet device has a forward thrust or force because some substance is emitted at the back.) The flow of steam causes a reaction, essentially like that of a jet engine, which causes the top sphere to rotate. This is a very simple example of a "reaction" turbine. Hero did not harness this device for any practical use.

Our second example, sketched in Figure 8–1b, is the basis of the first practical steam engine, built by Thomas Newcomen in 1712 to pump water from English coal mines. Coal was burned to produce steam which filled the cylinder above the boiler, forcing the piston to the top. The steam supply was then cut off, and water was sprayed into the cylinder, causing the steam to condense. When the steam condensed, atmospheric pressure outside the cylinder forced the piston down, resulting in the mechanical work used to operate the water pump. (We shall see this use of a spray of water to condense steam in a modern application in Chapter 10 on geothermal power.)

From this modest start, the steam engine has evolved over the past 250 years into a far more complex and efficient device. We trace a part of this evolution to indicate where we have come in the years since Newcomen.(3) Let us start with the simple system sketched in Figure 8–2.


## 8.2  TOWARD AN EFFICIENT PLANT

The system shown in Figure 8–2 will produce mechanical power which can be used to turn an electric generator. However, it will be extremely inefficient. The efficiency would no doubt be less than one percent, whereas modern steam engines have efficiencies of nearly 40 percent. How then do we alter this simple system, without changing its basic principle of operation, to achieve such efficiencies? We answer this question by considering the system in four parts:

1) The heating subsystem, including the fire

2) The steam subsystem, including the boiler and steam delivery system

3) The steam turbine

4) The used-steam disposal subsystem, including the condenser

The heating subsystem consists of those devices associated with getting the fuel to the boiler, burning it efficiently, and removing the products of combustion. The heating subsystem for a fossil-fuel plant is different from those of atomic or geothermal plants, but the other three subsystems are usually very similar if not identical for fossil-fuel, nuclear, and geothermal plants.

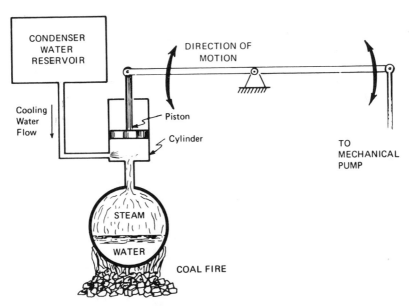

**Figure 8–1b.** Newcomen's Steam Engine (1712).

Figure 8–2 shows a very simple stationary fire. A practical large-scale fossil-fuel plant requires huge amounts of heat, and a way must be found to move in fuel and air efficiently and to remove combustion by-products. To see the magnitude of this problem, consider how much energy is available in typical fuels, and hence at what rate we must use such fuels.

Table 8–2 gives the "heating value" and the associated electric energy generation value of certain fuels. Heating value is the maximum amount of energy released when fuel combines with oxygen in a combustion process. It is commonly expressed in British Thermal Units (BTU) per pound (coal, oil) or per cubic foot (gas).

Modern steam power plants have actual efficiencies near 40 percent for fossil fuels and 33 percent for atomic fuels. These values and the above energy equivalence lead to the electric energy generation rates given in Table 8–2.

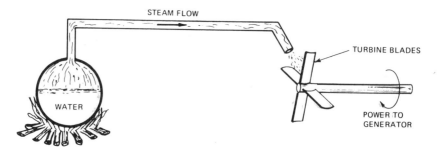

**Figure 8–2.** A Simple Steam Power System.

## TABLE 8–2

### Average Heating Values of Common Fuels

| Fuel | Heating Value | Electric Energy Generation Rate | Assumed Efficiency |
|------|---------------|--------------------------------|--------------------|
| Oil | 18,500 BTU/lb. | 2.15 KWH/lb. | 40% |
| Coal | 12,000 BTU/lb. | 1.4 KWH/lb. | 40% |
| Natural Gas | 1,000 BTU/cu. ft. | 0.12 KWH/cu. ft. | 40% |
| Uranium | 200,000,000 BTU/lb. | 17,500 KWH/lb. | 30% |

*Example 8–1*

A large modern coal-fired steam power plant, shown in Figure 8–5, was recently built near Centralia, Washington. The plant has a generating capacity of 1,400,000 kilowatts. The heating value of the coal used at this plant is 8,100 BTU/lb. Assuming an efficiency of 40%, find the tons of coal per minute needed to run this plant.

The energy produced each minute is:

$$1,400,000 \times \frac{1}{60} = 23,300 \text{ KWH}$$

The electric energy generation rate for this coal is

$$\frac{8,100 \times 0.4}{3,413} = 0.95 \text{ KWH/lb.}$$

Hence the amount of coal each minute is

$$\frac{23,300 \text{ KWH}}{0.95 \text{ KWH/lb.}} = 24,500 \text{ lbs.} = 12.25 \text{ tons}$$

This example clearly illustrates the enormous quantities of fuel required by coal plants. Large amounts of fuel are also used by plants burning other fossil fuels. It is apparent that large fossil-fuel plants must bring in, burn, and dispose of the waste of a great deal of fuel. Coal is usually brought in by train, or by conveyor belt if the plant is a so-called "mine-mouth plant." Oil is piped in or brought in by ship. Natural gas is presently piped in. However, it is possible to liquefy and transport natural gas at cryogenic temperatures by ship. In late spring of 1973, for example, the United States contracted with the Soviet Union to provide the United States with large quantities of liquid gas to be delivered by ship. In all cases the distance from the fuel source to the plant is an important economic consideration because of the cost of transportation. This factor becomes far less important with atomic plants because of their much greater energy concentration (see Table 8–2).

A very simple boiler or steam generator for a fossil-fuel plant is shown in Figure 8–3. The large outer vessel contains the fire. This vessel can be more than 100 feet in height and have a combustion chamber volume exceeding 100,000 cu. ft. The flame or hot gases heat the water which flows through many miles of tubing inside the chamber. Either coal can be introduced in chunks on a moving grate (C) or it can be blown into the chamber in a pulverized form (B). Oil or natural gas can be blown in through burners (A) on the sides of the walls. The burners look much like burners on a cooking stove, although they are much larger.

Wastes from the combustion process are released as gases

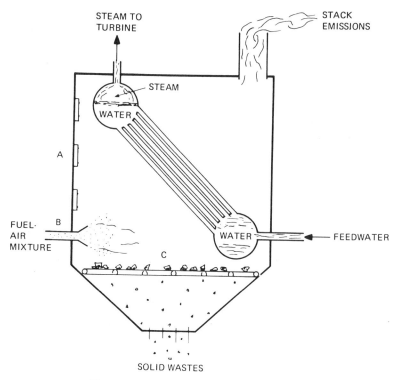

**Figure 8–3.** Boiler (Combustion Chamber).

from tall stacks and as solid wastes, such as ashes, into railroad cars for dumping.

The heat produced in the combustion process changes the water into steam. The steam flows through large pipes to the steam turbine. After it is used once, it is usually re-heated at least once and used again. We shall return to this process after discussing the steam turbine.

Today's steam engine is a multi-stage turbine. A part of such a turbine is shown in Figure 8–4. Steam enters the turbine on the left. A set of fixed blades (shown without cross-hatching) directs the steam to the moving blades (cross-hatched) which are attached to the main shaft. A typical turbine will have hundreds of blades of different lengths. The size of the turbine chamber increases from left to right—the flow direction of the steam in the drawing—because the steam is expanding as it does its work of driving the blades. In the simple steam engines we have already seen, work and steam expansion always go together. When the steam has done its work it is exhausted from the turbine into the condenser.

The purpose of the condenser is to cool the steam, causing it to condense back into water. It is then pumped back to the

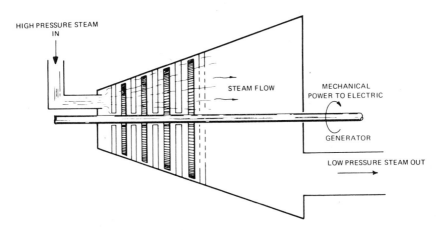

**Figure 8–4.** Modern Steam Turbine.

boiler to be made into steam again. Two very important and interesting questions come up at this point.

1) Why not just let the steam go out into the air and use some new water for new steam, thus avoiding the need to build a condenser?

2) Why cool off the exhaust steam when it is going to be reheated again by the boiler anyway?

There are at least three reasons for continually re-using the same water for steam. The first is that otherwise huge amounts of steam which would be released to the atmosphere would almost certainly cause very undesirable local weather conditions. The second is that new water would have to be introduced to the boiler continually. But water is often expensive or scarce. Many steam plants are located in areas which would not have new water available. The third reason for re-using water is that the water employed in a steam cycle must be very pure to avoid corrosion and mineral deposits in the system. It would cost entirely too much to have to purify new boiler water constantly. Saving the condensed water means saving money.

The answer to the second question above is related to one of the most fundamental laws of nature which man has been able to conceive: The Second Law of Thermodynamics, which states that it is impossible to construct an engine which, when operating through a complete cycle, will convert all of the heat supplied to it into work.

We use a condenser to cool and condense the steam because the work which can be accomplished by a heated substance operating in a closed cycle depends not only on the temperature of the gas but also on the temperature of the region into which the gas will be exhausted. The greater the difference between these temperatures, the greater will be the work which can be done. We discuss this in more detail in Section 8.3 below.

We shall want to say quite a bit more about the operation of the condenser later, since it is at the heart of one of our major environmental problems. But first we return to the steam cycle.

Recall that steam is generated in the boiler, piped to the turbine, and exhausted into the condenser. The resulting water is pumped back to the boiler. This is a very basic description of the fundamental steps. In fact a number of other things happen to the steam in its cycle in a modern plant. These added features are shown in Figure 8–6, along with most of the basic

**Figure 8 5.** Coal-burning power plant at Centralia, Washington. Two 700 MW units make up this huge fossil-fuel steam power plant. This plant, which went on line in 1972, is the first large steam plant in the hydroelectric-rich Pacific Northwest. It burns about 12 tons of coal each minute (see Example 8–1). The plant uses large electrostatic precipitators to eliminate particulate release, and it employs induced-draft cooling towers for condenser-water cooling. (Courtesy of Pacific Power and Light Co., Portland, Oregon.)

components already discussed. The primary purpose of most of these features is to increase plant efficiency. The simple system of Figure 8–2 has an efficiency much less than 1%. A modern steam power plant, using the features shown in Figure 8–6, will have an efficiency of nearly 40%.

First, consider the combustion system. Combustion requires fuel and air. Air is brought in cold as shown, and is heated by passing it through pipes in the stack. Heating the air improves the combustion process. We must be careful, however, not to remove too much heat from the stack gases. These gases contain water vapor from the combustion process. If the water condenses, it will combine with sulfur from the fuel to form sulfuric acid, which has a serious corrosive effect.

Hot air is fed to the combustion chamber to mix with the fuel. Again a critical balance is necessary. If too little air is introduced, the fuel cannot burn completely, causing waste and decreased efficiency. If too much air is introduced, work is wasted in pumping excess air, and also the excess air tends to cool the combustion chamber by absorbing heat released in the combustion process. All these processes must be monitored and regulated carefully for maximum efficiency.

We turn now to the steam generation system. Heat from combustion causes steam to form in the primary steam generation coils. The steam bubbles rise into the steam drum, where steam is temporarily stored. From the steam drum the steam goes to a superheater, which uses combustion heat to further heat the steam well above its previous temperature. This feature, with its important increase in steam temperature, is responsible for an important increase in steam engine efficiency. The steam next flows to the turbine. In modern plants the turbine has both high and low pressure stages. The steam flows first into the high pressure turbine, passing from one stage to the next past the turbine blades with a decrease in temperature and pressure at each stage. From the high pressure turbine the steam is fed back to the boiler where it is reheated, nearly to its former temperature, though at a much lower pressure. It then

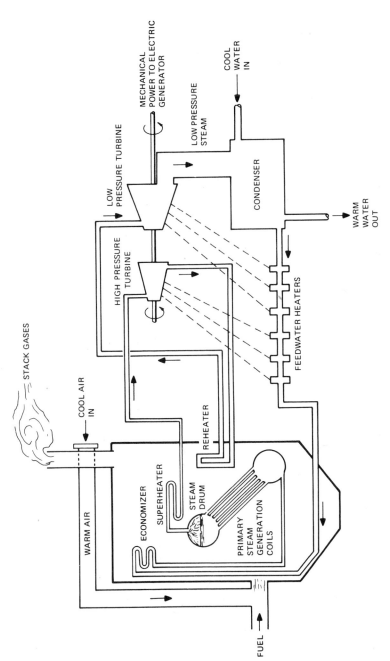

**Figure 8-6.** Modern Steam Power Plant.

175

goes to the low pressure turbine and then to the condenser. The feedwater (condensed steam) goes back toward the boiler. But it is now quite cold and it will require a great deal of heat to generate steam from it. Also the boiler would be seriously strained by the addition of this relatively cold water. Hence, it is desirable to heat the feedwater before returning it to the boiler. To accomplish this, a small amount of steam is bled off from successive turbine stages. Steam is taken from increasingly hotter stages as the feedwater gets hotter. Finally the feedwater is fed into the economizer, which is another set of tubes fairly high in the combustion chamber where the temperature has decreased somewhat. From here the feedwater goes to the boiler water drum and the primary steam generation coils where we started.

### Example 8–2

Find the rate at which steam flows in the Centralia coal plant mentioned in Example 8–1.

Each of two units at Centralia operates at 700,000 KW with an efficiency of 40%. This means that the equivalent power supplied by coal is:

$$\frac{700,000}{0.4} = 1,750,000 \text{ KW}$$

3,413 BTU is equivalent to 1 KWH. From this we see that 1 KW is equivalent to 56.9 BTU/min. Thus the heat supply rate from the fuel is:

$$1,750,000 \times 56.9 = 10^8 \text{ BTU/min.}$$

Steam tables show that for the temperature and pressure of the Centralia plant it takes about 1,400 BTU to heat each pound of water enough to cause the required steam to form. With this value and the heat supply rate we can determine the steam circulation rate for each unit.

$$\frac{10^8 \text{ BTU/min.}}{1,400 \text{ BTU/lb.}} = 71,500 \text{ lbs./minute} = 1,190 \frac{\text{lbs.}}{\text{sec.}}$$

Clearly the rate at which steam circulates through a major power plant is very large.

The final topic we shall discuss in this section is the condenser. It is the task of the condenser to cool the steam and condense it to liquid water since, as we saw earlier, the amount of work we can obtain from a given heat source depends on the reservoir, or reference temperature level available. The condenser decreases this reference temperature level. Even with a condenser, the efficiency of a modern fossil-fuel plant is around 40% and that of a nuclear plant around 30%. Of the 60% of the fuel heat which is lost in a fossil-fuel plant the great majority (50% to 55%) is carried away by the condenser. The remainder is lost in stack gases, leakage in the system, and mechanical losses. Thus the condenser must be able to carry away about 55% of the heat produced in the combustion process.

The condenser gets rid of this 55% of the fuel heat in fossil-fuel plants (or about 65% in atomic plants) by circulating "cool" water through pipes in the condenser chamber. These pipes with the cool water act as a sort of reverse radiator, cooling the condenser chamber, which leads to condensation of the steam. A condenser is shown in Figure 8–7.

Cooling water for condensers can come from a number of sources. Some are very cool and some not so cool. Common sources of cooling water include the oceans, rivers, lakes, manmade ponds, spray ponds, and cooling towers. Because the problem of disposing of a huge amount of heat in cooling waters is so critical, we shall devote Chapter 15 to the general problem of waste heat. Before we leave condensers, however, let us take a look at how much cooling water we will need.

### Example 8–3

What is the rate at which cooling water must flow in the Centralia plant of Example 8–2? Assume that the cooling water temperature rises 10°.

We need to recall that 1 BTU raises 1 lb. of water by 1° F. The

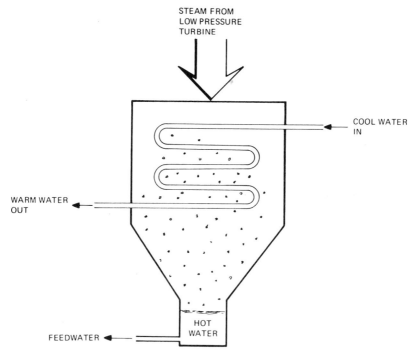

**Figure 8–7.** Steam Condenser.

heat which must be dissipated by the condenser is $0.55 \times 10^8$ BTU/min. which thus requires a cooling water flow rate of:

$$\frac{0.55 \times 10^8 \text{ BTU/min.}}{10 \text{ BTU/lb.}} = 5.5 \times 10^6 \frac{\text{lb.}}{\text{min.}}$$

Since water weighs 62.4 lbs./cu. ft. we can express the water flow rate as:

$$\frac{5.5 \times 10^6 \text{ lb./min.}}{62.4 \text{ lbs./cu. ft.}} = 8.82 \times 10^4 \text{cu. ft./min.}$$

$$= 1,470 \text{ cu. ft./sec.}$$

We shall leave to Chapter 15 the very important question of how we can dissipate the energy which the condenser's cooling water has picked up going through the condenser.

## 8.3 THE CONSTRAINTS OF THERMODYNAMICS

The Second Law of Thermodynamics states that it is impossible to construct an engine which, when operating through a complete cycle, will convert all of the heat supplied to it into work.

In this section we discuss this law in a little more detail, particularly as it applies to steam power plants. The most important general implication of this law is that, since the steam power plant is a heat engine, we cannot convert all of the energy released as heat in the combustion process into work. That is, the efficiency of the system must be less than 100%. As we saw in the previous section it is typically close to 40% for a fossil-fuel plant.

In the previous section we followed the steam through its path in the system, from boiler water into steam, out to the turbine, through the condenser and back into the boiler. This process can be referred to as a steam cycle. In the field of thermodynamics a number of ways have developed for studying this cycle. One is a plot of the pressure of the medium versus its volume, called a steam power pressure-volume (P-V) curve. A typical P-V curve is shown in Figure 8–8. The cycle shown here is a so-called ideal Rankine Cycle, which is commonly used as a standard of reference in analyzing the performance of steam power plants.

To assist in the explanation of the steam cycle, we relate it to a simple piston steam engine, also shown in Figure 8–8. Although this device looks different from a turbine or other steam engines we have discussed, its operation involves all of the same features of heat addition, steam expansion, heat subtraction, and recovery of feedwater.

The line AB in the diagram stands for the heating of the water in the boiler. There is very little volume change here. In this range, heat comes from an external source, the fuel in use. BC represents the process of evaporation or steam formation. At point C steam is released into the cylinder with the piston as far

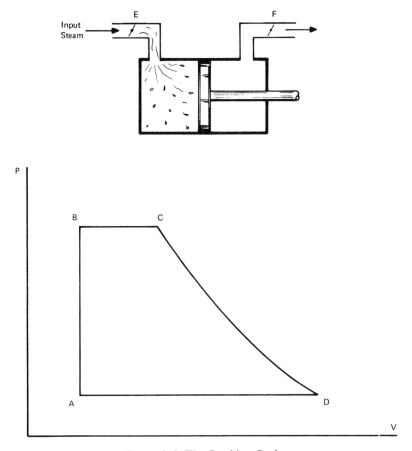

**Figure 8–8.** The Rankine Cycle.

to the left as possible. The line CD represents expansion of the
steam, and the corresponding decrease in pressure. As the steam
expands, it pushes the piston to the right, doing the work for
which the engine is intended. Now we are at a most interesting
point (D) in the cycle. Suppose we chose to leave the
now-expanded steam in the cylinder and repeat the process. We
would have to compress that steam back to its original pressure
and volume—that is, retrace the DC path. But to do so would
require the same amount of work just obtained in the expansion

stroke,* leaving us with a net zero external work. Clearly this will not do. We have a solution. At point D we open a valve (F) which releases the steam from the cylinder. Hence the piston moves back to the left without having to recompress the steam.

Now, what shall we do with the steam released at point D? We discussed this in the previous section and decided to run it into a condenser which will cool it and feed it back to the boiler. Faced with the argument as presented here, students often ask why we cannot pump the steam released through valve F back to the boiler without condensing it. One answer is that any way we chose to do this would require essentially the same amount of work as would have been required to recompress the steam in the cylinder. We would gain nothing. We must condense the steam and pump it back to the boiler as water. In condensing the steam we lose heat, which is released to the external environment in some form. There is no way to avoid this loss.

We accept this loss, undesirable as it appears to be, because of the net useful work obtained from the steam turbine. The turbine drives the electric generator. The generator in turn produces the electric energy which is the end objective of the system.

The unavoidable loss of heat is a manifestation of the Second Law of Thermodynamics. An obvious question arises. How efficient can a heat engine be? For all heat cycles the maximum possible efficiency is the Carnot cycle efficiency.[†]

$$e = \frac{T_1 - T_2}{T_1}$$

where $T_1$ is the highest temperature of the medium and $T_2$ the lowest temperature (the temperature in the condenser). Temperatures are in degrees Rankine (Fahrenheit + 460).

* Actually, a little *more* work would be required to overcome friction.

† Sadi Carnot (1796–1832), a French physicist, was one of the first persons to recognize the true nature of heat. He is best known for the ideal efficiency-temperature relationship that bears his name.

*Example 8–4*

What is the Carnot efficiency of a modern steam power plant operating at about 1,000° F? Assume that the condenser operates at about 100° F.

$$= \frac{1,460 - 560}{1,460} = \frac{900}{1,460} = 61.6\%$$

This is somewhat higher than the 40% suggested earlier. The Carnot efficiency is an ideal limit and many practical problems keep systems from reaching this limit.

## 8.4  COMBUSTION

Combustion is a rapid chemical reaction in which molecules of one substance combine with molecules of oxygen with an associated release of heat. Fuels used in the combustion process can be solid (such as coal or wood), liquid (crude oil or derivatives of crude oil, such as diesel oil) or gas (natural gas or manufactured gas).

The principal chemical elements which appear in these fuels, either in elemental form or in compounds, are carbon, hydrogen, and sulfur. The heat obtained from burning the sulfur is generally not very significant because the sulfur content is usually low in percentage. However, the sulfur does play an important role in the production of sulfur compounds, which are corrosive both in the power plant and outside it and are therefore environmentally undesirable.

Combustion takes place whenever any of these fuels is heated in the presence of oxygen to a sufficiently high temperature, called the *ignition temperature*. The latter may be as low as 470° F for sulfur or as high as about 1,200° F for methane ($CH_4$), an important constituent of natural gas. The ignition temperature is just high enough to sustain a chemical chain reaction. The heat released by one reaction must be enough to increase the energy of neighboring molecules so that they in turn react chemically with other fuel elements or oxygen, with the release of more heat. So the chain reaction proceeds. There are a great many chemical reactions which may occur. A few examples are:

Carbon to carbon dioxide
and heat $\qquad C + O_2 \rightarrow CO_2 + Q$
Hydrogen to water and heat $\quad 2H_2 + O_2 \rightarrow 2H_2O + Q$
Methane to carbon dioxide
and heat $\qquad CH_4 + 2O_2 \rightarrow$
$\qquad\qquad\qquad CO_2 + 2H_2O + Q$

Sulfur to sulfur dioxide
and heat $\qquad S + O_2 \rightarrow SO_2 + Q$

In all these reactions, Q stands for a quantity of heat released when the reaction occurs.

The reaction itself is a process in which atoms form new physical alignments and bonds resulting in new compounds, with less net energy than the pre-reaction substances. The net release of heat energy produces the steam required in the steam cycle.

In the chemical reactions above and in all conventional heat-producing reactions, the carbon, hydrogen, or sulfur comes from fuels. It is also necessary, of course, to provide a source of oxygen to the combustion chamber. Pure oxygen could be used, but it is expensive to obtain so we use ordinary air. The primary constituents are:

## CONSTITUENTS OF AIR

| Constituents of Air | Approximate Concentration | |
| | By Volume | By Weight |
| --- | --- | --- |
| Nitrogen | 78% | 76% |
| Oxygen | 21% | 23% |
| Argon | 1% | 1% |
| Others | Very Small | Very Small |

Air is clearly an excellent source of oxygen needed for combustion. It also contains nitrogen, which can combine with oxygen to form undesirable compounds, we shall see. As we mentioned in Section 8.2, it is important that the amount of air combined with the fuel be just right. Too little air leads to incomplete combustion and waste of fuel. Too much absorbs heat.

After the combustion has occurred, the resulting waste products are released to the atmosphere through stacks. The products released depend on which fuels are used. In general the important products are various compounds of nitrogen, carbon, hydrogen, oxygen and sulfur, including principally carbon dioxide, sulfur dioxide, water, and nitrogen dioxide.

In addition to the constituents important in chemical reactions, fuels also contain a certain amount of inert matter which appears as a combustion by-product in the form of ash or *particulate matter*. This is particularly true of coal and to a much lesser degree, oil. As waste, this matter appears either as an "ash heap" at the bottom of a combustion chamber, or as fine particles which are vented to the atmosphere with combustion gases.


## 8.5 THE ENVIRONMENT

Fossil-fuel power plants have a significant impact on the environment in three ways. First, they release about 60% of the heat available from their fuel as waste heat to the environment. Most of this is released from the condenser to cooling water. Second, they release miscellaneous undersired combustion by-products, in quantity and kind depending on the fuel burned and the heat of the reaction. An environmental advantage of fossil-fuel plants is that they can often be located much nearer to load centers (such as cities) than hydro or nuclear power plants. Nearby location decreases the need for unsightly transmission lines which dissipate some of the power transmitted.

We discuss the problem of waste heat, its effect on the environment, and ways of dissipating it, in detail in Chapter 15. Here we shall outline the problem briefly. Cooling water has usually come from rivers, lakes or the oceans. The most

**Figure 8–9.** Electrostatic precipitators. A bank of eight electrostatic precipitators is shown under construction at the coal-burning plant at Centralia, Washington, These hugh devices, which dwarf the workmen around them, remove over 99% of the particulate from the stack gases. Cost of these precipitators was $47 million, or about 18% of the total plant cost at this installation. (Courtesy of Pacific Power and Light Co.)

common system is "once-through" cooling, in which the cooling water is used once, and then returned to its source. The heated water causes a local increase in water temperature. The heat is then dissipated through mixing and evaporation. The effects of the local heating on the water environment are the subject of much controversy. Some environmentalists believe that added heat has been the cause of major environmental changes. They often refer to the effect as "thermal pollution." Others claim that there is little or no evidence of damage, and perhaps even some evidence of improved conditions due to heating.(4) Some have suggested that the effect might be called "thermal enhancement" or even "thermal enrichment." One compromise name, which seems reasonable for the time, is "thermal addition." We know that heat is added. We are not certain just what effect this heat has on the biological inhabitants of the cooling water source.

There are two major alternatives to once-through cooling. They are *cooling ponds* and *cooling towers*. Cooling ponds are simply holding ponds in which the heated water is allowed to evaporate. Cooling towers are devices which create a rain of hot condenser water, maximizing the contact of warm or hot water with cool air. In one form, called a wet tower, the cooling air flows past the hot water itself. In a second form, called a dry tower, the hot condenser water remains in radiating pipes, with the cooling air acting on the pipes, but not the water.

The second environmental problem relating to fossil-fuel plants is the problem of the by-products of combustion. Coal-burning plants emit huge amounts of smoke or particulate matter. This material can cover a wide neighborhood of the plant with dust. It is now possible to fit coal-burning plants with electrostatic precipitators which can remove from 99% to 99.5% of the particulate matter from the stack exhaust when they work properly. Such devices are fairly expensive. They are a good example of how the costs of "cleaning up the environment" must be paid for by the user of the product—electric power in this case. For example, the electrostatic precipitators at the 1,400 MW Centralia coal-fueled plant mentioned earlier cost just over $47,000,000 or about 18% of the total plant cost.(5) This cost must be passed on to the consumer. For a number of reasons, however, the increase in the customer's bill will be less than 18%.

The principal gaseous pollutants released from the stack are carbon dioxide, sulfur dioxide and nitrogen dioxide.

The effects of carbon dioxide are not clearly understood. It is required by plant-life for photosynthesis, but an excess may lead to undersirable effects, such as the "greenhouse" effect: A drastic build-up of $CO_2$ will raise the earth's temperature. To date there is not sufficient evidence to accept or reject the hypothesis of the greenhouse effect.

Sulfur dioxide is released principally from coal and oil, with amounts highly dependent on the original content of sulfur; this can vary significantly. Sulfur dioxide is very heavily studied as a pollutant. It is believed to have important detrimental effects on the lungs of human beings, particularly persons with other respiratory problems. It also has certain detrimental effects on some vegetation. At this time we are not certain just what effects sulfur dioxide has on the environment. One author(6) has recently suggested that such emissions may actually be beneficial under certain circumstances, particularly away from urban areas.

The major attack on the sulfur dioxide problem at this time is for government agencies to require that plants burn low-sulfur coal and oil, near one percent in content rather than three or four percent. Another partial solution is to use very tall stacks, over 1,000 feet in height. These have the effect of dispersing the undesirable gases. One disadvantage is that they are unsightly. Tall stacks are generally felt to be only a short-term solution. Other approaches are to remove the sulfur either from the fuel before combustion or from the the combustion gases after combustion. Both approaches face technical and economic difficulties at this time. Sulfur removal systems, either before or after combustion, may add as much as $50 to $125 per KW to plant cost.

Nitrogen dioxide is perhaps the major pollutant released from plants burning natural gas. The combustion process originally forms nitrous oxide (NO) as a result of the combination of nitrogen and oxygen from the air. The amount of NO formed increases with the flame temperature (at least 2,900° F is required for appreciable NO formation), and the time the combustion gases remain in the high temperature zone. The amount of excess oxygen also affects NO formation, but in conflicting ways. The amount of NO can be reduced significantly by adjusting the three factors listed above.

## 8.6  SOME THOUGHTS ON ENERGY AND POLLUTION

It is appropriate at this point to discuss briefly the problem of pollution, particularly as it arises from the generation and use of energy. There is no unique or unambiguous definition of *pollution*. We choose to define it as the side-effects or undesired consequences of any of man's physical actions which threaten the life or well-being of any living thing. Air pollution threatens the health of breathing animals, sometimes the health of plants, and the aesthetic view of observing man. Water pollution threatens the life of water-borne creatures and plants, and may make the water of no use to man. Noise pollution threatens man's tranquillity if not his eardrums. Land (aesthetic) pollution destroys the beauty of the land, taking from man a source of inspiration or relaxation, and from plants and animals a home. I imagine that we would all agree that pollution itself is bad. But there are some principles that should be understood before we leave the issue at that.

We should understand that pollution is natural. It is as natural as man. To exist is to pollute. Even man's most essential acts—breathing, eating, walking—tend to foul the air or the earth and to endanger some species. Mankind's more sophisticated acts seem to have ever greater impact on the environment. Man certainly cannot produce or use energy without causing various forms of pollution. We cannot ask that man act in a way which does not pollute. We can only ask if the level of the pollution produced can be tolerated in the light of the good which comes from the action. For many of man's activities, we have decided that the level of pollution is acceptable. However, we are beginning to question the acceptability of air pollution from cars and factories, water pollution from industries and power plants, noise pollution from airplanes near airports, and many more. We may change our views on the acceptability of given levels of pollution, but we should understand that we can never end pollution.

There has been talk in recent years of zero-release or zero-pollution systems. We should understand that in a global sense there is no such thing as zero-pollution. It *is* possible to build a treatment plant or a scouring system which would remove essentially all pollutants from a specific isolated factory or generation plant. But other plants in other locations must construct the pollution control equipment, and perhaps provide it with materials and power. All of this will pollute. We have some ability to move pollution from place to place, to isolate it, but never to eliminate it.

Finally, we must understand that it usually costs money to eliminate or abate pollution at a site or to exchange it for pollution at a less objectionable site. We will have to pay to be free of pollution. At some point there must be a compromise between our ability to tolerate pollution and our willingness to pay for its abatement. Life is of course a series of compromises, and pollution is a part of life.

## 8.7 THE ECONOMICS OF FOSSIL-FUEL PLANTS

In this section we review the economic considerations peculiar to fossil-fuel plants. The two basic cost factors, fixed costs and operation and maintenance costs, apply here as in hydroelectric plants. Also, the calculation of cost per KWH is as before. The major difference in the economic analysis of fossil-fuel plants, compared to hydro, is that fossil-fuel plants usually have somewhat lower fixed costs, but much greater operation and maintenance costs. The greater operation costs are due largely to the costs of buying and handling the fuel and handling the waste products.

Cost per kilowatt for construction of a fossil-fuel plant varies greatly with such factors as the location, size of the units, type of fuel, operating temperature and pressure, pollution control devices, and others. Average costs were close to $200 per kilowatt in 1974. Plants completed in 1977 may cost nearly $500/KW. Costs may continue to rise because of inflation and the need for new pollution-control devices.

These figures do not include the cost of cooling towers, which are being required in an increasing number of sites.

The estimated service life for modern high-pressure, high-temperature thermal units is about 30 years. This is the time period generally used in amortization calculations.

Other fixed charges include insurance and taxes, and a fund for interim replacements; that is, replacement of components which wear out during the 30-year life of the plant.

Also listed under annual capacity costs are carrying cost of maintaining a fuel inventory and operation and maintenance costs. Operation costs here include the fuel necessary for start-up or to keep the plant on the line, though not producing power. These costs are considered to be a part of fixed annual capacity cost.

The cost of energy used during generation periods is accounted for as a variable operating cost, dependent on the power demand on the plant.

These principles are illustrated by an example adapted from an FPC report(7) shown in Table 8–2. This example is for a 1,600 megawatt, coal-fired plant with a plant factor of 55 percent, fuel cost of $0.50 per million BTU, and a heat rate of 9,300 BTU/KWH. The heat rate is the number of BTU which must be supplied to obtain one KWH of electric energy. Estimates of 1975 costs are used.

The reader will note that the cost of money is accounted here in a way different from that in Chapter 4. Cost of money is indicated as 8% and depreciation as 0.9%. This assumes that the borrower pays the lender 8% of the total capital each year for

## TABLE 8–3

## Economic Analysis for a 1,600 MW Coal-Fired Plant

*Plant Factor: 55%; Fuel Cost: $.50/million BTU; Heat Rate: 9,300 $\dfrac{BTU}{KWH}$*

|  | Percent | Dollars Per Net Kilowatt |
|---|---|---|
| A. Plant Investment |  | $400.00 |
| B. Annual Capacity Cost |  |  |
| I. Fixed Charges |  |  |
| a. Cost of Money | 8.00 |  |
| b. Depreciation | 0.90 |  |
| c. Interim Replacements | 0.35 |  |
| d. Insurance | 0.25 |  |
| e. Taxes | 5.00 |  |
| Total Fixed Charges | 14.50 | 58.00* |
| II. Annual Cost of Fuel Inventory |  | 0.50 |
| III. Fixed Operating Costs |  |  |
| a. Fuel |  | 2.00 |
| b. Operation and Maintenance |  | 1.35 |
| c. Administrative and General |  | 0.80 |
| Total Fixed Operating Costs |  | 4.15 |
| Total Annual Capacity Costs |  | 62.65 |

|  | Mills/net KWH |
|---|---|
| C. Energy—Variable Operating Costs |  |
| a.Energy Fuel | 4.65 |
| b. Operation and Maintenance | 0.20 |
|  | 4.85 |

* 58.00 is obtained by multiplying 0.1450 by $400.

interest only. In addition the company puts 0.9% of the capital into a sinking fund. In 30 years this accumulated investment equals 100% of the capital, which is then returned to the lender. This is the same as if the borrower had paid 8.9% interest to the lender, in which case he would have paid both capital and interest at the same time. Hence, while the bookkeeping is different in this example, the effect is the same as it is in the example in Chapter 4. The reader can easily check this by noting in Table 4–1 that the yearly payment percentage, r, for an eight percent interest rate over 30 years is 8.9%.

The total annual capacity cost in Table 8–2 is seen to be $62.65. To find the capacity cost per KWH we divide by the number of hours of use, which is 8,760 (hours per year) times 0.55 (the assumed plant factor).

$$\text{Fixed Energy Cost} = \frac{\$62.65}{8,760 \times 0.55} = \$0.013 = 13 \frac{\text{mills}}{\text{KWH}}$$

It is seen that fuel costs and operation and maintenance show up a second time in Table 5–2 under "Energy-Variable Operating Costs." This section (C) represents costs for fuel expended in generating power, whereas section B accounts for fuel used in start-up and stand-by operations. The operation and maintenance accounting under fixed costs is that which is necessary to maintain the plant whether it produces power or not. The same item under section C accounts for special maintenance costs which depend on how much energy is produced by the plant.

Total energy costs are:

| | |
|---|---|
| Fixed Energy Cost | $13.00 \frac{\text{mills}}{\text{KWH}}$ |
| Variable Energy Cost | $4.85 \frac{\text{mills}}{\text{KWH}}$ |
| Total Energy Cost | $17.85 \frac{\text{mills}}{\text{KWH}}$ |

## REFERENCES FOR CHAPTER 8

1. News Release, Bureau of Mines, Washington, D.C., March 13, 1974.
2. News Release Number 20333, Federal Power Commission, Washington, D.C., May 24, 1974.
3. J.D. Storer, *A Simple History of the Steam Engine*, John Baker Publishers, London, 1969.
4. J.R. Adams, "Thermal Effects of Electric Power Plants," Pacific Gas and Electric Co., 1970.
5. D.G. Van Hersett, "Capital Requirements to Meet Environmental Criterion for Large Thermal Plants," Second Annual Thermal Power Conference, Washington State University, Pullman, Washington, October 8, 1971. (Supplemented by private communication subsequently.)
6. F.F. Ross, "What Sulfur Dioxide Problem?" *Combustion*, September, 1971, pp. 6–11.
7. Federal Power Commission, "Hydroelectric Power Evaluation," U.S. Government Printing Office, 1968.

## ADDITIONAL READING FOR CHAPTER 8

1. *Steam—Its Generation and Use*, The Babcock and Wilcox Co., New York, 1972.

    This is a very complete and detailed discussion of combustion systems written at a level such that the layman can understand much of the material and get from it a good idea of how such systems work.
2. J.D. Storer, *A Simple History of the Steam Engine*, John Baker Publishers, London, 1969.

    This is a very readable basic history of steam engines. The reader can learn much about the industrial revolution and about how man has harnessed steam.
3. H.C. Van Ness, *Understanding Thermodynamics*, McGraw-Hill Book Co., New York, 1969.

This is a very good short development of some of the simple thermodynamic concepts introduced in Chapter 5. Much of it can be read by persons lacking a background in physics.

4. H.F. Lund, *Industrial Pollution Control Handbook*, McGraw-Hill Book Co., New York, 1971.

This reference book provides an extensive and up-to-date review of pollution-control techniques and equipment and related control legislation. It is encyclopedic and technical, but many parts of it have value to the non-technical reader.

5. *The Economic Impact of Pollution Control*, Council on Environmental Quality, U.S. Government Printing Office, March, 1972.

This is a summary of recent studies on the cost of providing pollution control in a number of industries. It focuses on the problem of adding control costs to production costs, and it explores the implications of such actions.

6. J.C. Esposito, *Vanishing Air*, Grossman Publishers, New York, 1970.

A Ralph Nader study group produced this review of the causes, the threat, and some of the politics related to the problems of air pollution.

7. J.C. Redmond, J.C. Cook, and A.A.J. Hoffman, *Cleaning the Air: The Impact of the Clean Air Act on Technology*, IEEE Press, New York, 1971.

This is an excellent collection of engineering papers on air-pollution abatement.

## PROBLEMS FOR CHAPTER 8

*General Problems*

8.1. Find the volume of natural gas and the number of barrels of oil consumed each minute if the steam power plant at Centralia, Washington, mentioned in Example 4–1 were run on one of these fuels instead of coal.

8.2. How many acre-feet of coal are used each day by the

Centralia coal-fired plant? Assume coal weighs 85 lbs. per cu. ft. (9.5 acre-feet)

8.3. Assume a steam power plant has a condenser temperature of 100° F. Plot the Carnot efficiency as a function of the maximum steam temperature, which is $T_1$, for 100° F $\leqslant T_1 \leqslant$ 1500° F.

8.4. Write a short description of the combustion process in which carbon and oxygen are combined to produce carbon monoxide, carbon dioxide, and heat. Discuss the effects off heat, pressure and other important parameters.

8.5. Write a short paper on the effects of nitrogen oxides on plant and animal life.

8.6. Repeat the analysis of Table 8–2 for the following new conditions. Cost of money 10 percent. Plant Factor 60 percent. Fuel cost 6.00 mills/net KWH.

8.7. How many cubic feet of natural gas must be burned in a plant with efficiency 40 percent to run a 100 watt light bulb for eight hours?

8.8. Suppose that the addition of various pollution-control devices increases the capital cost of the plant of Table 8–2 by $75 per KW, and the variable operating costs by 0.2 mills/KWH. What is the new total energy cost?

## Advanced Mathematical Problems

8.9. *Heat rate* is the number of BTU which must be supplied to obtain one KWH of electric energy. Obtain a relation between plant efficiency and heat rate. Plot heat rate versus plant efficiency. On the same graph plot heat release to the condenser in BTU/KWH as a function of efficiency, assuming that 5% of the input energy is lost in the stacks or other non-condenser loss forms.

8.10. Consider a 700 KW oil-fired plant with a heat rate of 9,000 BTU/KWH. Assume that 1,300 BTU are required to heat each pound of water to the desired steam temperature and pressure. Find the steam circulation rate in pounds per second.

8.11. Consider Example 8–3. Plot the speed of the water flowing into and out of the condenser as a function of the condenser pipe diameter, for a diameter of 0 to 15 feet. What considerations affect the selection of the pipe diameter?

### Advanced Study Problems

8.12. One of the most controversial present fossil-fuel plant sites is at the Four Corners area in the Southwest. Obtain a number of references on this site. Discuss the reason for locating plants at this site, the markets for the power, and the environmental problems related to plants at this location.

8.13. Make a detailed study of methods presently available or proposed for removing sulfur from fossil fuels before combustion, or removing sulfur compounds after combustion. Find the fixed costs and the operating costs of these methods.

8.14. Write a paper on the physiological effects of sulfur and nitrogen compounds on man.

8.15. Discuss a way of deciding the maximum amount which ought to be spent on air pollution control.

# 9

# ELECTRIC ENERGY FROM NUCLEAR FISSION

*But thou shalt flourish in immortal youth,*
*Unhurt amidst the wars of elements,*
*The wrecks of matter, and the crash of worlds.*

Joseph Addison

At this writing, in the spring of 1975, nuclear fission is one of our fastest-growing sources of electric energy. (See Table 7–1.) Fission has two major advantages. First, it adds significantly to the fuels available for generating electric energy. Second, it does not lead to air pollution, as do fossil fuel plants. At the same time, nuclear energy creates an abundance of problems which need solutions, and it raises many questions which need answers. Critics and supporters alike agree that the debate over nuclear energy has not yet been concluded. The topic is

197

particularly controversial. The objective of this chapter is to describe the process and to present the arguments as fairly as possible.

By the end of 1974 there were 50 nuclear power plants, with a combined capacity of 33,000 MW, operating in the United States. About 70 more were in various stages of construction, and about 100 more were planned. As Table 7–1 indicated, the expected additions by 1983 amount to 190,000 MW. All of these data on future capacity are of course speculative, because plans change with new situations.

**Figure 9–1.** Diablo Canyon nuclear power plant. When completed in 1976 and 1977, each of the two Diablo Canyon nuclear units will produce 1,060 MW of power. The original cost estimate for the plant was $400 million, or about $200 per kilowatt. But escalating costs will raise that figure quite significantly by the time construction is complete, with an expected final cost near $450 per kilowatt. This Pacific Gas and Electric plant is on the Pacific Ocean between San Francisco and Los Angeles. It uses ocean water for once-through cooling. The cooling water outflow is shown under test. (Courtesy of Pacific Gas and Electric Co.)

Like the fossil-fuel plants discussed in Chapter 8, atomic fission power plants are thermal plants. They heat water to steam, which passes through a steam turbine, which in turn drives an electric generator. The steam cycle is essentially the same as for fossil-fuel plants except for the source of heat, which is a controlled nuclear reaction. In this chapter we shall emphasize that distinguishing feature, with little or no discussion of the basic steam cycle (Chapter 8) or the condenser cooling system (Chapters 8 and 15).

We start with an introductory look at nuclear physics, showing how energy can be obtained in a controlled way from certain nuclear, as opposed to chemical (fossil-fuel), chain reactions. We consider next how the atomic fuel is assembled in the "reactor core." We then look at a number of ways of building atomic reactors at this time. This leads us to what many people hope and expect will be the reactor of the future, the breeder reactor. Next we discuss the fabrication of the atomic fuel. We review the major environmental problems which must be faced as atomic power develops. Few environmental questions are so difficult to evaluate, and few are discussed as intently as are those relating to atomic power. At the end of the chapter, we take up some economic problems peculiar to the atomic energy power industry.

## 9.1 A SUMMARY OF NUCLEAR PHYSICS

Atoms are the basic building blocks of the things of nature. Atoms consist of a central nucleus containing protons and neutrons surrounded by rapidly moving light electrons. This structure is shown in Figure 9–2. The protons in the nucleus have a positive electric charge. The neutrons have no charge. The number of negatively-charged electrons surrounding the nucleus of a neutral atom (that is, one that has not been *ionized*), just equals the number of protons. Since both protons and electrons have the same unit charge, though it is of opposite sign in the two, the net charge of the atom is zero. At this point the

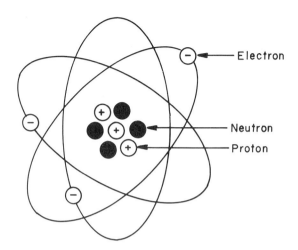

**Figure 9–2.** Atomic Structure.

atom is said to be electrically neutral—not ionized. The atom pictured in Figure 9–2 is enormously distorted in scale; the nucleus of a real atom is extremely small, with dimensions on the order of one trillionth $(10^{-12})$ of a centimeter; the centimeter is about 0.4 inches. The electrons surround the nucleus at distances about 10,000 times the dimension of the nucleus. Therefore, for the nucleus shown in Figure 9–2, the electrons should be drawn far beyond the edges of the paper.

Elements, of which there are over 100 in nature, are characterized by the number of protons in their nucleus. This number is called the *atomic number* of the atom. For example, the element hydrogen has one proton; carbon has six; silicon has 14, etc. The element uranium has 92. Their atomic numbers are 1, 6, 14, and 92 respectively.

It is possible for some atoms of any one element to have different numbers of neutrons in their nucleus, though of course the number of protons must be the same or they would constitute a different element. Atoms having the same atomic number (protons) but different numbers of neutrons are called *isotopes*. Isotopes are differentiated by their *mass number*, which is the sum of protons and neutrons in the nucleus. For example, there are 14 isotopes of uranium, three of which occur naturally. These three have mass numbers 234, 235, and 238. Their symbols are:

$$^{234}_{92}U$$

$$^{235}_{92}U$$

$$^{238}_{92}U$$

The lower left number is the atomic number; the upper left number is the mass number. The U is the letter symbol for uranium. Sometimes the lower left number is not used, since it repeats the same information as the letter symbol.

Uranium is of particular interest to us because it is the most important element used in nuclear fission energy generation today. The three isotopes mentioned above occur naturally in the following percentages:

| Isotope | Percent (by Weight) |
|---------|---------------------|
| $^{234}U$ | 0.006 |
| $^{235}U$ | 0.711 |
| $^{238}U$ | 99.283 |

Atoms can release energy in a process called *fissioning*, which can occur under certain limited circumstances. If the right isotope of the right kind of element is struck by a free neutron of the right speed (energy), the isotope can break up into two new elements, with the release of energy, and with the release of one or more additional particles or forms of radiation. It is the additional energy obtained in the fission process which can be harnessed in nuclear reactors. In order to obtain a significant amount of energy it is necessary to have the right materials under the proper conditions to set up a nuclear chain reaction, analogous to the chemical chain reaction required for combustion. In an atomic device, a chain reaction exists when sufficient neutrons are released and allowed to interact with other atomic nuclei to continue the fission—neutron release—new fission process or "chain." This chain reaction is essential if the fissioning material is to continue to release significant quantities of heat.

There are hundreds of isotopes in nature, but only a few of them can fission. Some of the most important are

$$^{232}_{90}\text{Th} \quad \underline{^{233}_{92}\text{U}} \quad \underline{^{235}_{92}\text{U}} \quad ^{238}_{92}\text{U} \quad \underline{^{239}_{92}\text{Pu}} \quad ^{240}_{94}\text{Pu} \quad \underline{^{241}_{94}\text{Pu}}$$

The four underlined isotopes have a special property. They can be fissioned by neutrons of any energy, down to zero. These isotopes are said to be *fissile*.

The three isotopes which are not underlined are said to be *fertile*. They can be fissioned only by neutrons with energies above about one million electron volts, written 1 MeV. (An electron volt is a measure of energy which an electron acquires as it passes from one point to another, with a positive electric potential of one volt between the points.) The fertile isotopes are called fertile because, when they capture a high energy neutron, they produce a fissile isotope after a short radioactive decay process.

Of all the hundreds of possible isotopes, *only* uranium-235 ($^{235}_{92}\text{U}$) *is fissile and occurs naturally*. This makes it a most important constituent of most atomic energy systems.

The process of fissioning $^{235}\text{U}$ is illustrated in Figure 9–3. A neutron is captured by $^{235}_{92}\text{U}$ transforming it to $^{236}_{92}\text{U}$, which is highly unstable. In about a millionth of a second or less the $^{236}_{92}\text{U}$ fissions (or breaks up) into two large "fission fragments," nearly equal in size, plus one or more neutrons, and gamma and beta radiation (which we will discuss shortly). The fission fragments are isotopes of new elements. There are at least 40 ways in which the original atom can fission, yielding over 80 different fission fragments. There is no way to predict which pair will be produced in a given fission. Furthermore, the resulting fragments are radioactive. That is, they emit radiation

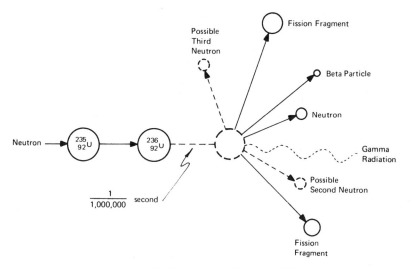

**Figure 9–3.** Fissioning of Uranium-235.

of some form, changing to a new isotope in the process. These changes continue in a chain through an average of about five states until they finally reach a stable non-radioactive state. The result of this process is that the fairly simple mix of $^{235}$U and $^{238}$U and possibly a very few other constituents originally put into a reactor becomes in time a complex of about 200 different isotopes, which may be considered waste products, although in their own right are considered valuable. Some are radioactive; some are not. Some are highly dangerous, biologically, for a long time; some are not.

This inventory of radioactive isotopes building up over months or years of plant operation is at the heart of most of the controversy related to nuclear power. It is essential that these waste products be contained, because they could be harmful or fatal to human beings if released in sufficient quantity.

Besides the fission fragments, indicated in Figure 9–3, there are also an average of about 2.4 neutrons released per fission for $^{235}$U. Some of these neutrons are lost to the reaction process, while others interact with other fissile atoms, continuing the chain reaction.Also, beta and gamma radiation are released. We shall return to a more detailed description of radiation shortly, but first we have to talk about the reason for building atomic reactors: energy.

When we add up the masses of all of the fragments and particles resulting from the fission process, we find that it is *less* than the mass of the original $^{236}_{92}U$. The mass which is lost has been changed into energy in accord with the famous relation postulated by Albert Einstein near the turn of this century:

$$E = mc^2$$

where E is energy (in ergs), m is the mass (in grams) and c is the velocity of light (about $3 \times 10^8$ meters/sec.). The energy increase resulting from the fissioning of a $^{236}_{92}U$ atom is about 200 MeV. Most of this energy (about 85%) goes into kinetic energy of the fission fragments. The rest is distributed among the other fission products, as shown below:

|                                              | Energy (MeV) |
| -------------------------------------------- | ------------ |
| Kinetic energy of fission fragments          | 168          |
| Kinetic energy of fission neutrons           | 5            |
| Energy of gamma rays                         | 11           |
| Energy of beta particles                     | 7            |
| Total heat energy                            | 191          |
| Neutrino energy (not available as heat)      | 11           |
| Total                                        | 202          |

The total heat energy is available to produce steam to drive the turbine of the electric power plant.

To see the significance of the release of 191 MeV of energy from an atom of fissile uranium, let us return briefly to the chemical reaction which takes place in combustion. When an atom of carbon combines with two atoms of oxygen to form $CO_2$, about four eV are released. This is smaller than 191 MeV by a factor of about 50,000,000.

Accounting for the difference in weights, we find that one pound of fissile material can release about as much energy as 1,400 *tons* of coal. When breeder reactors are developed, the ratio of required coal to fissile material will be far greater.

## Example 9–1

Assume that the percentage of fissile material (usually $^{235}U$) in reactor fuel is 2%. About how many tons of reactor fuel must be used each year in a plant equal to the size of the Centralia coal plant discussed in Chapter 8? How many cubic feet does this weight of reactor fuel equal? Assume a plant factor of 80%.

In Example 8–1 we saw that the Centralia plant requires 12.25 tons of coal per minute. Thus the coal required per year is:

$$12.25 \times 60 \times 8,760 \times 0.8 = 5,140,000 \text{ tons}$$

Since about 2 percent of the fuel is fissile, we require 1 lb. of uranium fuel for each $0.02 \times 1,400 = 28$ tons of coal. Thus the required uranium fuel is

$$\frac{5,140,000}{28} = 184,000 \text{ lbs.} = 92 \text{ tons}$$

Since uranium weighs 1,205 lbs./ft.³, the volume of 184,000 lbs. is:

$$\frac{184,000}{1,205} = 153 \text{ ft.}^3$$

These numbers assume complete burn-up of $^{235}U$, which does not occur in practice. Typically, a reactor of this size would have fuel replacement weights greater than the above but far less than for coal.

While it is certainly necessary that energy be released in the fission process, the neutrons released are of equal importance, because some of these neutrons will collide with other fissile atoms causing a new fission, with release of more energy and more neutrons. The object is to create a sustained chain reaction analogous to the chemical chain reaction required for combustion. There are a number of factors to consider in establishing and sustaining a safe chain reaction. We discuss some of these in later sections, and leave others to more detailed studies of nuclear reactor theory and practice.

## 9.2 RADIOACTIVITY

Radioactive materials spontaneously emit one or more of three types of radiation, called *alpha radiation, beta radiation*, and *gamma radiation*. This radiation is, in general, harmful to human beings, animals and plants, at least if the intensity is great enough. Such radiation occurs naturally in a number of forms, coming from the sun, from outer space, and from materials all around us. The world has always known such radiation, and it has always been at least potentially harmful.

Another source of radiation is in the decay of the 200 or so possible byproducts of a nuclear chain reaction. The difference between this radiation and that which the world has always known is that nuclear reactor radiation is far more concentrated, and thus potentially harmful or fatal if sufficient precautions are not taken.

We turn now to the three forms of radiation, considering their natures and their effects on man. An alpha particle consists of two protons and two neutrons. It is the nucleus of a helium atom. It is a heavy particle, capable of penetrating only a short distance into materials, depending on its speed or energy. It usually will not pass through a thin sheet of paper. It is not considered an external threat to the body. It can be very damaging if it gets inside the body. The effect of the alpha particle is to cause molecules to ionize. If this happens in a human body, unwanted chemical reactions follow and severe damage may take place.

Beta particles are electrons. They are much lighter than alpha particles. They also have a much greater ability to penetrate matter. A beta particle might be stopped by about one-half inch of aluminum. Again, this depends on the speed or energy of the particle. Beta particles also cause ionization, but, because they are lighter, they usually cause much less ionization than alpha particles. If particles have the same energy they cause the same ionization. We might ask just how much ionization a particle can cause as it moves through a material. Suppose the particle has an energy of five MeV. Since it takes an average of about 34 eV to form an ion pair, about 50,000 pairs can be formed by such a particle.

Gamma rays are essentially x-rays. They are electromagnetic waves, as are radio, television, and light waves, but x-rays are of much higher frequency. They have a very great ability to penetrate matter, requiring several inches of lead for adequate shielding. They cause the production of ion-producing particles, and they therefore can cause serious damage to the body.

It is important that we have a measure of the amount of radiation which the body receives, since this radiation can affect the health of the body. It is not a simple task to develop a universally useful unit because different forms of radiation have different effects.

The first generally accepted unit was the *roentgen*, which uses ionization produced in air as its basis. This unit relates directly only to x-rays or gamma radiation.

A more general measure of radiation is the *rad*. It is the amount of radiation which causes the absorption of 100 ergs of energy per gram of matter. This unit, however, does not take into account the relative intensity of biological damage caused by different forms of radiation.

A generally accepted unit which does consider relative damage effects is the *rem* (roentgen equivalent man).

The next obvious question is how many rems can a man be safely exposed to? This question is complex and controversial, particularly for low-level doses, as we shall see in Section 9.7 on environmental problems. For higher level doses, such as might be experienced from an atomic bomb, or from a very serious radiation accident, immediate effects are easier to predict. Doses from 0 to 25 rems would probably show no observable effect. Doses up to 100 rems would probably cause slight blood

**Figure 9–4.** Reactor-vessel delivery day. This huge 345-ton reactor vessel is the heart of one of the two 1,060 MW units at Diablo Canyon (Figure 9–1). The pipes on the near end (the bottom of the vessel) are for instrumentation. The large openings near the far end will carry pressurized water to steam generators. The vessel will rest in a concrete vault with walls six feet thick. This is the end of an 8,000 mile journey for the vessel, which was built in Chattanooga. It was barged down the Mississippi and shipped via the Panama Canal to the California site. (Courtesy of Pacific Gas and Electric Co.)

damage but little or no externally-observable effects. In the range 100 to 200 rems, "radiation sickness" may occur in some individuals, with vomiting in a few hours, fatigue, loss of appetite, and recovery in a few weeks. From 200 to 600 rems, radiation sickness will be more severe and may also be accompanied by loss of hair. Loss of life in a few weeks or months will occur for many, depending on the exposure and their state of health. More than 600 rems of exposure leads to massive radiation sickness, vomiting within an hour, severe blood change, hemorrhage, infection and loss of hair. Most persons exposed to this level die within two months.

The length of time that a material remains radioactive is usually expressed in terms of its *half-life*. Assume that a material has a certain number of radioactive atoms. These will decay spontaneously and randomly, the atom changing to some new isotope, with the release of some form or forms of radiation. The half-life of the material is defined as the time required for half of the atoms to decay. In one half-life, half of the atoms decay. In the next half-life, half of the remaining atoms decay. This process continues indefinitely. Half-lives of some radioactive isotopes are given below.

| Isotope | Half-Life |
|---------|-----------|
| Carbon-14 | 5,580 years |
| Plutonium-239 | 24,300 years |
| Plutonium-241 | 13 years |
| Uranium-239 | 23.5 minutes |

*Example 9–2*

If you start with one pound of carbon-14, how much is left in 27,900 years?

27,900 is 5 half-lives for carbon. Hence the weight is reduced by $1/2 \cdot 1/2 \cdot 1/2 \cdot 1/2 \cdot 1/2 = (1/2)^5 = 1/32$. Thus the weight is 1/32 lb.

## 9.3  THE REACTOR CORE

In this section we describe the basic structural form and components of a nuclear reactor. The essential parts of a reactor are the radioactive fuel, a moderating material, control rods, and a means of removing the heat from the reactor and getting it, eventually, to the steam turbine. (A simple core is sketched in Figure 9–5 below.)

The nuclear fuel, which is fabricated as described in Section 9.6, has the form of small cylindrical pellets about an inch in diameter and an inch and a half long. These pellets are placed in long thin cylinders and inserted into the reactor as a unit.

Fast neutrons are not easily captured by $^{235}_{92}\text{U}$, so a moderating material is required in the core of the reactor to slow down the neutrons produced by fission and needed for succeeding fissions. Neutrons are produced in fission processes with an energy close to two MeV. This must be reduced to a value

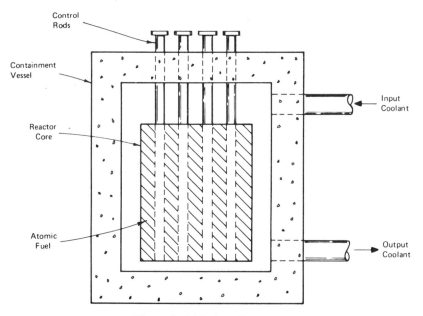

**Figure 9–5.** Nuclear Reactor.

near 0.1 eV. Moderators should contain light atoms which do not easily absorb neutrons. Water, hydrocarbons, beryllium, carbon, and some other materials make good moderators. Water is the least expensive and often the most convenient moderator. It is common practice to use the same water to carry heat from the atomic core to the steam generator.

Control rods are long cylindrical rods made of some material which absorbs neutrons, such as boron, or boron carbide and aluminum. When the control rods are inserted into the core, somewhat like pins in a pincushion, they capture neutrons, with the effect of slowing or stopping the chain reaction. Since they can be set in any desired position, they have the effect of controlling the reaction at the desired rate. They are also used as one of the safety mechanisms, since in case of an accident, they will stop the chain reaction when fully inserted into the core.

Heat is removed from the core by a circulating *coolant*. The coolant may be a gas, a liquid, or a molten solid. It is pumped through the core, where it makes contact with the hot fuel elements. It then carries the heat out of the core to be used eventually to drive the turbine. There are a number of possible forms for reactors; these are discussed in the following section.

## 9.4  FORMS OF COMMERCIAL NUCLEAR REACTORS

There are many forms in which a nuclear reactor may be built. We concentrate our attention here on the three basic forms which have been developed for commercial use in the United States. These are the *boiling water reactor* (BWR), the *pressurized water reactor* (PWR), and the *high temperature gas reactor* (HTGR). Only two of the 50 reactors in the United States are HTGR's. Of the remainder, about half are BWR's and half are PWR's. The basic form of the BWR is shown in Figure 9–6a. In this type of reactor steam is produced directly in the reactor and then fed to the turbine. This reactor operates at a pressure of about 1,000 pounds per square inch (psi). The PWR, shown in Figure 9–6b, has two loops, one in which the coolant remains inside the containment vessel. This loop uses a heat exchanger to transfer heat to a second loop, which then produces steam for the turbine. Pressures in the first loop are nearly 2,000 psi.

The BWR tends to have the higher radiation releases of the two because the coolant, which flows directly past the fuel

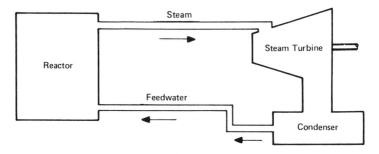

(a) Boiling Water Reactor (BWR)

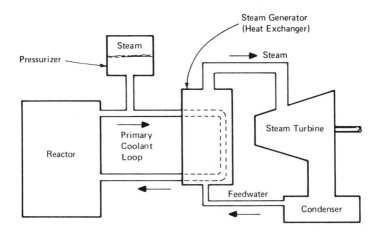

(b) Pressurized Water Reactor (PWR)

**Figure 9–6.** Forms of Water-Coolant Reactors.

elements, leaves the containment vessel to pass through the turbine. There is greater opportunity for release of small amounts of radioactive contamination from the BWR. (In the case of the PWR, the primary coolant loop is entirely within the containment vessel and the opportunity for release of radiation is reduced.)

On the other hand, the BWR is inherently safer because of the lower pressures encountered in the coolant loop. The BWR also has a safety edge because the boiling water, which itself moderates the chain reaction, becomes a poorer moderator as it turns to steam in case of an accident. This tends to slow down the reaction. Both forms have an efficiency of nearly 32%.

In addition to arguments suggested above, there are many other factors tending to favor one or the other of the two systems. Which, then, is the better of the two? There is no clear answer to this. It is not surprising that they share the commercial market almost equally.

The Atomic Energy Commission (AEC) encouraged the development of other reactor forms. One result is the High Temperature Gas Reactor (HTGR). The first commercial American HTGR (40 MWe*) was completed in 1967 in Peach Bottom, Pennsylvania. The only other HTGR (330 MWe) went into operation in 1974 at Fort St. Vrain, Colorado. A block diagram of the Fort St. Vrain facility is shown in Figure 9–7. The gas coolant is helium, which is heated to 1,300–1,500° F. Steam is produced at 1,000° F and 1,450 psi. The high steam temperature leads to an efficiency of about 40%, somewhat better than that of the PWR or BWR. Other advantages arise from better fuel utilization and longer periods between refueling. A disadvantage is a tendency for the HTGR to be more expensive, particularly for small units, than the PWR or BWR. Larger units are now available and increased interest in the HTGR is evident.

* The expression MWe stands for megawatts-electric. It is sometimes used to distinguish electric power out of a plant from thermal power into a plant.

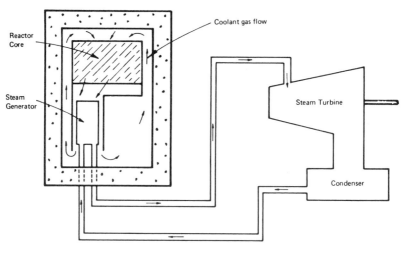

**Figure 9–7.** High Temperature Gas-Cooled Reactor (HTGR).

## 9.5 THE BREEDER REACTOR

The reactors discussed so far have been so-called "burners," because they burn up or exhaust their supply of $^{235}$U. They require a moderator to slow down the neutrons so that they can be captured by another $^{235}$U nucleus for another fission reaction. There are, however, other reactions which can take place. One reaction uses $^{238}$U, which is 140 times as abundant as $^{235}$U. It is fertile, however, and thus requires high-energy or "fast" neutrons. Such neutrons are present if we remove the moderator used to slow them down in burner reactors. One reaction with fast neutrons is:

$$n + {}^{238}U \rightarrow {}^{239}U \rightarrow {}^{239}Np \rightarrow {}^{239}Pu$$

| fast | 23.4 min. | 2.3 day | 24,000 year |
|------|-----------|---------|-------------|
|      | half-life | half-life | half-life |

Plutonium-239 ($^{239}_{94}$Pu), as we saw in Section 9.1, is fissile. This reaction, then, breeds an element which can become fissile fuel. If the reactor is to work satisfactorily as a breeder of fuel, it is necessary that more than two neutrons be emitted by the plutonium as it fissions. If, for example, an average of 2.5

neutrons are produced, one will fission an atom of $^{239}$Pu, continuing the chain reaction, and 1.5 will convert more fertile $^{238}$U to fissile $^{239}$Pu. The result is that more plutonium is produced than is consumed. The extra plutonium can eventually be used to fuel other reactors.

It must be emphasized that we are not breeding new fuel from nothing, but rather breeding fissile $^{239}$Pu from fertile $^{238}$U. Eventually we would use up all of our $^{238}$U, and also the fuel it has bred. The advantage of the breeder reactor is that it uses $^{238}$U. This increases the potential life of nuclear reactors as a power source from 30 to 100 years to perhaps thousands of years.

We cannot use water as a coolant in the breeder because it acts as a neutron moderator. One of the most popular designs presently under study uses liquid sodium. Other proposed breeders use other coolants, including gas. There are also other possible atomic reactions, including one using thorium-232 to produce uranium-233.

Much effort is presently underway to produce effective commercial breeders by the 1980s. Small breeders have been built, and some larger models have been built or are under study, particularly in the U.S.S.R. and in Great Britain. The United States effort centers on research and initial development in the 1970s. Commercial utilization has been planned for the late 1980s. However, prototype development has been experiencing very large cost overruns, such that the economic viability of the breeder has been questioned. The future of the breeder reactor program is not clear at this time.

## 9.6 FUEL FABRICATION, REPROCESSING, AND STORAGE

In this section we discuss how fuel is obtained from mines, processed for use in power plants, reprocessed after it is removed from the plant, and sent either to the original processing plants or to waste storage sites. This entire process is summarized in a block diagram in Figure 9–8.

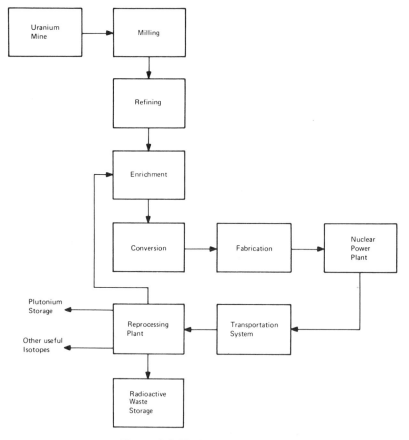

**Figure 9–8.** Nuclear Fuel Cycle.

The first step is to mine the uranium from the earth. Some is taken by open pit mining and some by underground mining. The earth's crust has a large amount of uranium, but most of it is widely dispersed. Principal sources of uranium are found in the United States, Canada, South Africa, France, Czechoslovakia and Russia. It appears in convenient concentrations in pitchblende or in uraninite, an oxide of the metal. Pitchblende has a greater concentration of uranium, but uraninite is more common. The latter provides about 95% of the uranium in the United States.

Uranium appears in uraninite in the form of an oxide of uranium, $U_3O_8$, which represents around 0.2 percent of the basic ore. The cost of producing one pound of $U_3O_8$ is about six to eight dollars at this writing. As $U_3O_8$ becomes less-easily mined and processed, the cost will go up. An important question in the nuclear power industry revolves about the amount of inexpensive uranium available. As the cost of uranium goes up, the cost of electric power generated from it will go up, but certainly not proportionally. The cost of uranium fuel is still a rather small fraction of the cost of delivered electric power. Another factor which complicates the cost analysis is that $U_3O_8$ will be far more valuable as a fuel in a breeder because utilization will be so much greater. We can afford to spend more to process fuel for breeders than for burners.

We turn now to a more detailed view of the steps involved in the fuel cycle shown in Figure 9–8. Uranium ore is slightly radioactive, and it requires some precautions in its handling. Prolonged breathing of the ore dust can be harmful. It is also necessary to handle the mine "tailings" or refuse with caution. In a recent incident a large number of homes were built in Colorado on ground using mine tailings for fill. The result is a slow release of low-level radiation in the area. (See Section 9.7.)

The $U_3O_8$ in the ore is concentrated in the milling step by a process which includes crushing, screening, washing and gravitational separation. This concentration step usually takes place near the source of the ore, so that the amount of valuable $U_3O_8$ which must be transported to other processing stages is small compared with that of the original ore.

The next step in the process is the refining step in which the $U_3O_8$ is chemically changed into either uranylnitrate hexahydrate (called "yellow cake" in the industry) or into uranium hexafluoride.

The enrichment step which follow is most important, since it is here that concentration of U-235 (normally 0.7%) is increased. This step is also quite difficult, because it involves separating isotopes which are chemically identical. Separation is accomplished by a complex process which takes advantage of the extremely small difference in mass between the isotopes U-235 and U-238. In the United States enrichment is accomplished in a gaseous diffusion process performed at plants at Oak Ridge, Tennessee; Paducah, Kentucky; and Portsmouth, Ohio. These plants are owned by the government but operated by private contractors.

The next step is to convert the enriched uranium to uranium dioxide powder ($UO_2$). This powder is pulverized and formed into small cylindrical pellets. These are the basic fuel pellets which are to be placed in the core of the reactor. At this point they are only very slightly radioactive and can be held in the hand without serious harm.

In the fabrication process the pellets are placed in long narrow cylindrical rods called *cladding*. The cladding must be strong enough to withstand many years of hot, high-pressure coolant flow. It also must allow neutrons to pass through it fairly easily without serious deterioration. Zircaloy, an alloy of zirconium, is widely used in water-cooled reactors. Fuel rods are collected in assemblies of perhaps a few hundred, with some rods left empty for control rod insertion. Fuel assembly fabrication is the most expensive processing step, and therefore it is the step in which major cost reduction is being sought.

Next the fuel assemblies go into the nuclear reactor, where they may remain for up to four years. About one fourth of the fuel is replaced each year or so. This process is necessary for a number of reasons. First, a small amount of fuel is burned up, possibly enough to slow or stop the reaction. Second, the fission byproducts tend to capture neutrons. Third, fuel elements and cladding suffer damage and distortion if left in place too long. There are at least two reasons for sending the *spent fuel* back to a processing plant rather than to *waste* storage, as we shall see shortly.

First let us consider the problem of transportation of spent fuel from the reactor to the processing plant. This is a critical step because we are now moving the highly radioactive fission products produced in the reactor core. Shipping of fuel assemblies is closely controlled by the AEC. Shipping casks must satisfactorily survive the following conditions:

1) Dropping 30 feet onto a hard surface
2) Dropping three feet onto a steel projection six inches in diameter.
3) Exposure to fire
4) Submersion in water

The reprocessing plant is the next step, first because unburned fuel can be salvaged and sent back to the processing plant, and second because plutonium and valuable isotopes can be recovered. Radioactive isotopes which are of no value and which cannot be released to the environment are sent to waste disposal sites where they will gradually decay at rates depending on their half-lives.*

The nature of the waste storage system depends on the degree of radioactivity of the waste. Highly radioactive material is stored in welded steel tanks with a capacity of 600,000 gallons. They are housed in concrete vaults, and covered with many feet of earth. Because the continued radioactive decay gives off heat, the liquid gives off heat, and it must be cooled continually. Present AEC plans call for converting wastes to a solid form for more convenient and safer storage.

There has been some suggestion in recent years that uranium fuel processing requires more energy than is produced by nuclear power plants. In fact, only about 5% of a nuclear plant's output would be needed to produce its fuel.(1) This is better than the 15% or so required for oil-fired plants and a little worse than the energy required for fuel preparation for coal-fired plants.

---

* The curious reader may wish to ponder the implications of this statement. Refer to the list of half-lives in Section 9.2.

## 9.7 ATOMIC POWER AND THE ENVIRONMENT

The major environmental advantage of atomic power plants is that they do not release large amounts of air pollutants (particulates and oxides of sulfur, carbon, and nitrogen). Fossil-fuel plants also require large quartities of fuel which in turn require many trains, pipelines, or oil tankers.

The problem of condenser-water heat addition (or thermal pollution) is the same in principle for atomic plants as for fossil-fuel plants, because both are thermal plants. However, as we shall see in Chapter 15, atomic power plants release to cooling water about 50% more heat than do fossil-fuel plants.

Four environmental problems are related to the use of nuclear power plants. These problems are:

1) Low-level release of radiation
2) High-level release of radiation
3) Diversion of atomic materials
4) Storage of waste materials

Low-level release of radiation may be expected and permitted by existing regulations, or it may be accidental. Such levels of radiation may be nearly harmless, although there is debate on this question. We refer to levels in the one to 500 millirem range. (A millirem is $1/1000$ of a rem.)

Radiation losses occur regularly in nuclear power plants because of leakages from the core or as a result of fuel or waste handling. They are relatively difficult to avoid. Typically, nuclear plants vent to the air or release into waterways radiation which would expose an individual near the plant to about one to 10 mrems per year.

Until 1971, AEC regulations permitted an exposure of 170 mrems per year to persons in the general population. The issue of the possible danger of such radiation levels was dramatically made public by two Lawrence Radiation Laboratory physicists, John Gofman and Arthur Tamplin.(2) They argued that exposing every person in the United States to these levels would result in an added 32,000 deaths per year from cancer and leukemia. Although the argument was not without flaws, it was no doubt very significant in influencing the AEC decision to reduce permitted exposure levels drastically. Present guidelines call for an exposure of five mrems per year for a person at the boundary of a plant and one mrem for large populations.

Normal background radiation and radiation from medical x-rays contributes about 100 to 200 mrems per year for each person. Hence the present guidelines would seem reasonable at this time.(1) However, these guidelines apply only to operating power plants, and not to processing plants. The latter could probably be controlled without too much added expense, and serious consideration should be given to bringing them under the above guidelines.

The second problem is that of high level release of radiation in the event of a serious accident in the plant or in various stages of processing or transportation. We do not refer here to atomic-bomb-like explosions, which are not possible with the very low concentration of fissile fuel in reactor cores. It *is* physically possible, however, to have serious or even catastrophic releases of radiation as the result of certain types of accidents. One serious and potentially dangerous accident is the loss-of-coolant accident, in which the lines carrying coolant to the reactor burst or the coolant pumps fail. This keeps the coolant from carrying heat away from the core. Control rods are immediately inserted into the core to stop the chain reaction. However, if the fuel has been in the core long enough to build up a sizable inventory of radioactive fission fragments or byproducts, this decaying radiation will contribute significant heat. The result may be a melt-down of the core. There is no material which can really contain this very hot core, and it will melt through containment structures into the ground. Where it will stop or spread to is not known. This possibility is sometimes referred to as the *China syndrome*.

Another possible accident involves the rupture of the outer

containment vessel when the coolant lines break. This could permit the release of massive amounts of radiation into the air.

These and other accidents *can* happen. But how probable are they, and how serious would they be? Both questions are essentially impossible to answer. We have had too little experience; the nuclear industry is changing far too rapidly, and there are many unknowns. However, in an attempt to answer the questions about reactor safety partially, in 1972 the Atomic Energy Commission (AEC) initiated the *Reactor Safety Study*. This study is so important to the story of reactor safety that it requires some detailed discussion.

The study was carried out over two years at a cost of three million dollars. About 60 persons worked on the team, headed by Professor Norman Rasmussen of the Department of Nuclear Engineering of the Massachusetts Institute of Technology. The study was sponsored by the U.S. Atomic Energy Commission, and was done principally at AEC headquarters. Ten team members were AEC employees. Others came from national laboratories, private laboratories, and universities. In August, 1974 the AEC released a draft report which is usually referred to, for brevity, as WASH-1400.(3)

The essential conclusion of the AEC's WASH-1400 is that " ... the risks to the public from potential accidents in nuclear power plants are very small."(3) To quantify the degree of risk in an understandable way, the report compares the probability of death from a nuclear accident with death from a number of other causes, including air crashes, fires, car crashes, explosions, tornadoes, earthquakes, and others. The AEC report finds that the probability of death from a nuclear accident is much less than the probability of death from any of these other causes.

The techniques used in the study are called *event trees* and *fault trees*. The basic principle is to itemize all of the components of a plant pertinent to reactor safety, to assign a probability of failure to each component, and to use mathematical logic and probability theory to deduce the probability of a given type of reactor accident. The mathematical analysis itself is usually not questioned, since it follows a prescribed set of mathematical rules which are relatively easy to accept or reject. Critics usually center their attention on the quality of the data used—the individual probabilities in this case—or the completeness of the analysis.

When the AEC issued its WASH-1400 draft in August of 1974, it invited comments from interested parties. Some expected critics responded immediately that they simply did not believe it. More serious analyses came in the weeks and months following. (See, for example, Reference 4.) The debate over WASH-1400 and reactor safety in general has only begun. The report has the great advantage that it has formalized and structured the debate over nuclear safety. Given the study, and the early response to it, we are left in the end with the basic conclusion that we do not really know how safe nuclear reactors are. Perhaps the final paragraph in the WASH-1400 summary best sums it up.

Decision making processes in many fields, and especially in safety, are quite complex and should not lightly be changed. This is especially true where a good safety record has already been obtained, as is so far true for nuclear power plants. The use of quantitative techniques in decision making associated with risk is still in its early stages and is highly formative. It appears that for the near future considerable additional development is needed in quantitative techniques before they can be used effectively in safety decision making processes.

The third problem we consider is the danger of diversion or stealing of nuclear fuel, particularly when it is being transported. This problem will become more serious with the introduction of breeder reactors, which will have significant supplies of plutonium-239. It would be relatively easy to use this material in the construction of a small atomic bomb. Such a device could be used by terrorist groups, small countries, or blackmailers. In 10 to 20 years huge amounts of spent fuels will be transported, with increasing opportunity for diversion.

Finally, we consider the problem of the storage of undesired nuclear wastes. Such wastes are radioactive and hot, and some of them must be stored for tens of thousands of years. The amount of such wastes will increase rapidly. We have the problem of finding a way to contain these wastes safely. Containment vessels tend to deteriorate because of the heat and

**Figure 9–9.** Floating nuclear power plants. One of the more imaginative solutions to the problem of siting nuclear power plants is shown here. The Public Service Electric and Gas Company of New Jersey has contracted with Offshore Power Systems to develop a pair of floating nuclear plants in the Atlantic Ocean, three miles off the New Jersey coast. The ocean here is about 40 feet deep. The plants are protected by an enormous breakwater 300 feet wide at the base and 30 feet wide at the top. The breakwater is designed to withstand winds, waves, and storms of much greater magnitude than have been observed in this location. Together, the plants will generate 2,300 MW. Condenser cooling will raise the temperature of a few acres of the surrounding ocean by about five degrees Farenheit. Power will be transmitted to the land by 345,000-volt cables buried beneath the sea. The cutaway drawing shows the reactor vessel and steam generators on the left, and the steam turbines and electric generators on the right. (Courtesy of Public Service Electric & Gas Co.)

radioactivity of their contents. Attempts are underway now to find a way to solidify wastes and to store them in underground vaults such as salt mines. Salt is relatively impervious to the flow of liquids. More exotic waste-disposal schemes suggest sending wastes into the sun in rockets. A final philosophical question is this: Does one generation have the right to create waste problems for dozens or hundreds of later generations to manage?

In the end we are left with the basic question of whether the dangers of atomic energy justify the good of additional energy. We might hope to answer the question by turning to the Atomic Energy Commission, which was the regulatory agency for nuclear power. Unfortunately, for most of its life the AEC played the role of promoter as well as regulator. As such its credibility as regulator was sometimes questioned. For example, in 1957 the AEC issued an analysis of the results of a major hypothetical accident.(5) The study suggested that in the very unlikely event of a major accident, deaths could occur up to 15 miles, and injuries up to 45 miles. About 3,400 people could be killed and 43,000 injured. Property damage could be as high as seven billion dollars. The report caused such a strong response that the AEC did not release another major safety analysis report until the above-mentioned Rasmussen Report (WASH-1400) in 1974.

In early 1975 the Atomic Energy Commission was broken up. Its regulatory duties were taken over by the newly-created National Regulatory Commission (NRC). Nuclear research and development responsibility was given to the new Energy Research and Development Administration (ERDA). We must assume that NRC and ERDA will pursue the question of nuclear safety vigorously.

No one can say today how safe nuclear reactors are. But we need to know the answer as accurately as possible. The stakes are too great. A catastrophic accident would have at least two serious effects. First, it would result in many deaths and much property loss. Second, it would strike a major blow at the use and development of atomic power in this country. The effect on a growing "energy crisis" would be another catastrophe itself.

## 9.8  THE ECONOMICS OF ATOMIC POWER

The cost of electric energy generated by nuclear power plants is, as with all power plants, the sum of fixed charges and operation and maintenance charges. These costs are very difficult to estimate for design of present-day nuclear plants, and even more difficult to predict for the plants of the future. Cost estimates are much more difficult for nuclear plants than for hydroelectric or fossil-fuel plants for a number of reasons. For instance, it is difficult to estimate the cost of building the plant. We have relatively few examples to give us experience, and some early plants were partially subsidized by the government so that their cost and construction time are difficult to estimate. Furthermore, some companies underbid costs of early plants to gain entrance into the business. Also, there has been a great deal of inflation, particularly of labor costs. Finally, rapid changes in technology have occurred, along with changes in environmental or safety standards or requirements.

Fuel costs are perhaps somewhat less troublesome to predict, but the estimation process is highly complex because the spent fuel has a recovery value. Some of it is directly useful as fuel; other elements have other immediate uses, while still others can be stored for future use.

The low point in nuclear energy costs occurred in 1966, when TVA decided to build a plant at Brown's Ferry at a cost of $116 per KW, with an energy cost of 2.30 mills per KWH.

Since that time costs have been rising steadily. Present plant construction costs fall in the range of about $450 to $600 for plants completed in 1976. Plants scheduled for completion in the early 1980s may cost as much as $1,000/KW. This might suggest that the competitive position of nuclear energy *vis-a-vis* other forms (primarily fossil-fuel in 1975) is declining. However, as we have seen, the cost of fossil fuels, as well as the cost of air

**Figure 9–10.** San Onofre nuclear power plant. The San Onofre generating station provides 450,000 KW of electricity for Southern California Edison Company and San Diego Gas and Electric Company—enough power to supply a city of well over half a million population. Nuclear components are housed in the steel containment sphere near the center of the picture. The Pacific Ocean, in the background, is the source for water for once-through cooling. Note the major excavation almost 70 feet down from the 100-foot bluff. Lowering the plant decreases the pumping head for ocean cooling water. (Courtesy of Southern California Edison Co.)

pollution control, is also rising rapidly. It is impossible to predict today the relative economic position of nuclear power in 1980 or 1985.

In Table 9–1 we show a calculation of fuel costs which indicates the relative cost levels.(6) We now use this figure in an example of total cost of energy for a hypothetical plant.

In Table 9–2 we calculate the total energy for a 1,000 MW plant, assuming a 60% plant factor. The final result of 17.50 mills/KWH is probably an acceptable (competitive) price in many parts of the United States at this time. Again, the reader is cautioned that nuclear energy costs are highly variable at present, and the examples given here should be considered only as expressing approximate relationships among the various cost factors.

## TABLE 9–1

### Nuclear Fuel Costs (First Core Fueling)

| | Mills/KWH |
|---|---|
| Raw Fuel ($U_3O_8$) at \$14/lb. | 0.08 |
| Conversion and Enrichment | 0.48 |
| Fabrication | 0.55 |
| Reprocessing and Shipment | 0.25 |
| Gross Direct Fuel Costs | 2.08 |
| Less: Spent Uranium Credit | −.15 |
| Plutonium Credit | −.28 |
| Total Credits | −.43 |
| Net Direct Fuel Costs | 1.65 |
| Fixed Charges and Interest | .40 |
| Total Fuel Cost | 2.05 |

## TABLE 9–2

### Total Nuclear Energy Costs

**Power = 1,000 MWe**　　　　　　　　　　　　　**Plant Factor = 60%**

| Fixed Charges | Capital Cost (\$1,000) | Cost of Money (%) | Annual Cost (\$1,000) | Unit Cost (mills/KWH) |
|---|---|---|---|---|
| 1. Depreciating capital —power plant, etc. | \$600,000 | 13 | \$78,000 | 14.85 |
| 2. Nondepreciating capital | | | | |
| a) Land | 500 | 11.5 | 580 | 0.01 |
| b) Operation and maintenance | 1,000 | 11.5 | 115 | 0.02 |
| c) Fuel cycle operations | 10,000 | 11.5 | 1,150 | 0.16 |
| 3. Liability insurance | | | 500 | 0.07 |
| Annual fixed charges | | | 79,823 | 15.11 |
| **Operating Costs** | | | | |
| 1. Operation and maintenance | | | 2,400 | 0.34 |
| 2. Fuel cost including capital cost | | | 11,530 | 2.05 |
| Operating costs | | | 13,930 | 2.39 |
| TOTAL ENERGY COST | | | 93,753 | 17.50 |

## REFERENCES FOR CHAPTER 9

1. R.E. Lapp, *The Nuclear Controversy*, Fact Systems, Greenwich, Conn., 1974.
2. A.R. Tamplin and J.W. Gofman, *Population Control Through Nuclear Pollution*, Nelson-Hall, Co., Chicago, 1970.
3. *Reactor Safety Study: An Assessment of Accident Risks in U.S. Commercial Nuclear Power Plants (Draft)*, Summary Report, U.S. Atomic Energy Commission, Washington, D.C., August, 1974.
4. "EPA Cites Errors in AEC's reactor Risk Study," *Science*, Vol. 186, No. 4168, Dec. 13, 1974.
5. "Theoretical Possibilities and Consequences of Major Accidents In Large Nuclear Power Plants, WASH-740," USAEC, March, 1957.
6. Federal Power Commission, *The National Power Survey*, U.S. Government Printing Office, 1970.

## ADDITIONAL READING FOR CHAPTER 9

1. G. Bryerton, *Nuclear Dilemma*, Ballantine Books, Inc., New York, 1970.

   This is an interesting and reasonably balanced summary of the promise and problems of nuclear power. It centers on a particular proposed plant in Oregon. Besides describing nuclear reactors in laymen's terms, it also discusses in some detail the political actions which were taken in Oregon by opponents of the plant. The result is interesting, informative, and highly readable.
2. D. Nelkin, *Nuclear Power and Its Critics—The Cayoga Lake Controversy*, Cornell University Press, Ithaca, N.Y., 1971.

   This book also discusses a particular controversy, this time in New York State. There is ample political discussion, and in addition this book is concerned to a significant degree with the heat addition (or thermal pollution) problem.

3. J. Stokeley, *The New World of the Atom*, Ives Washburn, Inc., New York, 1970.

This is a comprehensive review of the use of atomic energy in a wide variety of ways. Although it is written about the technical aspects of the problem, it is quite readable. It is suited to the non-scientific reader who wants to know more about atomic energy.

4. R. Curtis and E. Hogan, *Perils of the Peaceful Atom*, Ballantine Books, New York, 1970.

This is one of a large number of strongly written books with the thesis that nuclear power is perhaps too dangerous to use. After presenting its view of the truth, it closes by asking the question: 'Knowing this truth, do we dare continue gambling against Fate?"

5. A.W. Kramer, *Understanding the Nuclear Reactor*, Technical Publishing Co., Barrington, Illinois, 1970.

This is a fairly short, somewhat technical book, which expands on the material presented here in Sections 6.1 through 6.6.

6. Pederson *et al.*, *Applied Nuclear Power Engineering*, Cahners Books, Boston, Mass., 1972.

This is a technical book requiring an engineering or physics background. However, it is written at an introductory level and it is not hard to follow.

7. S. Glasstone and A. Sesonske, *Nuclear Reactor Engineering*, Van Nostrand Reinhold Co., New York, 1967.

This is a comprehensive graduate engineering text in nuclear engineering.

8. R.V. Moore, *Nuclear Power*, Cambridge University Press, 1971.

This partly technical book reviews nuclear technology but also discusses nuclear power from another country's viewpoint. It is of particular interest for this latter feature.

9. D.R. Inglis, *Nuclear Energy—Its Physics and Its Social Challenge*, Addison-Wesley Publishing Co., Reading, Mass., 1973.

This is a good general survey of the use of nuclear energy

in electric energy generation, atomic bombs, and medical purposes. Armament control, use of bombs and nuclear testing are discussed.

10. R.S. Lewis, *The Nuclear-Power Rebellion*, The Viking Press, New York, 1972.

The author wrote this non-technical book when he was also editor of the *Bulletin of Atomic Scientists*. In dramatic style he outlines some of the severe problems of nuclear power generation and shows how alert citizens have been able to challenge long-range expansion plans which could be or which are dangerous to the biosphere. For example, Chapter 6, "Boot Hill," describes in urgent terms what can happen when radioactive wastes leak, as they are now doing in Richland, Washington, and what can happen when bureaucracy decides to appropriate specific tracts of land for further waste storage.

11. Reference 1.

This is a very fine survey of the nuclear reactor controversy. It presents the major arguments raised against nuclear power, and then it gives responses to these arguments. It is interesting and easily read.

## PROBLEMS FOR CHAPTER 9

### General Problems

9.1. How many pounds of $^{235}U$ are there in one ton of uranium? (14 lbs.)

9.2. Explain what is meant by $^{239}_{94}Pu$. Indicate all of the information given.

9.2. What is the difference between fissile and fertile isotopes?

9.4. Make a chart of the three forms of radiation discussed in this chapter, comparing the structure, relative weights, ability to penetrate matter, and biological effects.

9.5. Explain the purpose of control rods, moderators, coolant, and containment vessels.

9.6. Explain the meaning of the term LMFBR, indicating the significance or meaning of each letter.

9.7. How many pounds of mine waste are produced to obtain one pound of $U_3O_8$?

9.8. What percentage of all the energy produced in 1964 was used by nuclear processing plants?

9.9. List the major advantages and disadvantages of nuclear power.

9.10. If a radioactive material has a half life of 10 years, what fraction of the material remains at the end of 40 years?

## Advanced Mathematical Problems

9.11. What is the approximate amount of mass lost by $^{236}_{92}U$ when it fissions?

9.12. How many half-lives are required for 99.9% of a radioactive material to decay?

9.13. Draw a logarithmic chart of the effect of various levels of radiation in mrems. Plot the mrems vertically, and indicate significant levels such as background radiation, AEC limitations, fatal exposure levels, and common power plant levels.

9.14. Assume that the percentage of power generated by atomic plants rises exponentially from 1 percent in 1970 to 50 percent in 2000. a) Find the percentage of power generated by atomic power of 1980 and 1990. b) Plot the percentage of power generated by atomic power from the year 1970 to 2000. Use semi-log plotting paper. c) What is the doubling time for percentage growth?

9.15. For the example given in Section 9.8, find the energy cost in mills/KWH if raw fuel costs increase from $14/lb. to a) $50, b) $200.

9.16. For the example given in Section 9.8, find the maximum acceptable cost of raw fuel if it is competing with fossil fuel available at 20 mills/KWH.

## Advanced Study Problems

9.17. Write a short paper indicating whether or not you favor the further growth of atomic power. Give your reasons.

9.18. Write a short paper on the history and future development plans of the breeder reactor. Include a forecasted timetable of development milestones such as date of first active large-scale plant, date when breeder plants could produce a significant amount of power (say 10 percent of U.S. capacity), etc.

9.19. Read at least two articles or books on reactor safety written by proponents (see, for example, power industry journals available in most libraries), and two written by opponents (environmental magazines, or Reading 4 or Reference 2 above). Compare specific points of disagreement, and decide whether you can make a decision about safety based on the evidence given. You will have to evaluate this evidence critically.

9.20. Study and report on the history and critical reaction to the AEC document WASH-1400. (See References 3, 4, and more recent developments which should become available.)

9.21. Read an Environmental Impact Report for a nuclear power plant. Summarize the most important factors of the report. Discuss how the report will be used by the government.

# 10

# GEOTHERMAL ENERGY

*A power is passing from the earth*
*To breathless Nature's dark abyss.*

William Wordsworth

The interior of the earth is a mass of very hot and sometimes molten rock. The heat from this region is a huge potential source of natural energy which can be used for the generation of electric power at many places in the world. In this chapter we talk about where geothermal development is possible and why. We then center our attention on the major development presently underway in the United States.

The basic principle of geothermal generation is that steam is used to drive a turbine, as in thermal plants fueled by uranium or by fossil fuels. The essential difference in geothermal power is that the source of heat which produces the steam is the earth's interior. This heat is tapped by wells drilled as much as two miles into the earth.

## 10.1  PANGAEA AND TECTONIC PLATES

One of the most fascinating aspects of geothermal power is that it is closely linked to a newly-evolving and extraordinary hypothesis about the earth's geological history. Scientists now believe that the world once had only one land mass called Pangaea (all lands), and that the present continental land masses resulted from the breakup of Pangaea and the movement of certain earth masses over the past 200 million years.[1] South America broke away from Africa, North America from Europe, and in perhaps the most spectacular dash of all, India raced from Antarctica at a speed of perhaps inches per year, until it smashed into Southern Asia, creating the Himalayas.

The earth has an outer shell or crust (or *lithosphere*) about 50 miles thick. This is broken into perhaps ten major pieces called *tectonic plates*. For reasons which are not clear these plates move with respect to each other, thereby rearranging the earth's land masses. The boundary lines between plates, which are thus cracks in the earth's crust, are called "rifts." Along these rifts tearing or scratching takes place as one plate moves past the other. When such tearing occurs it is felt as an earthquake on the surface of the earth. One such famous rift area is near the west coast of the United States. The San Andreas Fault, whose movement caused the disastrous 1906 quake in San Francisco, is associated with this rift. (According to present theory Los Angeles should drift along the west coast rift area as far north as San Francisco in about 10,000,000 years.) Other major rifts are located near other parts of the world which typically experience severe earthquakes. These include Japan, western South America, Turkey, and many others.

If the moving plate theory and some of its implications are

true, then it is no coincidence that most of the earth's geothermal power sites are located near rifts. Or, to tie in the factor above, geothermal sites are often located in major earthquake zones. Volcanic activity is also common in such areas.

There is an explanation in the plate theory justifying geothermal sites near rifts. It is theorized that at cracks or rifts in the earth's crust, hot molten material can seep or well up from the earth's interior to within a couple of miles or so of the earth's surface. Here the hot material may encounter underground water, resulting in steam or hot water. Sometimes this steam or hot water reaches the earth's surface naturally, appearing as geysers or hot springs. At geothermal sites, wells are drilled to reach the best steam or water available.

## 10.2  GEOTHERMAL ENERGY

Geothermal heat almost certainly originates with magma (molten rock) which is relatively near the earth's surface, probably for the reasons suggested in the previous section. Figure 10–1 suggests how the earth's interior heat may be converted to steam or hot water. The lower layer is the hot magma. It is covered by an impermeable crystalline rock perhaps one to two miles thick, which transfers heat up to a layer of porous rock. This layer is topped by a layer of less-permeable matter. Water finds its way down to the porous rock, and because of the heat transferred up from the magma, the porous rock region acts almost like a boiler in changing the water into hot water, wet steam, or dry steam. Sometimes this water or steam escapes to the earth's surface, appearing as fumaroles (emissions of hot gases or steam) or geysers (emissions of a mixture of steam and hot water).

Geothermal steam or hot water is obtained by drilling down into the porous rock "boiler." The best possible product of a geothermal well is steam that is hot, dry, and clean. It should be

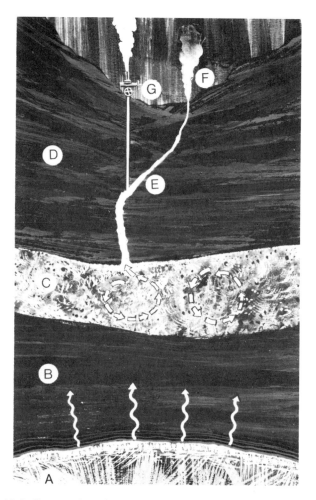

**Figure 10–1.** Cross section of geothermal region. In certain places throughout the world, nature provides just the right combination of circumstances to produce steam which can be used for geothermal power production. Hot magna (A) wells up within a few miles of the earth's surface, near crustal fracture lines. Heat from the magma passes through a region of low-permeability (that is, nearly solid) rock (B) up to a zone of porous rock (C). Region C is nature's boiler. Here, water that has seeped down, usually over decades, is transformed into steam. A low permeability layer (D) caps the boiler to hold the steam. Thin breaks (E) in the cap let steam escape and appear at the surface as geysers or fumaroles (F). Then man drills a well (G) to capture the steam for use in a geothermal plant. (Courtesy of Pacific Gas & Electric Co.)

hot to make the thermal plant efficiency high. It should be dry—containing few water particles—to minimize the heat loss to the water and the corrosion resulting from wet steam. Finally, it should be clean; that is, it should contain as few mineral impurities as possible, because impurities cause turbine corrosion and leave undesired mineral deposits on the earth's surface.

The quality of the medium varies greatly from one site to another. The best sites produce fairly hot dry steam; the poorest produce hot water with a high concentration of minerals. The likelihood that a site can produce economically feasible geothermal power is closely related to the quality of the medium.

At some sites the steam or water, pumped up from one to two miles down, is as much as 50 to 100 years old. That is, it has taken that amount of time for surface water to seep down through the low-permeability top layer into the steam-producing porous-rock region. This suggests that steam beds may be exhausted in time since replacement water is so slow in reaching the underground "boiler." Artificial insertion of water through old wells or dry wells may or may not turn out to be practical. At the only site where geothermal plants have been operating for many years, wells have dried up in 20 to 30 years. There is not sufficient experience or thorough understanding of the mechanism to predict how long new wells may produce steam. When a well does dry up, it is often possible to drill a new well in the same general vicinity. In other cases a particular steam field may become exhausted. This uncertainty factor is important in an industry which is responsible for meeting the power demand of its customers reliably.

## 10.3 GEOTHERMAL POWER AROUND THE WORLD

The rifts or breaks in the earth's 30 mile deep crust are widely spread over the earth's surface. Hence it is not surprising that geothermal power has been developed or is being considered in many countries around the world.(2) Ten countries have developed or are constructing geothermal plants. An additional 14 or more countries are also seriously considering this form of power. The ten active countries are shown in Table10–1 below. (Adapted from References 2, 3, and 4.)

Use of geothermal heat for space heating certainly predates man's earliest histories. The first important generation of geothermal *electric* power came in Larderello, Italy in 1904. At first this source lit only a few lightbulbs. In time, however, it became the major source of power for Italy's electric railroads. Today (1975) it is the second largest operating geothermal source in the world. The Geysers system north of San Francisco in the United States has moved into first place in capacity with 502 MW in mid 1975. It is anticipated that about 100 MW will be added at the Geysers each year for at least the next few years.(4) The fields at the Geysers and at Larderello, plus one at Matsukawa in Japan, are the only three active sites presently producing dry (slightly superheated) steam.

Other nations are developing plants with lower-quality steam. Such plants tend to be more costly than dry steam plants. It is impossible to give a comprehensive picture of world geothermal activity because new fields are constantly being

## TABLE 10–1

### Active Geothermal Production

| MW  Country | 1974 MW | Planned Additions | Total |
|---|---|---|---|
| El Salvador | 0 | 60 | 60 |
| Iceland | 3 | 32 | 35 |
| Italy | 390 | 0 | 390 |
| Japan | 32 | 150 | 182 |
| Mexico | 75 | 75 | 150 |
| New Zealand | 170 | 0 | 170 |
| Taiwan, China | 0 | 10 | 10 |
| Turkey | 0 | 30 | 30 |
| USSR | 5 | 26 | 31 |
| United States | 306 | 506 | 902 |

explored and ways to utilize low quality heat are being sought. The prospects for world-wide development are truly extraordinary, but it is too early to say where these prospects lead. Rather than try to summarize the world picture, we turn now to a discussion of the United States, where a highly successful geothermal power plant complex has been developed in a dry steam field, and where solutions are being sought in a very wet and very contaminated field.

## 10.4 GEOTHERMAL POWER IN THE UNITED STATES

Development and exploration of geothermal power in the United States have been largely limited to the State of California. Some important exceptions include the discovery of some dry steam in Yellowstone National Park (Wyoming), development of a 10 MW plant near Brady, Nevada, and the use of geothermal heat in about 400 buildings in Klamath Falls, Oregon. A large number of other sites, particularly in the western United States, no doubt justify and will experience exploration.

The major success in the United States is The Geysers in northern California, which we describe in detail in the next section.

A plan under study in the United States calls for exploding an atomic bomb deep beneath the surface of the earth and using the trapped heat to generate steam.(3)

Without a doubt the greatest interest in an untapped potential geothermal source is in the Imperial Valley—Salton Sea area of southern California. Estimates have been made that this region might yield as much as 20,000 to 30,000 MW of electric power, nearly equal to the present *total* power capacity in the State of California. Study of this potential is being spurred by the successful development of the Cerro Prieto plant (75 MW) just 20 miles or so south of the border in Mexico. Cerro Prieto steam is relatively wet and contaminated by minerals. To the north in the United States the geothermal medium tends to be much more contaminated in wells drilled to date. Such wells, in this region, offer three opportunities for commercial development. The first is geothermal electric power. The second is the production of minerals from the medium, including potash, lithia, salt, calcium chloride, manganese, copper, lead, and silver. The third is the production of desalinated water in a very dry region. Obstacles to development include the corrosive effect of the minerals and the necessity of getting rid of the residue, probably by pumping it back down a dry well.

The extraordinary heat reserves in southern California have recently led to great optimism about the prospects for this region. Evidence of heat concentrations in the area south of the Salton Sea comes from infra-red satellite photographs, surface temperature tests, and some preliminary drilling. A Bureau of Reclamation document describes a very ambitious plan for research and development over a seven-year period.(5) This would be followed by a demonstration program which would combine power generation and water desalination. One hundred twenty five thousand acre-feet of water would be pumped from the Salton Sea; 100,000 acre-feet of desalinated water would be returned to the Salton Sea to control the salinity of that body. Twenty five thousand acre-feet would be used in cooling towers (see Chapter 15) for 420 MW of geothermal power. Power cost would be a highly attractive five mills per KWH. The final stage of the project would deliver 2.5 million acre-feet of desalted water annually to the Colorado River and would produce 10,500 MW of power.

A recent *Wall Street Journal* article indicates an optimism for development in this area suggested by major land leases and well drillings by large energy corporations.(6)

Will this great potential resource be developed? The answer hinges principally on whether the technological problems can be solved at a cost which is competitive with alternative generation schemes. It will certainly be most interesting to watch this area.

## 10.5  THE GEYSERS

The Geysers area, located about 75 miles north of San Francisco, California, is the fastest-growing geothermal power producing region in the world. In 1975 it had a capacity of 502 MW. Future development could lead to a total capacity of 1,000 MW by 1980. Estimates of the final capacity of the field range from 2,000 to 4,800 MW.

All of the power presently generated at this site belongs to the Pacific Gas and Electric (PG&E) Company. The present capacity represents a little less than 4% of the company's present total generation capacity. This figure will increase by about one percent of total capacity per year for at least the next two years.

Units built in recent years have been 55 MW plants. Each such plant receives steam from about 10 wells. In 1974 a single 110 MW plant was built. In general, geothermal plants tend to be smaller than other thermal plants because of the lengths of steam pipes required to feed a large plant. Wells must be separated by some minimum distance to avoid overlap of steam demand. Between 20 and 40 acres are typically dedicated to each well. If a very large plant were built it would be necessary to pipe steam in from greater distances with a corresponding loss in heat and increase in pipe costs.

Wells at The Geysers are drilled to depths ranging from 3,000 to 9,000 feet. The bottom of the producing field has not yet been reached. Also, it is not known whether or not there is a single large reservoir about seven miles in length by two miles in width or a series of smaller pockets of steam. Steam wells produce from 50,000 to 150,000 lbs./hr. of dry steam. Gaseous impurities average about 1% of the steam flow. The most noticeable gas released is hydrogen sulfide, which causes a slight odor of rotten eggs in some parts of the region. The steam also contains a small amount of rock dust.

It is believed that the wells at The Geysers can and will be depleted. Accordingly, capital investment is being amortized over the expected (or guessed-at) life of the reservoir.

Steam at The Geysers is supplied to PG&E by three independent companies: Union Oil, Thermal Power, and Magma Power. They make geological studies, drill wells, build roads, build steam lines to the plants, and return certain waste products back into the ground via dry wells, as will be discussed later.

We see how PG&E uses the steam obtained from its suppliers

**Figure 10–2.** The Geysers geothermal site in Northern California. Far below the surface of the earth, the immense heat of the earth's core creates great pockets of steam which can be used to drive turbines. Steam at the Geysers site is hot and clean, making it a very attractive source of energy. The life of such steam pockets is very difficult to estimate. Other sites are under exploration in the United States and around the world. (Courtesy of Pacific Gas and Electric Co.)

through a discussion of a typical Geysers geothermal power plant, sketched in Figure 10–3.

Hot dry steam comes in at the upper left from suppliers' pipelines. It is first passed through centrifugal separators which remove any rock particles or dust from the steam. (At other sites around the world such separators may be used at this point to separate steam from water or water vapor, if the medium is fairly clean and dry. At more contaminated sites the geothermal medium is not used directly in the turbine but is used to produce steam in a closed loop through some kind of heat exchanger.)

The hot steam next passes through a rather low pressure steam turbine. The pressures available here are not comparable to the much greater pressures generated in conventional modern thermal plants. The expanded steam passes out of the turbine. At The Geysers it goes to a condenser. A reasonable question is why we do not simply vent the used steam into the air, since there is no problem here of recycling the steam-water as in most thermal plants. There are two answers. The first is that the expended steam contains impurities which are undesirable in the environment. The second reason is that the condenser works at a *back pressure* (4″ Hg. compared to atmospheric pressure near 30″ Hg.). This back pressure is like a high quality, though not perfect, vacuum which helps "suck the steam out of the turbine." This has the effect of increasing the efficiency of the plant. Even with the condenser, efficiency is low (around 15 percent) because steam pressure and temperature are low. Thus relatively more steam must be used here to generate a given amount of power, compared to a modern thermal plant. But the steam is inexpensive and no boiler or fuel is needed, so the cost turns out to be competitive with that of conventional plants.

The condenser used is a so-called "barometric condenser." Steam flows into the condenser, where it encounters a spray of cool water which condenses it by contact. This is the same basic principle used in Newcomen's engine (see Figure 8–1b). When the steam condenses, it leaves behind a high quality vacuum. The effect is that the condenser acts much like a huge water

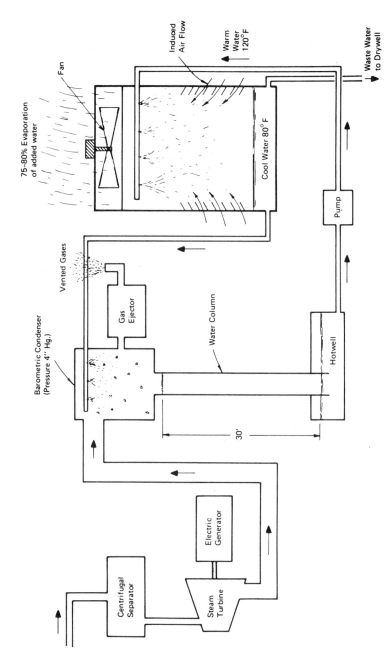

**Figure 10–3.** Typical Geothermal Power Plant at the Geysers.

75–80% Evaporation of added water

Fan

Induced Air Flow

Warm Water 120° F

Cool Water 80° F

Waste Water to Drywell

Pump

Vented Gases

Gas Ejector

Barometric Condenser (Pressure 4" Hg.)

Water Column

Hotwell

30'

Electric Generator

Centrifugal Separator

Steam Turbine

barometer, with the water column in the barometer's pipe standing about 30′ above its "hotwell" pool, which is at atmospheric pressure.

### Example 10–1

On the earth's surface atmospheric pressure is about 30″ of mercury (Hg.). That is, a column of mercury in a cylinder with an evacuated and sealed top and a bottom immersed in mercury which is exposed to the atmosphere will rise to a level of about 30″ at sea level. Find the height of water in a water barometer at sea level.

The specific gravity (in comparison with water) of mercury is 13.546. Since water is this factor lighter than mercury, we would expect it to rise by that factor more than mercury.

$$30'' \times 13.546 = 407'' = 34'$$

Since the back pressure in the condenser above is 4″ we can expect a water rise of:

$$26'' \times 13.546 = 353'' \cong 30'$$

The steam from the ground contains a certain amount (about 1%) of gases which do not condense. If these were allowed to accumulate in the condenser they would gradually destroy the vacuum. A three-stage, steam-driven, gas ejector is used to remove these gases. The ejector requires about 5% of the steam used in the plant.

From the hotwell at the bottom of the condenser, water is pumped to the top of a forced-draft wet cooling tower. (See also Section 15.3.) The water is sprayed down (at 120° F) over baffles which slow its descent, as air is pulled in from the sides by a fan (which looks much like a propeller) at the top of the tower. By the time the water reaches the bottom of the cooling tower, which is 50–75′ in height, its temperature has been reduced to about 80° F. About 75–80 percent of the water circulated through the tower is evaporated into the atmosphere. Of the remaining cooled water a part is pumped back to the barometric condenser to use as the spray water in the condensation part of the cycle. About 20% of the water, containing most of the undesired contaminants, is returned to the ground.

## 10.6 ENVIRONMENTAL FACTORS

From an environment standpoint, geothermal power is generally considered to be quite "clean," or desirable. It is necessary, however, to take certain precautions to protect the environment, depending on the local conditions.

One advantage of geothermal power is that it does not use up irreplaceable fuels, unless we consider the heat lost from the earth's interior. This heat, however, is so huge that there is no way that significant amounts could be taken from the earth by geothermal power even if it were developed at many times its present level for hundreds or thousands of years.

A second advantage is that relatively small areas of land are used compared to land use in the other "free-fuel" systems, namely hydro- or solar power. Large fields with well-heads, steam pipes, power plants, and cooling towers might cover a few square miles. There is sometimes excessive noise due to escaping steam, and minor odors from escaping gases. These factors as well as aesthetic concerns may make geothermal plants undesirable as near neighbors, but the effects should not extend to very great distances.

A major potential problem concerns the possible destructive effects of contaminated waste water. Fortunately, it is usually possible to dispose of such wastes, when necessary, in an acceptable way. As an example, early in the history of The Geysers, waste waters were released to a nearby creek. It was found that these wastes contained ammonia, which is harmful to fish, and boron, which is harmful to plants. Today all waste water at The Geysers is returned to the earth through non-productive wells. Other areas must deal with wastes in similar or alternative ways, as appropriate.

Another possible problem is *land subsidence* (sagging or falling of land) resulting from the removal of large amounts of steam or water from the ground. Relatively little evidence is available as yet on the likelihood of subsidence. Some subsidence has occurred at oil field sites, and at geothermal sites in Mexico and

**Figure 10–4.** Geothermal exploration. Engineers drill for geothermal steam near Mono Lake in Eastern California. It has been estimated that major parts of the western United States may yield geothermal energy. But first we must find the steam, and then harness it. Whether geothermal power will make major contributions to the nation's energy needs or not is one of the questions for the rest of this century. (Courtesy of Southern California Edison Co.)

New Zealand. One approach to the problem is to re-inject water into the the ground.

Similarly, little is known about possible seismic effects. Earthquakes could be triggered by geothermal activity such as water re-insertion. Conceivably, however, the opposite effect may occur. Water insertion in seismic areas has often been suggested as a way to reduce the danger of major earthquakes by inducing minor quakes. The water acts as a lubricant to help the tectonic plates slide.

Geothermal plants will release a large amount of waste heat to the environment. Whether or not this release is environmentally serious is difficult to say.

So it appears that there are some important questions about the environmental effects of geothermal power production. On balance, however, this approach to generation is perhaps as attractive as, or more attractive than, any present alternative.

## 10.7  GEOTHERMAL POWER ECONOMICS

It is difficult to summarize the economic status of geothermal power because costs are highly dependent on the country where the site is located, and on the quality of the steam or water available. In determining whether geothermal power is economically desirable, it is of course also necessary to consider the costs of alternative generation schemes. These costs vary greatly from one region to another. In countries where hydro power is plentiful, geothermal power may not be competitive. However, we can say fairly generally that geothermal power, using good quality steam, is quite likely to cost less than any conventional thermal process, atomic or fossil.

At Larderello, Italy the KWH cost is about 3.2 mills.(2) At Matsukawa, Japan costs range from 4.6 mills/KWH for a 20 MW plant down to an expected 3.1 mills/KWH for a second plant. At The Geysers in the United States costs have varied from 4.5 to 5.0 mills/KWH in the initial plants. More recent costs are somewhat higher. The capital costs of new units are increasing because of inflation in construction costs. Steam costs have also increased.

Steam can be obtained by the utility company producing the power, or it may be purchased by them from independent companies. The latter arrangement may be convenient or perhaps even necessary if the steam fields are not owned by the utility, or if regulations prohibit the utility from speculative explorations.

At The Geysers, the steam is owned by three independent companies and sold to PG&E for a price which includes the cost of returning waste material to the earth. The price which PG&E pays for steam is related in a complex way to the cost of thermal energy from other sources used by PG&E. Because the cost of fossil fuels has risen dramatically, the cost of steam has also risen. In 1972 steam cost about 2.7 mills/KWH. In early 1975 the cost was 7.39 mills/KWH.(4)

The total fixed and operating costs of geothermal electric energy at The Geysers in early 1975 was about 12 mills/KWH. This was certainly much higher than the cost in 1972, but it is much lower than fossil fuel energy costs. Only hydroelectric energy is less expensive.

## REFERENCES FOR CHAPTER 10

1. R.S. Dietz and J.C. Holden, "The Breakup of Pangaea," *Scientific American*, October, 1970, pp. 30–41.
2. G. Facca, "General Report on the Status of World Geothermal Development," *United Nations symposium on the Development and Utilization of Geothermal Resources*, Pisa, Italy, 1970.
3. P. Kruger and C. Otte, *Geothermal Energy, Resources, Production, Stimulation*, Stanford University Press, Stanford, California, 1973.
4. Personal communication, Pacific Gas and Electric Co., San Francisco, California, March 4, 1975.

5. "Geothermal Resources Investigations—Imperial Valley, Calfornia," Bureau of Reclamation, January, 1972.

6. E.C. Gottschalk, Jr., "Steam Below Ground Seen Giving Big Boost to U.S. Energy Supplies," *Wall Street Journal*, March 20, 1975.

7. D.B. Barton, "The Geysers Power Plant—A Dry Steam Geothermal Facility," Geothermal Resources Council Meeting, El Centro, California, February 16–18, 1972.

## ADDITIONAL READING FOR CHAPTER 10

1. *Continents Adrift*, W.H. Freeman and Co., San Francisco, 1973.
      This is a very interesting collection of readings from *Scientific American* on continental drift and its relation to various phenomena such as earthquakes and the earth's heat. Geothermal power is not discussed directly.

2. D. Tarling and M. Tarling, *Continental Drift*, Anchor Books, Doubleday and Co., Garden City, N.Y., 1971.
      This book also discusses geologic factors relating to geothermal power, but does not consider such power directly.

3. M. Goldsmith, "Geothermal Resources in California—Potentials and Problems," *Environmental Quality Laboratory Report No. 5*, California Institute of Technology, December, 1971.
      This is an excellent general review of the geothermal potential in California. It is written at a semi-technical level.

4. "The Economic Potential of Geothermal Resources in California," Geothermal Resources Board, State of California, January, 1971.
      This report stresses economic factors relating to geothermal development. It also reviews briefly some of the potential areas of future growth.

5. J.R. McNitt, "Exploration and Development of Geothermal Power in California," *Special Report 75*, California Division of Mines and Geology, 1965.
      This document is not as up-to-date as 3 and 4, but it does

have an interesting historical and geological review of California geothermal power development. It also includes some technical material on geothermal power plant configurations.

6. Reference 3 above.

This is an excellent general reference on geothermal energy. It is a set of technical papers from a conference held in 1972. Even though there is much detail for the engineer working in the field, there is still much that can be understood by any student wishing more information on geothermal energy.

## PROBLEMS FOR CHAPTER 10

### General Problems

10.1 Consider Figure 10–3. If 75–80% of the condensed steam ends up being evaporated and vented by the cooling tower, what advantages are there over simply venting the steam out of the turbine?

10.2. List the possible environmental problems related to geothermal power and indicate solutions where such exist.

10.3. At The Geysers power plant, forced-draft cooling towers are driven by 150-horsepower fans (or propellers). Five such towers are required by each 55 MW plant. Determine the approximate percentage of the 55 MW generated that must be used to drive these fans. (About one percent)

10.4. What factors might tend to increase the costs of geothermal power in areas where the medium is hot, dirty water rather than dry steam?

### Advanced Mathematical Problems

10.5. What would be the height of a column of methyl alcohol in a barometer at sea-level pressure (say about 30″ Hg.)?

10.6. For the example given at the end of the chapter, plot the cost of energy versus plant factor for a plant factor ranging from 50 to 90%.

## Advanced Study Problems

10.7. Discuss the role geology plays in the generation of power by hydro, fossil-fuel, nuclear, geothermal and tidal schemes. That is, describe how geology affects each scheme.

10.8. Construct a table of locations on the earth where two or more of the following phenomena are common: earthquakes, geysers or fumaroles, volcanos, geothermal power exploration, any other correlatable phenomena. Note that you are not *proving* a necessary connection by this identification, but only pointing out where certain phenomena coincide. Such evidence is certainly not sufficient to prove any major geological hypothesis about the earth's crust, though it might be used in partial support of a theory.

10.9. Describe in more detail than is given here the most recent commonly accepted concept or hypothesis about the form of the earth's interior, its source of heat, its major components, and its history.

# 11

## *SOLAR POWER*

*The clouds dispell'd, the sky resum'd her light,*
*And Nature stood recover'd of her fright.*

John Dryden

Energy from the sun gives life to the earth. Without it we would have no vegetation, no winds, no rain, no life. Earth would be a dead and barren planet. But of course the sun does warm the earth continuously, and man has always made use of the sun's energy. It is the ultimate source of all of our energy, with the exception of nuclear energy and, possibly, geothermal energy.

The solar power which falls upon the earth is an immense 177 trillion KW ($1.77 \times 10^{14}$ KW), which is 500,000 times the electric power capacity of the United States. Hence the available energy from the sun is far in excess of our foreseeable future needs. Can we find a way to harness this energy, though? That is the question we shall explore in this chapter. We consider three schemes which have been developed to some extent or which have been proposed.

1) Small heating and cooling systems
2) Orbiting space stations
3) Ground-based thermal plants

These examples do not exhaust the possible configurations, but they are representative of projects presently under consideration or development.

## 11.1  SOLAR-POWER DENSITIES

Table 11–1 lists the approximate solar-power density incident upon the earth, above the atmosphere as well as at the earth's surface. The energy from the sun near the earth but beyond the atmosphere is expressed in terms of a *solar constant*.(1) Even this presumably constant value varies slightly, depending on the condition of the sun (number of sunspots, distance from sun to earth, and so forth). The second row in Table 11–1 gives the solar-power density for a clear day with the sun directly overhead.(2) The third row accounts for the fact that the sun is not directly overhead very long; the row entries, therefore, average the power over eight hours of the sun's apparent motion. Finally, the fourth row takes account of the fact that, over a year's time, the sun varies considerably in its noontime angle from an overhead position. The figures given assume a latitude of about 40°.

Still other factors, which have not been considered, will decrease the average available power still further. These include cloudy days, air pollution or smog conditions, averaging over night-time hours, and the conversion efficiency of the

## TABLE 11–1

### Approximate Solar-Power Densities

| Condition | Watts per sq. in. | Watts per sq. ft. | Watts per sq. yd. | MW per sq. mi. |
|---|---|---|---|---|
| In space near earth (solar constant) | 0.90 | 130 | 1,170 | 3,630 |
| On Earth, sun overhead; clear day | 0.64 | 92 | 830 | 2,570 |
| On Earth, sun overhead; clear day, 8 hour average | 0.54 | 78 | 710 | 2,180 |
| On Earth, 40° Latitude; clear day, 8 hour average | 0.37 | 53 | 480 | 1,490 |

proposed solar power plant system. All such factors must be examined in the initial study of a potential system at a given site.

## 11.2 SMALL HEATING AND COOLING SYSTEMS

According to Table 11–1, on a clear day one-half KW or more may be incident on each square yard in a middle-latitude region. A typical home may have available perhaps 10 to 100 square yards (on a roof, for example) which would permit collection of about 5 KW to 50 KW of power averaged over eight hours. A larger building, such as a school or a commercial building, may have as many as 1,000 or more square yards available. The school shown in Figure 11–1 has more than 500 square yards of solar collector area.

Solar heating of small buildings is established and rapidly growing in the United States. The National Science Foundation recently funded two successful proof-of-concept experiments, providing solar heat for a grade school in Timonium, Maryland (Figure 11–1), and a high school in Dorchester,

**Figure 11–1.** Solar energy in action. This solar scheme, installed in an elementary school in Timonium, Maryland, was one of two proof-of-concept experiments sponsored by the National Science Foundation in 1974.(3,4) Ten banks of solar panels, with over 5,000 square feet of surface area, collected enough solar energy to supply 90% of the heat required by this wing of the school in the spring of 1974. It is expected that systems of this type will be economically feasible as alternate fuel prices rise and solar-system construction costs decrease. (Courtesy of AAI Corporation.)

Massachusetts (3,4). Other medium scale experiments are under way in many parts of the country. On a smaller scale, scores of houses in the United States use solar energy.(5)

The basic concept or application of solar heating is quite simple. Let us start with a very basic system, and work up to a practical solar heating system available today.

Most people have observed that a garden hose which has been left out in the sun emits warm or hot water for a few seconds when the faucet is turned on, until all the water standing in the hose has passed through. Perhaps the simplest of "solar plants" employs a suitable length of black hose (to absorb radiation) placed in the open sun. Such a system will produce a bit of warm water, depending on the weather conditions, which could be used for bathing or washing clothes or dishes. System cost is the cost of an old black hose.

The next step is to build a box to hold the hose, and to cover it with one to three sheets of glass which allow solar radiation to enter but trap most of the infrared heat energy produced by the sun. This is essentially the *greenhouse effect* (4) which is used to grow plants, and which also operates on a global scale with carbon monoxide acting as an atmospheric trap for infrared energy. This system will cost quite a bit more money and produce quite a bit more heated water than the black hose for the same collection area. This is an excellent example of a *capital-intensive* system, in which the initial investment is very important to the success and effectiveness of the system, and operating and maintenance costs are of little importance. In this case, of course, there is no "fuel" cost, but it will be necessary to perform occasional maintenance tasks such as cleaning the glass, removing corrosion from the pipes, and painting the system. Such costs should be a small fraction of the energy costs for this system.

The system above can be modified almost indefinitely, increasing the efficiency and the cost with changes in the shape of the collector, its orientation with respect to the sun, the convective losses of the water pipes (formerly black hose), and many more.

A typical plumbing diagram for such systems is shown below in Figure 11–2. This is actually the diagram for the Timonium School pictured in Figure 11–1. The solar collectors, seen as slanted panels in Figure 11–1, collect the heat energy from the sun. Insulated pipes carry the hot water to a well-insulated storage tank. From the storage tank, water is delivered to classrooms as needed. Heat storage is crucial to the success of solar heating systems, because the sun's energy is not available at night and on cloudy days. As a general rule, adding storage to solar heating systems increases both their value and their cost.

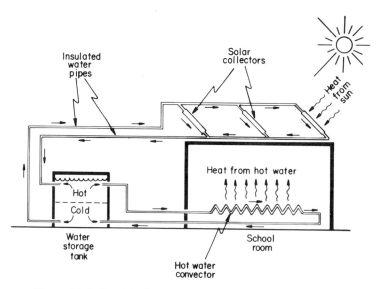

**Figure 11–2.** Graphic Representation of Solar Heating System.

The Timonium Elementary School solar heating system was designed, manufactured, and installed in 45 days. This provides dramatic evidence of the relative simplicity of such systems. Simplicity permits their rapid installation. In a number of previous chapters, we have observed that it will take years or decades to develop major new central power plants or new energy industries. In the case of small solar heating systems, however, the technology already exists, and it can be implemented readily.

The economic viability of such systems is not yet clear, however. The Timonium experiment indicated that installation costs were about double those necessary for the system to compete with oil fuel systems. If fuel costs increase and solar heating system costs decrease, solar heating may be economically feasible. The school installation above is only one example, of course. Many systems being built around the country appear to compete successfully with other sources of energy.

So far we have emphasized only heating. A solar cooling or refrigeration cycle is also quite credible, although somewhat more complicated. A cooling cycle will require additional equipment, with its added costs, but will also save the energy of electric air conditioners.

There are not as yet any economically viable solar schemes for producing electricity at small local sites. To date solar electric panel costs and storage battery costs have been prohibitive.

## 11.3  SPACE SYSTEMS

In the previous section we saw that small local solar plants have not been widely adapted to electric power generation, and are also sensitive to the presence of sunlight. A highly imaginative scheme has been proposed by Glaser(7) to convert solar power to electric power on a continuous basis.

Glaser proposes the use of a huge satellite, far above the earth's surface, in a *synchronous orbit*. That is, the satellite would be at such a height (22,300 miles) that its speed of rotation around the earth would be just equal to the speed the earth rotates. In this way the satellite is always over the same place on earth. A very large solar panel would be used to collect the sun's energy and convert it into electricity. One way to accomplish this task is to use a solid-state semiconductor diode, a relative of the transistor, which converts solar energy to electric energy. (See also Reference 8.) Such solar cells have an efficiency of about 10 to 15 percent. The electric energy generated by these solar cells would be used to drive a powerful microwave beam which would be transmitted to earth. The scheme is outlined in Figure 11–3.

This scheme has four critical components: 1) the solar panel, which must collect the sun's energy efficiently and convert it into electricity; 2) the satellite controller, which must maintain the position of the satellite panel with respect to the sun and

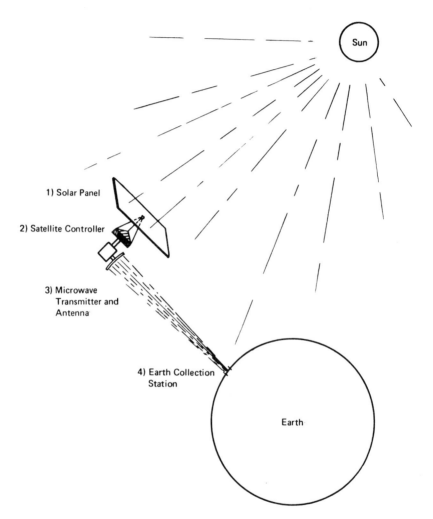

1) Solar Panel

2) Satellite Controller

3) Microwave
Transmitter and
Antenna

4) Earth Collection
Station

Sun

Earth

**Figure 11–3.** A Solar Power Plant in Space.

antenna with respect to the earth; 3) the microwave transmitter and antenna, which must change the available electric energy into microwave electromagnetic energy and transmit it in a highly concentrated and directed beam back to earth, and 4) the earth's receiving antenna site. Each of these critical elements presents serious technological problems which must be solved before the scheme can be implemented. We consider each of these problem areas briefly.

First we consider the solar collection panel. Such devices have been used for years to provide electric power for satellites. Power to run a satellite may allowably be very expensive, but commercial power must be competitive in the marketplace. So we must expect any proposed system to be able to produce energy at perhaps six to 10 mills per KWH. Economy of scale effects suggest that we will probably wish to build very large solar plants, of perhaps 10,000 to 25,000 MW. The cost of solar cells is presently about $400 per square foot.

## Example 11-1

Consider a plant of the type described above, with a total overall efficiency of 8%, a desired power output on earth of 12,000 MW, and a plant factor of 80%. Find the cost of energy due only to the capital costs of the solar cells.

An output power of 12,000 MW and an efficiency of 8% requires an input power of:

$$\frac{12,000}{0.08} = 150,000 \text{ MW (solar)}$$

Referring to Table 11-1 we see that the solar power intensity near the earth is about 3,000 MW/sq. mi. The required collection area is 50 square miles, which means a square panel about seven miles on a side, or a round panel of diameter about eight miles. Solar cells now cost about $400/sq. ft. or about $10,000,000,000 per square mile. Hence the total cell capital cost is approximately $500,000,000,000 (500 billion dollars).

Assume we amortize the capital (if we could find it) over 50 years at 6%. Referring to Table 4–1 we see that an annual payment of 6.3 percent, or $31,500,000,000 is required. A plant factor of 80% means the number of hours per year the plant is used is:

$$8,760 \times 0.8 = 7,008 \text{ hours}$$

Hence the total energy produced is:

$$7,008 \times 12,000,000 \text{ KW} \cong 84,000,000,000 \text{ KWH}$$

Finally, to find the energy cost per KWH due to the capital cost of the panels alone we divide capital cost by energy

$$\frac{\$31,500,000,000}{84,000,000,000} = \frac{\$0.375}{\text{KWH}} = 375 \text{ mills/KWH}$$

It is clear from the above example that solar panels are prohibitively costly and inefficient at this time. It will be necessary to reduce costs drastically or increase efficiency of panels before such plants can become financially feasible. It is not obvious at this time that this can be done, but there are some possible alternatives to present cells, such as organic cells, or vastly improved inorganic single-crystal semiconductors, which may in the future permit the cost-efficiency combinations necessary to justify commercial solar cell panels.(9)

The reader will note that we have not, of course, completely analyzed the costs of orbiting 50 square miles of solar panels. The weight of such a panel might be 10,000 to 50,000 tons. Shuttle systems presently under consideration could build such space stations. The costs of orbiting and building are very difficult to estimate, but they would certainly be quite significant.

We consider next the problem of the position of the satellite. It would be necessary to provide constant control to maintain the correct synchronous orbit, as well as panel and antenna orientation. Such control would be essential and probably within the present state of technology.

A second problem related to satellite position is that for short periods during the year, near the equinoxes, the satellite is in the earth's shadow. That is, it does not see the sun. During these periods it would not be able to transmit power back to earth. It has been suggested that a solution to this problem is to place two satellites in orbit such that one is always in the sun. The theory is that power would then never be interrupted at the receiving site. This approach appears to have a serious economic flaw. Most of the capital cost of the system would probably be in the satellite system, rather than the ground receiving station. Hence, once a satellite is orbited, it is highly desirable to use it as much as possible. We would no doubt want to have both satellites transmitting energy back to earth, using this as baseload. The problem then is that when one satellite is shadowed, the baseload drops by 50 percent. Hence the problem has not changed significantly from that of the single-satellite problem.

The third problem concerns the microwave transmitter and antenna. No single microwave transmitter tube can handle anywhere near 10,000 MW, but 10,000 of them might generate 1 MW each with only a fairly minor extension of the state of the art. The antenna would need to be about one mile in diameter to concentrate a beam which would radiate onto an area on earth of perhaps 20 square miles.

### Example 11–2

If 12,000 MW are transmitted to an area of 20 square miles on earth, what is the power density of the beam in watts/square inch?

The area in square inches of 20 square miles is:

$$20 \times 5,280^2 \times 12^2 = 80,289,792,000 \text{ sq. in.}$$

The beam intensity is approximately:

$$\frac{12,000,000,000}{80,000,000,000} = 0.15 \text{ watts/sq. in.}$$

Microwave power intensities near that of the above example may be somewhat but probably not severely damaging to living things. It would no doubt be desirable or necessary to restrict human access to the receiving antenna region, to restrict aircraft flights through the beam, and to have a highly reliable way of turning off the beam if it were misdirected to some other region on earth.

Finally, we turn to the problem of the earth's receiving station. The station would act like a huge antenna, made up of dipoles connected to very high efficiency solid state rectifiers. The rectifiers would change the incoming microwave (alternating current) signal to a direct current (DC) signal which would be fed to transmission lines and eventually transmitted to appropriate load centers. Research on networks such as this has been initiated, but it is not clear at this time exactly how such a station would be developed.

A solar station in space is certainly a most exciting proposal. It also is one with many difficult technological challanges. Whether the technology and the economics will ever justify such development is impossible to predict.

Meanwhile, as this approach is reviewed and studied, our attention turns back to earth to other proposals for harnessing solar power.

## 11.4 GROUND-BASED CENTRAL POWER PLANTS

If we wish to avoid the problem of building and orbiting a huge satellite, we can of course think of using a ground-based station. That avoids the problems discussed in the last section. In their place it introduces a new series of problems, primarily concerned with loss of sun at night; weather, and atmospheric attenuation.

One possibility is to put the solid-state solar panel of the last section in a ground configuration. However, this system is far too costly at this time, as we saw in Example 11–1, and is also rather inefficient at this time. The search turns to some alternative scheme which might offer hope for acceptable efficiency and cost while avoiding the problems of a space station. One scheme has been proposed by Aden Meinel of the University of Arizona.(10)

The Meinel scheme (Figure 11–4) calls for a large network of glass pipes containing liquid metal (sodium or a mixture of sodium and potassium) to be heated by the sun. The pipes would carry heat at about 560° C to a large combination heat storer and exchanger. This device plays the dual role of storing heat during times when the sun is not on the pipes, and transferring heat to a steam generator for interface with a conventional steam power plant.

The group of heat-carrying pipes and associated reflector panels at the top of Figure 11–4 would actually be a "solar farm" in the desert, many square miles in area. The hot liquid metal would be pumped to very large cylindrical underground tanks which contain an appropriate mixture of salts (such as NaCl and MgCl). The hot metal would transfer its heat to the salt in the tank through a heat exchanger. Heat would then be stored within the tank, until it is needed, for as long as weeks.

In the lower loop of Figure 11–4, water is pumped into the heat storage chamber; it leaves as high pressure steam. The steam drives a conventional steam-turbine electric generator to produce electric energy. The steam leaving the turbine must of course be condensed for the same reasons as gven in Chapter 8. The Meinel scheme uses a thermal cycle, whereas Glaser's space station employs a direct conversion scheme from electromagnetic radiation to electric energy.

The important implication of Meinel's thermal cycle is that condenser cooling water is required. This would require major sources of cooling water in the arid deserts of the Southwest. The waste heat could be used to desalinate sea water from the Pacific Ocean or from the Gulf of California, however. This would produce a valuable byproduct. The combination of electric power and fresh water in desert areas would open up

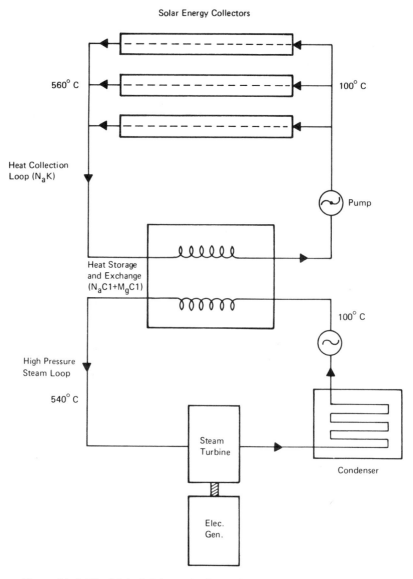

Solar Energy Collectors

560° C

100° C

Heat Collection
Loop (N$_a$K)

Pump

Heat Storage
and Exchange
(N$_a$C1+M$_g$C1)

100° C

High Pressure
Steam Loop

540° C

Steam
Turbine

Condenser

Elec.
Gen.

**Figure 11–4.** The Meinel Scheme for Land-Based Solar Power Generation.

some rather extraordinary opportunities for new development. The implications or effects of such development are not clear at this time. We will discuss below some of the possible effects. First, let us turn to the question of dimensions of our plant.

It is clear from our study of solar plants in space that solar energy is quite diffuse, and a given power plant size will require a relatively large surface area. We saw in Example 11–1 that a plant of 12,000 MW size, operating at eight percent efficiency, would require close to 50 square miles. On earth the area would be even larger because of the loss of energy through the atmosphere, during night time, and on cloudy days.

Meinel has made a rough calculation of the amount of land required to produce 1,000,000 MW, which is about half of the projected U.S. power demand in the year 2000. The result is in excess of 13,700 square miles, or about 14 percent of the U.S. desert area.

A number of problems arise. First, do we want to use this amount of land to "farm" energy from the sun? One answer is that we presently cultivate far more land for farms which grow food, at a much lower efficiency level. A second answer is that while this approach may not be ideal, it may be better than any of the alternatives, and the sacrifice of land should be made. A third answer, offered by many conservationists, is that the sacrifice is too great.

A second question is whether the system would have significant effects on the weather conditions of the Southwest. The answer is not really known.

To get a better idea of the magnitude of the project, consider Figure 11–5.(10) In this figure we see the proposed Meinel solar farm area, which is located in the desert country of the Southwest. Large areas on either side of the Colorado River would be "farmed" for solar power. Along the river a greenbelt area would no doubt develop, with major new industry, housing, irrigation, and vegetation. Industry would be attracted to the new source of power, and it might even be necessary to keep energy costs down. People would be required to operate

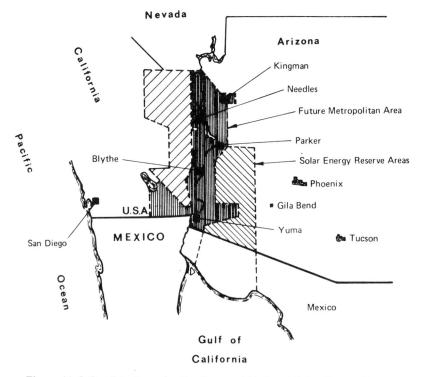

**Figure 11–5.** Possible Areas for the Proposed National Solar Energy Reserve, Including the Resulting Colorado River Metropolitan Area.

the power system and new industries. The Meinels have estimated that as many as one to two million people would be needed to operate and provide services related to a one-million megawatt system.(8)

A development of this magnitude certainly would have an effect on local and possibly also on regional weather conditions. Such effects would be observed as the project grew in magnitude. Obviously any change which altered the presence of clear skies would be undesirable or unacceptable. It might be necessary to restrict the use of gasoline-driven vehicles in the vicinity because of the resulting smog and its effect on the solar collectors.

Another factor which would have to be considered is the interaction with other major new projects in the area, such as the proposed Salton Sea geothermal project. (Reference 5, Chapter 10.) Both of these projects involve extensive desalination programs.

The Meinel approach is called a *distributed collector system*. An alternative *central receiver system* uses a large number of mirrors, called *heliostats*, which reflect the solar energy to a single receiver and thermal converter.(9) These two systems are similar in most respects, excepting collection.

Regardless of which solar central power plant is developed, the interrelated questions of land use, weather changes, and related projects will have to be reconsidered at each stage of the basic development.

Another consideration is that of raw materials. Many of the needed materials are abundant; others are much less so. It remains to be seen exactly what kinds of materials, and in what quantities, will be required.

Finally, there is a question concerning what would be done if the region experienced a long string of cloudy days. There would be no backup system, apparently, to bail out customers who depended upon solar energy. The result of cloudy periods might be significant cutbacks in power. Recall that the proposed scheme, if fully developed, would represent more than 50 percent of the nation's power capacity. Reliance on such a system would require us to consider temporary power shortages and curtailment; we would probably also need new systems of storage of energy.

These are just a few of the problems which must be faced and solved. The approach in this case almost certainly will be cautious and relatively slow. Some additional initial studies are necessary. They will probably be followed by a small pilot plant, and later a significant commercial plant if no major obstacles arise. Only very slowly will we need to decide whether we have the ability, the economic feasibility, and the desire to cover much of our desert land with solar collecting plates.

## 11.5 CONCLUSIONS

The major lessons of this chapter are that the energy of the sun is immense, and that it is very diffuse. The former offers us an extraordinary opportunity to obtain electric energy without the sacrifice of depletable fuels. The latter leaves us with the sobering challenge of trying to find an acceptable way to harness this diffuse source. In the years between 1975 and 1990 we should find out if we are able to harness the sun. If we are, we shall then have to decide if we wish to do so.

### REFERENCES FOR CHAPTER 11

1. J.I. Yellott, "Solar Energy," in *Standard Handbook for Mechanical Engineers* (Baumeister and Marks, Editors), Seventh Edition, McGraw-Hill Book Co., New York, 1967.
2. N.C. Ford and J.W. Kane, "Solar Power," *Science and Public Affairs*, October, 1971, pp.27–31.
3. "Solar Heating Proof of Concept Experiment for a Public School Building," AAI Corporation, Baltimore, Maryland, June, 1974.
4. "Solar Heating Experiment on the Grover Cleveland School, Boston, Massachusetts," NSF-RA-N-74-064, General Electric Space Division, Philadelphia, Pa., July 15, 1974.
5. D.S. Halacy, Jr., *The Coming Age of Solar Energy*, Harper and Row, New York, 1973.
6. J.S. Sawyer, "Man-made Carbon Dioxide and the 'Greenhouse Effect,'" *Nature*, Vol. 239, September 1, 1972, pp. 23–26.
7. P.E. Glaser, "Power from the Sun," *Mechanical Engineering*, March, 1969, pp. 20–24.
8. R.J. Smith, *Circuits, Devices, and Systems*, John Wiley and Sons, Inc., New York, 1971, pp. 463–464.
9. *Solar Energy, Task Force Report, Project Independence*, National

Science Foundation, U.S. Government Printing Office, Washington, D.C., November, 1974.

10. A.B. Meinel, "A Proposal for a Joint Industry-University-Utility Task Group on Thermal Conversion of Solar Energy for Electrical Power Production," University of Arizona, April 27, 1971.

11. A.B. Meinel and M.P. Meinel, "Is it Time for a New Look at Solar Energy?" *Science and Public Affairs*, October, 1971.

## GENERAL READING FOR CHAPTER 11

1. "Power from the Sun" from General Reading Citation 5 in Chapter 813.

This chapter of W. Ley's book on the dreams of engineers is a very interesting review of some of man's efforts to harness the sun.

2. B. Chalmers, *Energy*, Academic Press, New York, 1963.

This partly technical book has a considerable amount of material on solar energy as well as most of the other forms of energy discussed in the present work. Most of the material can be understood by the average reader.

3. F. Daniels, *Direct Use of the Sun's Energy*, Yale University Press, New Haven, 1964.

This is a complete and competent discussion of all the major aspects of solar energy. It includes some history, theory, and a good many applications. It is written at a relatively low level of difficulty, and it contains many references.

4. J.Hoke, *Solar Energy*, Franklin Watts, Inc., New York, 1968.

This simple introductory work on solar energy emphasizes pictures and elementary explanations. It illustrates a number of examples of use of the sun's energy.

5. D.D. Halacy, Jr., *The Coming Age of Solar Energy*, Harper and Row, New York, 1973.

This is a good contemporary discussion of solar energy. It

contains detailed material on a number of existing or proposed processes, including the Glaser scheme for a space station and the Meinel scheme for farming the desert. The level of difficulty is not high.

6. Reference 9 above.

This is a rather complete (exhaustive?) semi-technical government report on solar energy prospects. It can be read by the non-technical student. It has much material for extended study, and it is a bit dry.

## PROBLEMS FOR CHAPTER 11

*General Problems*

11.1. A home solar power plant is set up at a location in latitude 40°. Assume that, because of 24-hour averaging and some cloudy days, the average solar power density is 100 watts per square yard. A 25 square yard panel is set up on the roof. If the conversion efficiency of the system is 10%, what is the available average power, energy per month, and the value of that energy at a rate of $.03 per KWH? (250 watts, 180 KWH, $5.40)

11.2. Consider the previous example. If the total system efficiency were increased to 100%, would the plant become feasible?

11.3. Suppose that the Meinel scheme were fully implemented, with the development of 1,000,000 MW of power. About how much capital could we afford to spend on such a facility?

11.4. Indicate some additional problems which might arise in the implementation of the Meinel scheme.

11.5. Which states have an area roughly equal to that of the proposed Meinel solar farm?

### Advanced Mathematical Problems

11.6. What is the energy cost due to the solar panel if the efficiency is increased to 70% and the cost reduced to $2.00 per square foot? (The plant factor is 90% and the cost is amortized over 40 years at 5% interest.)

11.7. Write an equation for the solar power density as a function of the angle of incidence of the sun's rays on the earth. Assume that when the sun is directly overhead, the density is $P_o$. What do you have to assume to write this equation? How could you alter the equation to compensate for this assumption?

### Advanced Study Problems

11.8. Build a small solar plant of any form. Test it, and, if possible find a way to measure its efficiency.

11.9. Read Reference 5, particularly Chapter 1, for one author's sense of the sun's role in providing man with energy. Discuss Claude Summers' "thermal ceiling." How is this concept related to concentrating people in relatively small areas?

11.10. Read Reference 9 above on the costs relevant to solar central power stations. Summarize the basic cost problem, particularly with respect to other energy systems.

# 12

# NUCLEAR FUSION

*So let us melt, and make no noise,*
*No teare-floods, nor sigh-tempests move ...*

John Donne

There is perhaps no potential source of electric energy yet conceived that offers greater promise or greater challenge than does nuclear fusion. Of fusion we can say:

1) Its fuel sources are essentially limitless.

2) It is inherently less dangerous than fission power.

3) Storage of fusion waste products is less difficult than storage of fission waste products.

4) We don't know how to make it work.

In this chapter we explore both the promise and the challenge

277

of fusion. We have a second objective in this chapter. We will also show that it can take decades from the time a power generation scheme is proposed until it can generate very large (significant) amounts of electric power.

## 12.1 NUCLEAR FUSION REACTIONS

There are two important nuclear reactions which involve the release of energy. They are *fission* and *fusion*. Fission, which was discussed in Chapter 9, is the splitting or division of a heavy atom (or isotope) into two atomic (or isotopic) fragments of nearly equal mass, plus some radiation products. Fusion is the joining of two light nuclei with a release of energy. In this chapter we discuss how this process may some day be harnessed to produce electric energy.

A number of fuels have been proposed for possible forms of fusion reactors. The most important are the two heavy isotopes of hydrogen, deuterium ($^2_1D$) and tritium ($^3_1T$). Deuterium occurs quite commonly in heavy water, $D_2O$. It occurs in the ratio of about one part to each 6,500 parts of light (ordinary) water in the sea. Tritium is a radioactive (electron-emitting) isotope which does not occur naturally in any abundance. It is, however, the by-product of some possible reactions.

Deuterium is a highly attractive fuel not only because it is abundant in sea water, but also because it is relatively easy to separate from light sea water. Heavy water has a mass more than 5% greater than that of ordinary water. This is far greater, for example, than the mass difference between U-235 and U-238, which must be partially separated in a crucial stage of nuclear fission fuel processing.

Many possible light nuclei reactions lead to fusion energy. One of the most important is presented here as an example.

$$^2_1D + {}^2_1D \rightarrow {}^3_2He + n + 3.2 \text{ MeV}$$
$$^2_1D + {}^2_1D \rightarrow {}^3_1T + p + 4.0 \text{ MeV}$$
$$^2_1D + {}^3_1T \rightarrow {}^4_2He + n + 17.6 \text{ MeV}$$
$$^2_1D + {}^3_2He \rightarrow {}^4_2He + {}^1_1He + 18.3 \text{ MeV}$$

He represents helium, n a neutron and p a proton. This chain of reactions can be summarized as follows:

$$6^2_1D \rightarrow 2^4_2He + 2p + 2n + 43.1 \text{ MeV}$$

The byproducts are $^4_2He$, a stable isotope of helium; two protons, which are simply nuclei of the principal hydrogen isotope, $^1_1H$; and two neutrons. The 43.1 MeV of energy may seem small compared to the 200 MeV released in the fissioning of a heavy isotope like $^{235}_{92}U$. However, the energy released per mass of fuel is actually greater for the fusion case.

One important problem with the reaction above is that the D-D reaction rate is fairly low. An alternative cycle takes advantage of the greater reaction rate of D-T.

$$^2_1D + ^3_1T \rightarrow ^4_2He + n + 17.6 \text{ MeV}$$
$$n + ^6_3Li \rightarrow ^4_2He + ^3_1T + 4.8 \text{ MeV}$$

where Li is the element lithium.

The D-T reaction is more challenging to harness techno-logically in some ways and less challenging in other ways. The net result is that it is likely that a D-T reaction will be developed first, but that the D-D reaction will in time supplant it, assuming, of course, that fusion power is someday harnessed.


## 12.2  CRITERIA FOR NUCLEAR REACTIONS

The fuel in a fusion reactor is in the form of a gas. The reactions indicated in the previous section require extremely high temperatures, of perhaps 50,000,000° K to 200,000,000° K. (The sun is a lukewarm 20,000,000° K by comparison.) The reason for these high temperatures is that the nuclei are identically charged, and therefore have a tendency to repel each other. Only if the kinetic energies of the nuclei are extremely high will they be able to approach close enough to fuse. At the very high temperatures indicated above, atoms are stripped of their orbiting electrons. The gas becomes ionized

—separated into positive and negative charged particles. In this state the gas is called a *plasma*.

In addition to the requirement of high temperature, a reactor which is to produce net power must have an acceptable combination of particle density, or nuclei per cubic centimeter, n, and particle confinement time t in seconds. The Lawson criterion requires that the product nt be equal to $6 \times 10^{13}$ for the D-T reaction and $2 \times 10^{15}$ for the D-D reaction. In Section 12.3 we discuss how plasma confinement may be accomplished.

The very significant factor of almost 30 times between the Lawson criteria for the D-T and the D-D reactions is the major reason why the D-T reaction is likely to be developed first.

Figure 12–1 is a plot of particle density versus temperature for a number of important plasmas.(1) Many of these plasmas should be familiar to the reader. The ionosphere, which is above the earth from an altitude of roughly 50 to 1,000 miles, is relatively cool and tenuous (non-dense). Even though its temperature is sometimes quite high relative to the earth's surface, its density is so low that an object such as a spaceship can pass through it without "burning up." A candle "flame," on the other hand, has a greater density and temperature, and it can burn some materials.

Temperatures and densities far greater than those for these last two examples are necessary for today's controlled fusion experiments and tomorrow's proposed fusion reactors. These regions are in the upper right hand corner of Figure 12–1. We turn now to the very difficult task of confining plasma particles with densities and temperatures in these regions.


## 12.3  PLASMA CONTAINMENT

It is not possible to contain a very hot plasma within a solid vessel made of steel, concrete, wood, etc. We would not have to worry about the containment vessel melting. The plasma density here is still so low that the vessel could absorb the heat without being destroyed. However, contact with the wall of the vessel would essentially quench the plasma, bringing the temperature of the gas down close to that of the vessel. In addition, local heating of the vessel would vaporize small

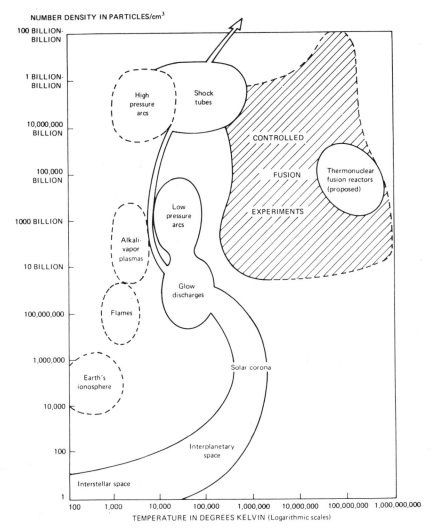

**Figure 12–1.** The World of Plasmas.

fragments of it, producing contamination which would inhibit the reaction process. Hence, it is critical that the plasma be contained away from the walls of the reactor.

The solution to containment lies in the fact that the plasma consists of electrically-charged particles. Charged particles which move in a magnetic field experience forces which can be used to confine or contain the particles away from the walls of the reactor. We must design a kind of magnetic prison in which particles are held not by steel walls but by invisible magnetic field lines, like those produced by a child's toy magnet. Not just any prison will do. Escape must be very improbable. The basic task we have in fusion research today is to find a magnetic system which can contain a plasma of sufficient density and temperature for a sufficient length of time.

The physical theory of operation of the possible containment schemes is beyond the scope of this text. The interested reader may consult References 2, 3, 4, and 5. Here, we shall only briefly describe the most important general forms.

Three major containment schemes are presently under study. These include:

1) Stabilized mirror containment
2) Toroidal (doughnut-shaped) containment
3) Theta pinch containment

The stabilized mirror system being tested at the Lawrence Radiation Laboratory uses a magnetic field which is squeezed together at the ends so that the field lines come closer to each other, as shown in Figure 12–2. The effect is to cause the charged particles to reflect from or mirror back from the region in which the lines converge. In this way the particles continually bounce back and forth from one end of this "magnetic bottle" to the other. This is essentially the same phenomenon as that experienced by charged particles which are trapped in the earth's Van Allen Belt. These particles travel from one pole to the other in about 1.5 seconds, only to be reflected back again by the earth's converging magnetic field lines. This process continues until situations are such that any individual particle "leaks" out at one of the earth's poles.

In the magnetic bottle the plasma particles must be contained long enough to permit a significant amount of power to be generated. This may be a fraction of a second. One experiment at the Lawrence Radiation Laboratory yielded a density of $n = 5 \times 10^{13}$ particles/cm$^3$ and a temperature $T = 80,000,000°$ K. However, the containment time was only about 0.3 msec, which is about one thousandth of the required time.

The toroidal configuration has been under study at the Kurchatov Institute of Technology in Russia and at Princeton University. The Russian device is called a Tokamak, the Princeton device a Stellerator. To date the Tokamak has had much greater success. In fact, the Princeton device has been converted to the Tokamak form. The principle is to force the charged particles to follow a circular path inside a toroidal structure. Figure 12–3 shows the basic Tokamak configuration, and Figure 12–4 is a picture of the Princeton Tokamak under test.

A theta pinch experiment is in progress at the Los Alamos Laboratory. The objective is to obtain a very rapid compression of an existing low-density, low-temperature plasma. The compression causes heating which leads to the necessary conditions for sustaining a reaction. Many other variations of containment schemes have been proposed. Some are under study at this time.(2–5)


## 12.4 FUSION BY LASERS

Recently it has been proposed that fusion power may be obtained without magnetic containment through use of a high-powered *laser*.(6) The laser is a device which can focus a very high intensity light beam on a small region for a short period of time. In one scheme a deuterium-tritium pellet is dropped into a sphere or reaction chamber. When the pellet reaches the center of the chamber the very high intensity laser beam heats the pellet to fusion temperatures and a fusion reaction follows. Energy is deposited in a lithium shell as heat. This is drawn off through a heat exchanger to produce steam for a conventional turbine.

There are two major problems facing this scheme. The first is

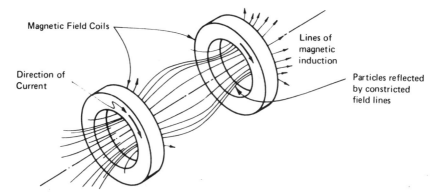

**Figure 12–2.** Magnetic Mirror Confinement Scheme.

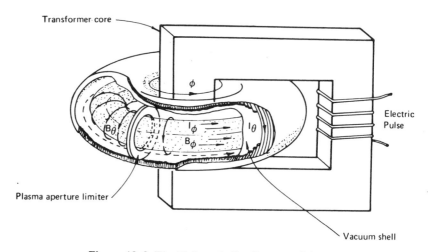

**Figure 12–3.** The Tokomak Confinement Scheme.

**Figure 12–4.** The Symmetric Tokomak, a controlled fusion research device in toroidal geometry, located at Princeton University Plasma Physics Laboratory and sponsored by the U.S. Atomic Energy Commission. The photograph suggests the toroidal, or doughnut-shaped, configuration of the Tokomak. According to *Survey of USAEC Program in Controlled Thermonuclear Research*, " ... this machine was built to attack three main goals. The first, already accomplished, is to verify that such devices do produce hot, dense plasmas. The second goal is to determine the essential features of the confinement process and to evaluate the differences, if any, between Stellarator and Tokomak confinement. The third goal is to move beyond the present parameters, especially in the direction of higher ion temperatures." The third goal is being successfully attacked by present research. The Princeton team has injected a stream of deuterium atoms into the plasma in such a way that the pre-compression temperature of the plasma has been raised from about 3.5 million degrees to 4.5 million degrees. After compression, the plasma temperatures are about 10 million degrees without deuterium injection, about 12.5 million degrees with deuterium injection. Fusion reactors will require temperatures in the range of 180 million degrees. (Courtesy of Princeton University Plasma Physics Laboratory.)

that there are presently no lasers of sufficiently high power to trigger the reaction. The second problem lies in containing and harnessing the sudden release of energy which occurs in a shock wave form, and which might otherwise damage or destroy the containment vessel. The problems facing the laser approach seem at least comparable with those facing magnetic containment.

## 12.5  ELECTRIC POWER PLANT

So far our attention has centered on the fusion reaction itself. We turn now to the problem of using thermonuclear energy, released in that reaction, to generate electric energy. Two basic approaches have been conceived, one using a thermal (steam) cycle, and one which converts reactor energy directly to electric energy. In addition, a number of proposals have been made for combining the fusion reactor with one or more secondary devices.

Figure 12-5 shows one form of a thermal cycle. A cross section of a toroidal reactor is shown on the right. In the center of the toroid the contained plasma moves in a vacuum. We have cut across the doughnut of the toroid; imagine that the plasma is flowing out of the surface of the page. Neutrons released in the reaction are absorbed by the liquid lithium, which carries heat to a heat exchanger steam generator. The rest of the system to the right of the heat exchanger is essentially identical to the steam system studied in Chapter 8. Since neutrons react with lithium to produce tritium, which is needed in the D-T reaction, the tritium is separated out from the liquid lithium and reinjected into the reactor.

A direct energy conversion scheme, shown in Figure 12-6, has been proposed by Dr. Richard Post of the Lawrence Radiation Laboratory. A mirror containment device is used, as shown on the left. Some particles escape through the mirror on the right into a charge collection region. Electrons would be

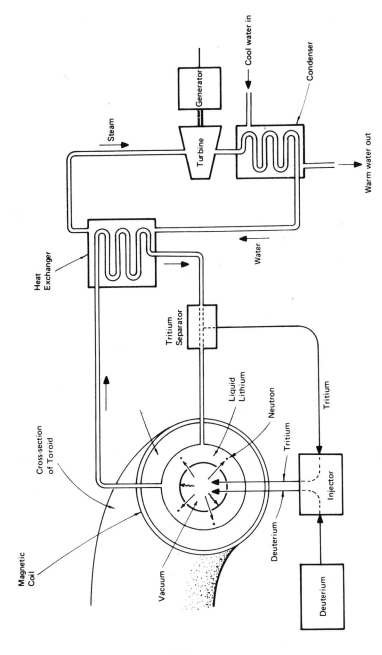

**Figure 12–5.** Fusion Reactor in a Thermal Generation Scheme.

287

removed by electric collecting plates, much as they are in a vacuum tube. These electrons would then appear as an electric current in an external circuit.

A novel extension of the fusion reactor is the fusion torch, which would use the very hot plasma available from a reactor to burn refuse completely, reducing it to its basic elemental constituents.(1)

## 12.6 DEVELOPMENTAL PROBLEMS

At the present time we are in a stage of research directed at showing that acceptable containment is possible. Sometimes this is called a phase of scientific research. This is perhaps a misnomer. The scientific credibility of thermonuclear reactions has been established on the earth, and is demonstrated in the continued life of the sun and the stars. In a sense we are now trying to solve the first of a series of engineering challenges to achieve practical application of theory. Some experts (see, for example, Reference 4) believe that we may reach the minimum criteria for an energy-producing reaction in a few years. In recent years funding to this end has been increasing, but is still somewhat less than research groups believe could be used effectively.

After we have reached the minimum physical criteria, we must then turn to a very wide range of serious application problems. We should anticipate that these will require many years to solve. The following partial list of major technical problems will suggest the magnitude of the task ahead. (8,9)

1) Large, high-strength magnetic fields produced by super-conducting magnets will be needed. They must be developed and they must run at relatively low power levels.

2) Vacuum chambers that can withstand severe temperatures and neutron bombardment must be developed.

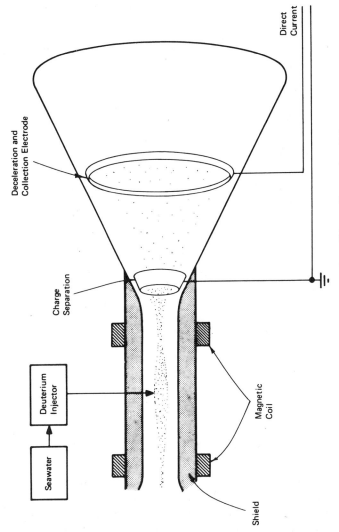

**Figure 12–6.** Fusion Reactor in a Direct Conversion Scheme.

289

3) Tritium handling apparatus must be developed.

4) Technology must be developed for fueling and refueling reactors, recovering unburnt fuel, and handling waste products.

5) Schemes must be developed for start-up, shutdown, and load-following.

## 12.7  ENVIRONMENTAL QUESTIONS

Inevitably the fusion reactor is compared with its potential competitors. The breeder reactor, probably an advanced model, may be a major middle-term competitor. Solar power may compete eventually. Geothermal power seems only an outside prospect at this time, considering the very large amounts of energy that might be produced by fusion.

The first fusion plant will probably be a thermal plant, with the same basic thermal pollution or heat addition problems as those of any other thermal plant. In time, however, a direct conversion scheme could lead to major reductions in waste heat release.

The major radioactive materials in fusion reactors are tritium and the radioactive isotopes produced by neutron bombardment of the reactor's structure. The prospects of a major nuclear excursion seem very slight, since, if anything goes wrong in the reactor, the plasma will probably be quenched quite quickly by the reactor walls. If the reactor is catastrophically ruptured, the release of radioactive materials is far less serious by a factor of perhaps one million in fusion than in fission reactors.

The radioactive waste storage problem with a fusion reactor is much less severe than with fission reactors. Therefore, on environmental grounds, the fusion reactor seems quite attractive.

## 12.8 IS FUSION IN OUR FUTURE?

The history of fusion power is one of ebbing and flowing tides of optimism and pessimism. Today we ride the crest of a flow, if not a flood, of optimism. Many experts are beginning to predict in terms of "when" instead of "if." But most agree that the timetable for development is not short. One general schedule suggests five years to show that minimum criteria can be met. Another 10 years would be required to iron out the technical problems discussed in Section 12.6, and still another 10 years to develop the first full scale plant. That brings us up to the year 2000. Some say such a timetable is too optimistic; others say that is unduly pessimistic and that a major increase in research funds should be made; they would greatly shorten the time-table.

It has been suggested by some that we bypass the breeder reactor and proceed with all due speed to fusion. It does not seem likely that this will happen. Industry and government have essentially committed us to development of the breeder reactor. It is the surer device. We essentially know how to do it. Fusion is more of a gamble; the stakes are high, though, the rewards are great.

It seems that we ought to wager more on the fusion scheme. The extra millions we spend today on feasibility determination and on the simultaneous attack on technical problems may yield huge gains in environmental protection as well as economic gain on some earlier tomorrow.

## 12.9 A FINAL THOUGH ABOUT FUSION

The problems we face in developing fusion power have one thing in common with any major new generation scheme. The timetable is long. It takes years to show technical feasibility, more years before the new scheme carries any large proportion of the load. Even though nuclear fission power was shown to be feasible over 30 years ago, and the first plants produced power over 15 years ago, nuclear power still produces less than 8% of our electric energy (1975). The coal and oil and nuclear plants we build today will be producing power 30 and 40 years from now, when fusion may be just coming on line. Nonetheless, it seems to this writer that we ought to spend more today on this great prospect. We might shorten by years, perhaps by a decade, the time to realization of fusion power.(10,11)

## REFERENCES FOR CHAPTER 12

1. W.C. Gough, "Why Fusion?" U.S. Atomic Energy Commission, 1970, U.S. Government Printing Office.
2. W.C. Gough and B.J. Eastlund, "Prospects of Fusion Power," *Scientific American*, February, 1971, pp. 50–64.
3. L.M. Lidsky, "The Quest for Fusion Power," *Technology Review*, January, 1972, pp. 10–21.
4. D.J. Rose, "Controlled Nuclear Fusion: Status and Outlook," *Science*, May 21, 1971, pp. 797–808.
5. S. Glasstone, *Sourcebook on Atomic Energy*, Third Edition, Van Nostrand Reinhold Company, New York, 1967.
6. M.J. Lubin and A.P. Fraas, "Fusion by Laser," *Scientific American*, June, 1971, pp. 21–33.
7. M. Kenward, "Fusion Power Politics in the U.S.," *New Scientist*, May 18, 1972, pp. 380–382.
8. S.H. Schoor, *Energy Research Needs*, Resources for the Future, Inc., National Technical Information Service, Washington, D.C., October, 1971.
9. H. Hurwitz, Jr., "Comments on the Prospects of Fusion Power," General Electric Company 71-C-217, July, 1971.
10. R.L. Hirsch and W. L. Rice, "Nuclear Fusion Power and the Environment," *Environmental Conservation*, Vol. 1, No. 4, Winter, 1974, pp. 251–262.
11. R.G. Mills, "Current Expectations for Fusion Power from

Toroidal Machines," Paper T14 097-2, IEEE Power Engineering Society Winter Meeting, New York, January, 1974.

## GENERAL READING FOR CHAPTER 12

1. A.S. Bishop, *Project Sherwood—The U.S. Program in Controlled Fusion*, Addison-Wesley Publishing Co., Inc., Reading, Mass. 1958.

   This is an interesting historical account of the early years of fusion research. It also acts as a good introduction to many of the basic problems which still plague development in this field.
2. W.C. Gough, "Why Fusion?" U.S. Atomic Energy Commission, 1970, U.S. Government Printing Office.

   This is an interesting short review of the general problems of energy need which provide the impetus for fusion research.

## PROBLEMS FOR CHAPTER 12

### General Problems

12.1. Explain briefly why the D-T reaction is likely to be developed before the D-D reaction.
12.2. What is the number of electrons, protons, and neutrons in one atom of each of the following elements? $^1_1H$, $^2_1D$, $^3_1T$, $^6_3Li$?
12.3. According to the Lawson criterion, how much confinement time is necessary in the D-T reaction if the particle concentration is 100,000 billion nuclei per cubic centimeter?
12.4. Explain why it may be possible under certain circumstances to place your hand in a very hot gas without being burned.

### Advanced Study Problems

12.5. In 1961 the United States committed itself to a crash program to "put a man on the moon." How does this problem differ from the fusion problem? It is extremely unlikely that we could solve our energy problems in 10 years with fusion power. Why?

12.6. Using references above, and more recent documents, list and categorize according to form of operation all of the major proposals of fusion reaction forms. Show estimates where available of the effectiveness of each form.

12.7. It has been recommended by some that we should bypass the breeder reactor and proceed to a major effort to develop the fusion reactor. Discuss this recommendation in detail, considering such factors as economic and environmental risks, time scales, etc.

12.8. Read Reference 1. Discuss the implications of the "fusion torch" for man's way of life.

# 13

# MISCELLANEOUS ELECTRIC GENERATING TECHNIQUES

*Many are called, but few are chosen.*

Matthew 22

We have not exhausted our study of all the ways by which man can generate electric energy, or by which he may dream to do so. In previous chapters we discussed six ways of generating electric energy. Included were the most important present techniques and some which may never be important, at least on a large scale.

There are many approaches which we have not discussed. We cannot hope to do full justice to all of these. And yet some deserve mention because they are important or because they are interesting. So we have gathered together in this chapter, for brief discussion, nine more generation schemes which are listed below. Some are operating today, some are under serious study, and some are only dreams.

A. Operating systems

    1. Gas turbines
    2. Diesel Engines
    3. Tidal Plants

B. Systems under serious consideration or development

    4. Magnetohydrodynamics (MHD)
    5. Fuel cells

C. Speculative schemes

    6. Thermal particle devices
    7. Thermal sea power
    8. Wind machines
    9. Wave machines

## 13.1 GAS TURBINES

A gas turbine is an engine which operates much like a steam turbine except that the medium which flows past the turbine blades, causing them to turn, is the gaseous product of a combustion process. A *simple cycle* gas turbine is shown in Figure 13–1. The turbine drives both the electric generator and also a compressor whose function is to compress input air to a relatively high pressure before it is mixed with gas or liquid fuel in the combustion chamber. The exhaust gases are released to the air after passing through the turbine.

The major advantage of the gas turbine is its inherent simplicity. It has no boiler or steam supply system, no condenser, and no waste-heat disposal system. The result is that capital costs are low: about 100 to 125 $/KW. However, the efficiency is lower than that of modern steam plants, so

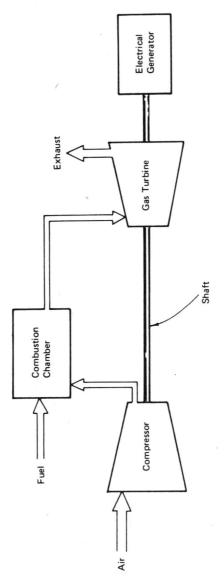

**Figure 13–1.** Gas Turbine-Electrical Generator.

297

operating (fuel) costs tend to be high. Gas turbines can be started quite rapidly, with synchronization and power delivery in five to 20 minutes. The low capital cost, high fuel cost, and short starting times suggest that the primary uses for gas turbines will be for peak-power and standby sources. Recently, however, some utilities have found it desirable or even necessary to use gas turbines for an increasing number of hours each year. This is largely a result of the lack of availability, and increasing costs, of other base-load and intermediate-load plants.

Recent years have seen rapid growth of gas turbine use in the U.S. By the end of 1973 the total installed capacity of gas turbines was 32,877 MW.(1) This represents a very significant 7% of total U.S. capacity.

A number of factors have led to a major new interest in gas turbines. One of the most important of these is the growing shortage of capacity, resulting from construction delays, delays due to environmental restrictions, insufficient planning, and failures of other units. Gas turbine units as small as five MW or as large as 200 MW can be installed in six to eight months. Many are being installed on an emergency basis to meet critical demand needs. In addition, a wide variety of fuels can be used in gas turbines, including natural gas, process gas, distillate oil, residual oil, crude oil, naphtha, and kerosene.(2)

Gas turbines have some environmental advantages compared with other thermal power plants. Since they do not employ a steam cycle, they do not cause heat addition to water. Exhaust heat is vented from a short stack into the air. They are relatively small plants, so they tend not to disfigure their sites, and they require little ground space.

Simple cycle gas turbines have an efficiency of about 20% to 30%.(3) In a regenerative cycle (Figure 13–3) the compressed gas is pre-heated, and the resulting efficiency is close to 36%.

Finally, there is much interest at this time in combining the best features of gas turbines and steam power plants, producing a so-called "combined cycle" plant. The combined cycle plant uses the hot exhaust gas from a gas turbine to provide heat to a boiler for a conventional steam generator-turbine. The gas turbine and the steam turbine drive separate electric generators. The efficiency of this device is about 40%. One manufacturer anticipates that combined cycle efficiencies will reach 45% to 50% by 1980.(3) (See also Section 5.2.)

## 13.2 DIESEL ENGINES

Diesel engine generator units have been built for many years in the range of two to six MW. They are more efficient than gas turbines, and can be started and brought on-line faster than

**Figure 13–2.** Gas turbine. One of four 156-MW floating General Electric Gas Turbine Power Blocks under way from Newport News, Virginia, to Consolidated Edison Mooring in New York City. Standard units such as this can be delivered to a customer in as little as one to six months, depending on availability of a required package. Land-based plants can be installed in six to eight months depending on size. These short installation times are an important factor in the attractiveness of gas turbines in meeting demand quickly. (Courtesy of The General Electric Co., Gas Turbine Products Division.)

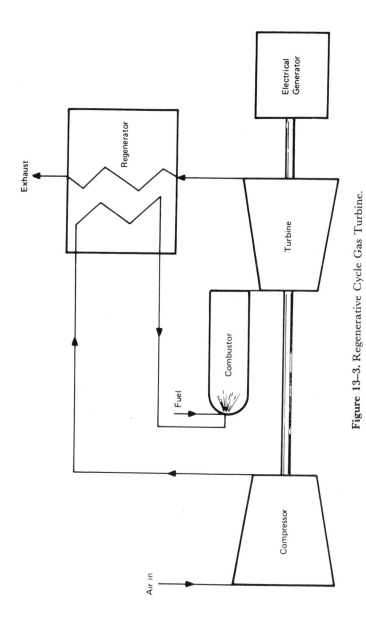

**Figure 13-3.** Regenerative Cycle Gas Turbine.

300

any unit except hydroelectric generators. Capital costs, at $100/KW, are excellent. Diesel units are particularly attractive for very small loads and for emergency standby systems. The major drawback of the diesel unit is its small size. The total capacity of diesel generators in 1973 was about 4,800 MW, or just over 1% of the total U.S. power capacity.

## 13.3 TIDAL POWER

Man has used the tides as a source of energy for countless centuries. The Domesday Book (11th century) mentions a tidal mill at Dover, England. Salem, Massachusetts had a mill in 1635. Tides successfully drove a pump that supplied London with its water until its demolition in 1842. In more recent years many potential sites around the world have been considered for electric power plants. Some, such as the Passamaquoddy site on the U.S.-Canada border, have been studied very extensively. One major plant, at La Rance in France, was completed in 1966. But this represents very little total development. We must ask why the apparent promise of the tides has not led to very much development. It is a common experience that many projects which seem attractive develop slowly if at all. We start by looking at the physical background of tidal power.

The originating source of tidal energy is in the kinetic energy of the orbiting and rotating earth, moon, and sun. As long as these bodies move relative to one another, the waters of the earth rise and fall due to changing gravitational effects.

Energy is available because water changes its level or height. This is equivalent to the development of a head in a hydro-electric project. There are at least three ways in which tidal energy might conceivably be harnessed. These ways are indicated in Figure 13-4.

The first way of harnessing tidal energy is simply to place a water wheel in a tidal stream, as shown in Figure 13-4a. This is

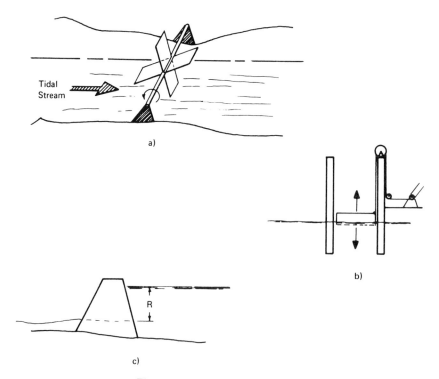

**Figure 13–4.** Using Tidal Energy.

analogous to using a water wheel in a river. The problem with this scheme, as with the water wheel in the river, lies in the variability of the tidal stream flow. A tidal wheel may be acceptable for some applications, such as pumping water or milling grain, but it is almost certainly unsatisfactory for electric energy generation.

The second possible scheme is shown in Figure 13–4b. A large floating object such as a barge is raised by an incoming tide; it is constrained between pilings. It can then be held and dropped later or allowed to fall with the tide. In either event, as it falls it drives an electric generator. To determine the practicality of such a scheme we consider a specific example.

*Example 13–1*

Consider a ship of 20,000 tons displacement, with a tidal rise of 15 feet. What is the average power which can be generated?

The average power in foot-pounds per second is $P = HW/T$, as given in Equation 7–2 where H is the head or change in level in feet, W is the weight in pounds and T is the time over which the average is taken in seconds. We assume that the time between tides is about 12 hours (43,200 seconds).

$$P = \frac{15 \times 20,000 \times 2,000}{43,200} = 13,900 \text{ ft.-lbs./sec.}$$

$$= 25.3 \text{ HP}$$

$$= 18.85 \text{ KW}$$

Hence our 20,000 ton barge can generate about enough power for a few private residences. This won't do, of course. Let's stop and take a look at the situation and see why we are not getting more power. Recall our basic hydraulic power equation:

$$P = \frac{HW}{T}$$

One problem here is with T. The available energy (HW) must be averaged over 12 hours. The result is that P is very small. We can't do anything about T since it is fixed by orbits of the earth and moon. The only way we can increase H is by going to some place on the earth where the difference between high and low tides is greater. This we can try to do. Next our attention centers on W. One approach is to use more barges. Clearly, however, if one large barge yields only 19 KW, we shall need far too many barges to obtain a reasonable level of power. Barges are not the answer.

Raising and lowering the barge is equivalent to raising and lowering the amount of water displaced by the barge. The obvious solution is to work with the moving water rather than

**Figure 13–5.** The Rance River tidal power plant. The only major tidal power plant in the world (in 1975) is at La Rance on the west coast of France. This 240,000 KW plant harnesses what appears to be "free energy." But the reader must realize that the building costs—$100 million in this case—make the energy anything but free. The cost of harnessing "free energy" must always be considered. In this photograph, the water which had entered with the rising tide, and had been trapped in the river basin to the left, is now being released through the dam, in which it turns turbo-generators. (Courtesy of Electricite de France.)

with an object floating on the water. We can do this by building a low dam (Figure 13–4c) across the mouth of a bay or tidal estuary. As the tide comes in, gates are opened in the dam and water flows into the bay or estuary. At high tide the gates are closed. When the tidewater outside the bay recedes, a head develops which is used to turn hydraulic turbines as in a hydroelectric plant.

The weight of the water stored behind the dam, from the high tide level to the low tide level, is RSw, where R is the tidal range in feet (or difference between high and low tide levels), S is the average surface area of the storage pond or reservoir in square feet, and w is the weight density of water in pounds per cubic foot. Consider again Figure 13–4c. We would like to run this weight of water RSw through the turbine, but we cannot assume the head is R because as water flows out of the reservoir, the level of the reservoir decreases. The energy actually available can be obtained by taking the head as the average difference in water level. This average value is 1/2 R. Hence the available energy is:

$$E = \frac{1}{2} R \times W = \frac{1}{2} R \times RSw$$

$$= \frac{R^2 Sw}{2}$$

The average power is obtained by dividing by T.

$$P = \frac{R^2 Sw}{2T}$$

The value we use for T here depends on the form of the system. In some configurations both incoming and outgoing tides are utilized. In this case T can be taken as six hours (21,600 seconds).

*Example 13–2*

Consider a tidal reservoir with an area of 10 square miles and a tidal range of 17 feet. Assume T = 6 hours. Find the average power.

$$P = \frac{R^2 Sw}{2T} = \frac{(17)^2 (10 \times 5,280^2)(62.4)}{2(21,600)}$$

$$= 116,400,000 \text{ ft.} = \text{lb./sec.}$$

$$= 209,000 \text{ HP } (158,000 \text{ KW})$$

This is a fairly respectable average power, and the example goes a long way in support of our intuitive sense that there's a lot of free energy going to waste in the tides. This is the kind of statement we often hear in regard to tidal power. Similar statements are made with respect to many other apparently attractive schemes. Why don't we have hundreds or thousands of tidal power plants? It is true that sometimes technological "progress" is constrained by a lack of imagination or the courage to try something new. But the history of electric energy generation is full of examples of great engineering challenges met in the face of great opposition and formidable technical obstacles.

The basic problem with the development of tidal projects is that the energy is *not* free, at least not as electric energy. Dams must be built in salt water basins, usually in the presence of massive amounts of rapidly flowing water. It is often very expensive to build such facilities. We cannot argue, of course, that once the facilities are built, the energy is free, because we must pay for the capital investment over the life of the project, as we saw in Section 4.2 in our discussion of the economics of hydroelectric plants. The initial cost of the plant may be so great that the cost of energy per KWH is greater than that available from alternate generation methods.

In seeking a potential site for a tidal power plant the following four criteria provide a first-order evaluation:

1) The tidal range R should be large.

2) The storage area S should be large.

3) The site should allow the development of the necessary plant for reasonable cost.

4) Construction of the plant and impounding of the tidewater should not have an unacceptably adverse effect on the environment of the surrounding region.

It is not easy to satisfy all of these criteria. The world's first major tidal electric power plant was completed in 1966 at La Rance in France, on the English Channel. Figure 13–5 shows water flowing out from the La Rance tidal power plant to the channel and the ocean. The capacity of the La Rance plant is 240,000 KW. Power is generated on incoming as well as outgoing tides. The maximum flow rate is nearly 650,000 cfs. Tidal ranges vary from 20 to 47 feet. La Rance uses a single-pool concept, and it has 24 generator units. The dam across the narrow estuary mouth is a 2,300 foot long hollow reinforced-concrete structure. The cost of the plant was about $100,000,000.

The 240,000 KW La Rance plant can be called moderate in size. It makes a contribution to France's generation capacity (about two percent) and yet it is far smaller than some proposed plants. It must be considered an experimental plant if for no other reason than that it is the first major tidal plant, and many agencies considering tidal plants will no doubt be watching it closely.

The second tidal example we will consider has been proposed but never built.

The Passamaquoddy site is on the U.S.-Canadian border (Maine-New Brunswick). Almost 50 years ago an American engineer, Dexter P. Cooper, proposed a two-basin scheme. The financial catastrophe of 1929 was too much for this proposal and it died, only to be resurrected in somewhat different form by a federal public works program in 1935. An end of Congressional appropriations terminated the study two years later, though not before valuable data for later studies had been gathered.

In 1948 an International Joint Commission was set up to review the concept. Its report in 1950 led to additional work from 1956 to 1959. Following these studies, the Department of the Interior developed plans for a 1,000 MW plant. The plan envisages 100 10 MW turbogenerators and seven miles of rock-filled dams (some in depths of 125 to 300 ft.). Many of the engineering problems have no precedent. After five years of study, ending in 1961, the IJC reported that the project was economically unfeasible by a wide margin, that the project could not produce power at a price competitive with the price of power available from alternative sources.

But Passamaquoddy does not die easily. President Kennedy asked the Secretary of the Interior to reopen the study. The subsequent study by the Interior Department found that the project could be feasible if operated as a peaking power source.(4) The proposed configuration for the plant is shown in Figure 13-6. Passamaquoddy Bay forms a 101-square mile high pool with the smaller Cobscoo Bay acting as the low pool. The total project would require seven miles of dams, 160 water gates for emptying and filling pools, and a number of maritime locks.

Capital cost of the Passamaquoddy Project was estimated, in 1963, at about $750,000,000, with energy costs about four mills/KWH. Inflation would certainly have greatly increased those costs if the project were initiated today.

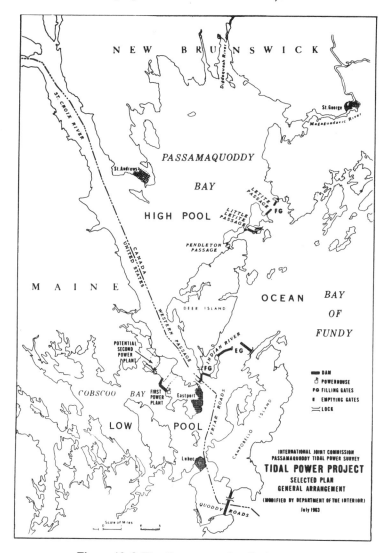

**Figure 13–6.** The Passamaquod . ' Project area.

After the Interior Department report was released in 1963, the investor-owned utilities in the area retained Charles T. Main, Inc., a Boston engineering consulting firm, to study the project. The Passamaquoddy project would of course be a government project, and would be a competitor of the private utilities. Main's analysis indicated that tidal power would actually be more costly than that from alternative sources. There is no clear answer as to which party is right. Each seems right from its own viewpoint; the feasibility argument is at a standoff.

Why is there today a tidal power plant at La Rance, but not at Passamaquoddy? The public power-private power issue is no doubt a major factor, but one must also be impressed by the differences in the engineering challenge at the two sites. We have seen in the previous section that, in many ways, the technical problems at La Rance were *relatively* simple.

At Passamaquoddy the technical problems are far greater than at La Rance. In addition, the presence of the Passamaquoddy site on an international boundary introduces a whole new range of problems.

In asking for a new study at Passamaquoddy, President Kennedy observed, "Each day a million kilowatts of power surge in and out of Passamaquoddy Bay." This is true, but it is not a complete justification for development. As we saw in Chapter 4, every project must be economically justified and financially feasible. Whether Passamaquoddy or any of the world's other great tidal sites someday meet these criteria is a question for the future.

## 13.4  MAGNETOHYDRODYNAMICS

A magnetohydrodynamic (MHD) generator uses an ionized gas or *plasma* moving through a magnetic field to produce an electric potential. Figure 13–7 shows the basic physical action of the generator. An ionized gas is produced in a burner to the left

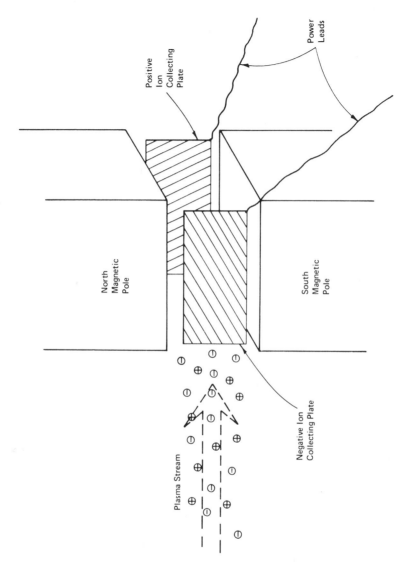

**Figure 13-7.** The Magnetohydro-dynamic Principle.

Power Leads

Positive Ion Collecting Plate

North Magnetic Pole

South Magnetic Pole

Negative Ion Collecting Plate

Plasma Stream

of the figure and is blown past a magnetic field, perpendicular to the ion flow. The field deflects the positive ions to one metallic collecting plate and the negative ions to the other metallic collecting plate. The principle is simple. The application of the principle in a large efficient generator, however, has so far eluded researchers. There are a number of possible forms of a working MHD generator. The MHD unit can be developed alone or combined with a gas turbine, or with a conventional steam generator.

Figure 13–8 shows one possible complex generator using an MHD cycle and a steam cycle. Fuel is introduced to the burner along with a *seed* material such as potassium. The purpose of the seed is to increase the conductivity of the gas sufficiently to permit practical operation of the device. The magnet deflects some of the ions to the plates, which become charged, producing a DC electric potential. This voltage can be used in this form or changed to AC. The exhaust gas passes first through an air heater which heats outside air which has been compressed by the compressor attached to the steam turbine. The heated air is then used in the burner. The hot exhaust gases from the MHD generator then pass into the steam generator, where they produce steam to drive a conventional steam turbine. The steam turbine drives both the compressor and an electric generator. The exhaust gases continue on through a seed recovery stage where the seed is captured and fed back to the burner. Since the recovery is not perfect, some make-up seed must be added. Next, the exhaust gas passes through a nitrogen and sulfur removal stage before being released by the stack.

The primary advantages of the MHD unit are its simplicity —it has no moving parts—and its high operating temperature, which leads to a high overall efficiency of perhaps 50% to 60%. This will provide major savings in fuel utilization and in condenser cooling.

Many problems must be solved before practical systems are developed. The burner must be designed to burn an abundant

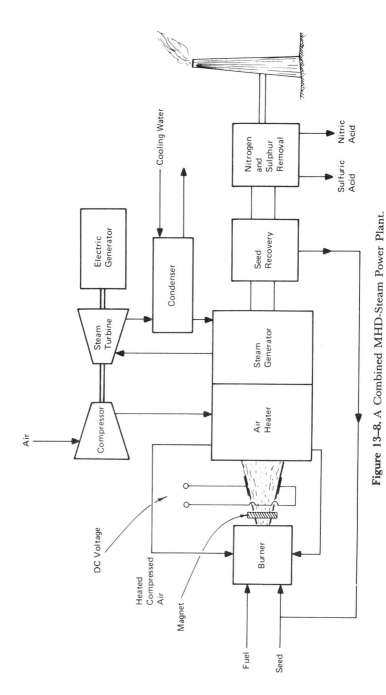

**Figure 13–8.** A Combined MHD-Steam Power Plant.

fuel, such as coal, which is dirty. To date acceptable high-volume burners operating under acceptable conditions do not exist. The very high temperatures out of the burner present new technological challenges in the design of gas channels, electrodes, and air heaters. Magnets of acceptable size and strength must be developed. As we saw in Chapter 8, high combustion temperatures lead to the production of oxides of nitrogen which must be removed. Adequate systems to remove sulfur and nitrogen oxides are still under study.

Other MHD cycles, including a liquid instead of gaseous medium, are also being considered. Some small experimental MHD systems are under development.(5,6,7) It remains to be seen whether this approach can be developed well enough to make an important contribution to the generation of electric energy.

## 13.5  FUEL CELLS

Fuel cells are somewhat like batteries in physical form. They have two electrodes, called the *anode* and the *cathode*, and an acid *electrolyte*. Unlike batteries, however, they have a continuous fuel input. One possible fuel is Hydrogen, which is quite expensive. If the fuel cell is to be successful commercially, it will have to be able to use an inexpensive and abundant fuel such as coal or natural gas. Fuel cells have been used in space but the cost has been very great. Research is under way to reduce the cost of fuel cells substantially.(8)

Fuel cells appear to have an important potential as power supplies in remote locations, supplying small loads to single homes or apartments or small industries. In addition, there has been some recent study of the possibility of using fuel cell systems in small (perhaps 20 MW) central power plants.(8)

Fuel cells should be quite attractive environmentally, compared with many existing systems.

## 13.6   THERMAL PARTICLE DEVICES

Related to each other in a sense are a trio of devices which make use of heated particles to generate electric energy directly.

The electrogasdynamic generator uses a moving neutral gas, with its kinetic energy, to force charged particles to move against an electric field, thus increasing the potential of the charged particles. This increased potential is then tapped off as from a battery.

The thermionic generator is an extremely simple device in which one electrode is heated enough so that electrons boil off it and flow to a nearby second electrode. A potential then exists between the two electrodes, which can be used as a source of DC electric energy.(9)

The thermoelectric generator makes use of the long-known Seebeck principle that a potential exists between two joined dissimilar conductors which are heated.

All three of these approaches are being studied but none is seriously expected to be developed in any but the distant future for central station use. The latter two may perhaps see applications in space.

## 13.7   THERMAL SEA POWER

We saw earlier in this book that work can theoretically be accomplished when two bodies are available at different temperatures. The greater the temperature difference, the greater the efficiency of heat-work conversion, following the Carnot efficiency relation. The oceans provide vast amounts of water at differing temperatures as a result of the sun's heat. At locations such as the Caribbean Sea, tropic waters meet and flow over arctic waters, with a temperature difference of perhaps 35° to 40° F over a separation of 1,500 to 2,500 feet.

## Example 13–3

Suppose that sea water layers are available at 45° F and 75° F. What is the Carnot efficiency?

From Chapter 4, the Carnot efficiency is $e = T_1 - T_2/T_1$ where the temperatures are in °K.

$$e = \frac{535 - 505}{535} = 5.6\%$$

Because of practical problems such as losses and the energy required to lift the water, the actual efficiency would be closer to 2% to 3%.

This low efficiency should not dissuade the developer. The warm and cold waters are not fuels for which he must pay. He does, however, have to pay for the equipment required to run the plant. This can be quite significant because of the necessity of moving a great deal of water to generate a reasonable amount of energy.

A number of schemes for applying the principle exist, and some pilot plants have been developed. Some have failed because of corrosion, equipment breakdown, and other reasons. Like the tides, interest in thermal sea power ebbs and flows.(10,11) Perhaps someday we may harness this immense source of energy.

## 13.8  WIND MACHINES

The wind's energy has been used to do work for man since before recorded history began. Windmills have ground grain for centuries. It is not surprising that much thought would be given to using the winds to generate electric energy.(12) Two major factors have inhibited the development of wind machines for electric energy generation. First, the winds are greatly variable. They even compare poorly with a flowing stream as a source of continuous and dependable energy. Second, a very large

**Figure 13–9.** An experimental wind machine. The energy of the winds has been used for centuries in wind machines. Today a number of fairly small wind machines generate electric energy, usually to pump water or charge a storage battery. Experiments continue to seek better energy conversion, primarily for remote low-energy sites. The device above is an experimental 500-watt machine which has been tested at Oklahoma State University in Stillwater, Oklahoma. (Courtesy of School of Electrical Engineering, Oklahoma State University.)

machine or many machines together are required to provide sufficient energy to justify most proposals. Wind machines so far are therefore best suited to some intermittent tasks such as the pumping of water from a well.

Wind machines can be used profitably by combining the intermittent input energy with a storage system which can be tapped at some later time to provide dependable electric energy. One such storage system is a simple battery. This scheme is used in Sweden to supply electricity to remote automatic telephone exchanges. The system includes sensing devices to control the charge delivered to the battery so that it is not overcharged. Another possible storage scheme is a water storage or pumped-storage hydro system. The major problem in this case may be obtaining enough energy to justify the installation costs. Once again, "free" energy may just be too expensive.

Nonetheless, serious research is presently underway in an attempt to find useful ways to harness the energy of the winds. It is very possible that we will see some small systems developed in the years ahead.

## 13.9   WAVE MACHINES

Both the winds and the waves contain extraordinary quantities of kinetic energy. The energy of the waves is perhaps even more dramatic, since it produces rolling, crashing breakers. It is certainly not surprising that man would try to harness this source, as he has. In 1909 the California Wave Motor Co. built Alva Reynold's "Ideal Wave Motor," a contraption using panels moving under water to transfer the energy of the waves to an electric generator. The device worked! Improvements were promised, and the device was to revolutionize the power industry. But the improvements didn't work out. For years the device lighted lamps on the wharf at Huntington Beach, until one day a storm washed away the machine. The power industry looked elsewhere for its revolution.

Interest in wave machines did not die with that storm, but neither has it led to major new triumphs. Experiments continue now and again along the coasts. It is difficult to believe, however, that large sections of ocean shores would ever be dedicated to this form of electric energy generation, whether it is financially feasible or not.

## 13.10  CONCLUSION

There are many more ways in which the energy of nature might be harnessed to do man's work. It seems unlikely that the search for a new Ideal Machine will ever cease. Some will be tried and will fail. Some will be limited successes for special applications. And some may truly revolutionize the energy industry. But none will be free. Two questions will always demand answers:

Can it be done?
Is it worth the price?

### REFERENCES FOR CHAPTER 13

1. News Release No. 20426, Federal Power Commission, Washington, D.C., June 24, 1974.
2. A.D. Foster, "Gas Turbine Fuels," *Combustion*, April, 1973, pp. 4–14.
3. N.R. Dibelius and E.W. Zeltman, "Gas Turbine Environmental Impact Using Natural Gas and Distillate Fuel," Report No. 73-GTD-6, General Electric Company, Schenectady, N.Y., February, 1973.
4. U.S. Department of the Interior, "The International Passamaquoddy Tidal Power Project and Upper Saint John

River Hydroelectric Power Development," Report to President John F. Kennedy, July, 1963.

5. M. Petrick, "Liquid-metal Magnetohydrodynamics," *IEEE Spectrum*, March, 1965, pp. 137–151.

6. D. Bienstock *et. al.*, "Environmental Aspects of MHD Power Generation," Proceedings of the 1971 Intersociety Energy Conversion Engineering Conference, Boston, Mass., August 3–5, 1971.

7. A.M. Bueche, "An Appraisal of MHD-1969," Office of Science and Technology, Washington, D.C., February 3, 1969.

8. W.J. Lueckel *et. al.*, "Fuel Cells for Dispersed Power Generation," Paper No. T72–235–5, *Proceedings of the IEEE Winter Meeting*, New York, Jan. 30–Feb. 4, 1972.

9. V.C. Wilson, "Thermionic Power Generation," *IEEE Spectrum*, May, 1964, pp. 75–83.

10. S. Walters, "Power in the Year 2001, Part 2—Thermal Sea Power," *Mechanical Engineering*, October, 1971, pp. 21–25.

11. H. Ting, "A Possible Breakthrough of Exploiting Thermal Power from the Sea," *Combustion*, August, 1970, pp. 16–19.

12. J. McCaull, "Windmills," *Environment*, Vol. 15, No. 1, Jan./Feb. 1973, pp. 6–17.

## GENERAL READING FOR CHAPTER 13

1. *The 1970 National Power Survey—Part 1*, Federal Power Commission, U.S. Government Printing Office, December, 1971.

Chapters 8 and 9 review a number of the schemes mentioned in this chapter. The material is descriptive and easily understood.

2. S.W. Angrist, *Direct Energy Conversion*, Allyn and Bacon, Inc., Boston, 1971.

This textbook provides much technical detail in areas such as thermoelectric, photovoltaic, thermionic, magnetohydrodynamic and fuel cell generators.

3. B. Chalmers, *Energy*, Academic Press, New York, 1963.

This text, less technical than the previous listing, discusses many of the topics of this chapter.

4. H.C. Hottel and J.B. Howard, *New Energy Technology—Some Facts and Assessments*, M.I.T. Press, Cambridge, 1971.

This book has some fairly technical details on recent work in gas turbine and magnetohydrodynamics technology.

5. W. Ley, *Engineers' Dreams*, The Viking Press, New York, 1958.

This is a very fascinating account of a number of fantastic projects that men have visualized in different parts of the world. Some are forerunners of great future projects. Some are already obsolete or too incredible to consider seriously —perhaps. Included are projects on solar, geothermal, tidal, and wind power; harnessing of the Mediterranean; construction of huge lakes in Africa; taming volcanoes, and many more.

6. A. Defant, *Ebb and Flow*, The University of Michigan Press, Ann Arbor, Michigan, 1958.

This is a short book on the tides: what causes them, how they are measured, their force, and more. This book does not contain material on tidal power projects. It is not highly technical, and it can be read with relative ease.

7. A.J. Ippen, *Estuary and Coastline Hydrodynamics*, McGraw-Hill Book Co., New York, 1966.

This is a highly technical, detailed study of ocean waves, tides, and estuaries. It is appropriate only for the serious student of ocean-water motion and its effects. It has no information on tidal electric power.

8. T.J. Gray and O.K. Gashus, Editors, *Tidal Power*, Plenum Press, New York, 1972.

This is a collection of technical papers on the use of the energy of the tides. It is not appropriate for the general reader, but it may be of substantial interest to the technical student.

## PROBLEMS FOR CHAPTER 13

*General Problems*

13.1. Suppose that a tidal basin has a surface area of 10 square miles and a tidal range of 25 feet. Assume that the basin is filled and the tide then recedes to its low value. What energy is potentially available in the impounded tidewater? Express your answer in ft.-lbs. and the equivalent KWH. ($5.42 \times 10^{12}$ ft.-lbs.; 2,050,000 KWH)

*Advanced Mathematical Problems*

13.2. For the student acquainted with simple electronic circuits, a fascinating analogy exists between a halfwave rectifier circuit with a parallel resistor-capacitor load and the two-basin tidal scheme. (See, for instance, R.J. Smith, *Circuits, Devices, and Systems*, John Wiley and Sons, Inc., New York, 1971, p. 396, for a discussion of rectifiers, and see General Reading #8 for a discussion of two-basin tidal schemes.) Develop the analogy by showing what elements of the two systems are analogs. How does the analogy fail?

*Advanced Study Problems*

13.3. Find in a recent article or book a newly proposed scheme for generating electric energy. Discuss its basic physical basis, its energy source, and the problems associated with its development. Also, estimate its prospects for significant development.

13.4. Compare in detail the relative air pollution produced by gas turbines and other fossil-fueled power plants. Evaluate the prospects for reducing air pollution from these systems in the future.

13.5. Discuss in detail the problem of evaluating fuel cells as a prospective source of electric energy at remote sites with small energy demands. What other schemes would be competitive in such a market? Consider the economic evaluation of competing schemes as well as you can.

13.6. Find additional literature on wave machines and write a brief history of this approach to electric energy generation. What factors have inhibited the growth of this form of power?

13.7. Repeat 13.4 for wind machines.

13.8. Make a comparative study of tidal and hydroelectric power plants. How are they similar, and how different? Discuss as many properties or factors as you can.

13.9. Read "Islands Afloat," from *Engineers' Dreams* (Reference 1). Discuss some of the reasons that this dream has never been brought to fruition.

13.10. Determine through a search of recent periodical literature the status of tidal power plant development in the United States and elsewhere.

# 14

# *WASTE HEAT*

*Doth a fountain send forth at the same place sweet water and bitter?*

James 3

We saw in Chapters 8 and 9 that huge amounts of energy are lost as waste heat in fossil-fuel and nuclear power plants. In this chapter we restrict our attention to the heat given up in the condenser and ignore other losses.

These losses are often called *thermal pollution*. They are so important, and they differ in many ways from other forms of pollution, that they deserve the extra attention of a special chapter.

We start with some calculations of the amount of heat wasted. This leads us to a consideration of the effect which added heat has on the biological world. Next we consider the ways in which heat can be dissipated, finishing with a study of the economic and environmental considerations relevant to each of the cooling schemes.

The first parts of this chapter are rather mathematical. The non-mathematical reader can ignore the development of equations and concentrate on the resultant magnitudes of energy loss and the methods of dissipating heat.

## 14.1  CONDENSER COOLING REQUIREMENTS

We want to know how much heat must be carried off by condenser cooling water. This will give us a sense of the magnitude of the problem before we ask what effect this heat has, and then what we might do about it.

Burning fuel in a thermal power plant (either fossil or nuclear) produces a certain amount of heat energy, $E_f$. A fraction $\eta$ of this energy is available as electric energy $E_g$ ($= \eta E_f$). A fraction $(1 - \eta)$ of $E_f$ is lost as waste heat. In a fossil-fuel plant about 85% of this waste heat is carried off by the condenser cooling water, and 15% is lost in stack gases and other miscellaneous forms. In nuclear plants about 95% of the waste heat is carried off by the cooling water. Hence the total energy dissipated by the condenser is:

$$E_c = r(1 - \eta) \, E_f \qquad\qquad (14\text{--}1)$$

where:

$$r \cong \begin{array}{l} 0.85 \text{ for fossil-fuel plants} \\[6pt] 0.95 \text{ for nuclear plants} \end{array}$$

In the discussion to follow we shall be concerned with the *time rate* at which heat energy is: (a) produced; (b) transformed into electric energy, and (c) lost as waste heat.

Working with the rate of heat flow is convenient because it

permits a direct relation to the electric *power* generated by a plant. We shall represent heat rates by $\dot{E}$ where the dot stands for a time rate. Also we shall commonly refer to $\dot{E}_g$ as $P_g$, the generator power. (Recall that in Chapter 2 we defined power as the time rate at which energy is made available or work is done.) Using these conventions we write:

$$P_g = \dot{E}_g = \eta \dot{E}_f \qquad\qquad (14\text{--}2)$$

$$\dot{E}_c = r(1 - \eta)\,\dot{E}_f \qquad\qquad (14\text{--}3)$$

where:

$\dot{E}_f$ = rate of heat production by the fuel
$\dot{E}_g$ = generator power
$\dot{E}_c$ = rate at which the condenser cooling water carries off heat
$\eta$ = efficiency of the plant
$r$ = fraction of waste heat carried off by the condenser

The units of these heat rates are KW. The relationships above are summarized in Figure 14–1.

Next, we seek a direct relation between the condenser waste heat rate and the generated electric power. This relation is available by solving Equations (14–2) and (14–3) to eliminate $\dot{E}_f$. This yields:

$$\dot{E}_c = r\,\frac{1 - \eta}{\eta}\,P_g \qquad\qquad (14\text{--}4)$$

### Example 14–1

Find the condenser cooling water waste heat rate for a modern 1,000 MW fossil-plant with an efficiency of 40%. Compare this with the power dissipated by the same size (same $P_g$) nuclear plant with an efficiency of 33%.

Fossil:  $\dot{E}_c = 1,000 \times \dfrac{1 - .4}{.4} \times 0.85 = 1,275$ MW

$$\text{Nuclear: } \dot{E}_c = 1,000 \times \frac{1 - .33}{.33} \times 0.95 = 1,930 \text{ MW}$$

The very interesting and important result shown in Example 14–1 is that, for these assumed efficiencies which are reasonable modern plant numbers, *nuclear plants must dissipate about 50 percent more condenser waste heat than fossil plants.*

Now that we have the condenser waste heat rate, in Equation 14–4, we shall want to find out what the flow rate of condenser cooling water must be. With the equivalence relation 3,413 BTU = 1 KWH, we can write (14–4) as:

$$\dot{E}_c = 3,413 \frac{r(1 - \eta)}{\eta} P_g \frac{\text{BTU}}{\text{Hour}} \tag{14–5}$$

where $P_g$ is expressed in KW.

### Example 14–2

What is the answer to the problem in Example 14–1 expressed in BTU/Hr.?

Fossil:     $\dot{E}_c = 4.36 \times 10^9$ BTU/Hr.

Nuclear: $\dot{E}_c = 6.59 \times 10^9$ BTU/Hr.

Before we can proceed further we need to know how many degrees we can or should increase the cooling water temperature. The amount of cooling-water temperature increase depends on the construction of the condenser and the rate at which water passes through the condenser. For technical reasons too complex to discuss here, the temperature increase should not be less than about 10° F nor more than about 20–25° F. A typical change is 15° F. We shall call this change $\Delta T$.

Recall that one BTU raises the temperature of one pound of water one degree F. Hence if we divide $\dot{E}_c$ in Equation 14–5 by $\Delta T$ we have the required water-flow rate in lbs./hr. To convert this to cubic feet per second we divide by

$$3,600 \ \frac{\text{sec.}}{\text{hr.}} \ \times 62.4 \ \frac{\text{lbs.}}{\text{cu. ft.}}$$

Introducing these three factors into Equation 14–5 yields:

$$Q = \frac{0.0152r \ (1 - \eta)P_g}{\eta \Delta T} \ \text{(cfs)} \qquad (14\text{--}6)$$

## Example 14–3

Determine the required flow rate of cooling water in a 1,000 MW nuclear power plant with an efficiency of 33%. Assume a condenser temperature change $\Delta T = 15°$.

$$Q = \frac{0.0152 \times 0.95 \ (0.67) \times 10^6}{0.33 \times 15}$$

$$= 1,950 \ \text{cfs}$$

## Example 14–4

Calculate the cooling water in acre-feet per year required by the plant described in Example 14–3.

$$Q = 1,950 \times (3,600)(8,760) = 6.15 \times 10^{10} \ \frac{\text{cu. ft.}}{\text{year}}$$

$$= \frac{6.15 \times 10^{10}}{43,560} = 1.41 \times 10^6 \ \frac{\text{ac. ft.}}{\text{year}}$$

It is clear from the above examples that thermal power plants require very large water flow rates for cooling. In the past it has been common to use river, ocean, or lake water run through the condensers once and then returned to the source. This is called *once-through cooling*. In recent years, however, there has been increasing concern about the effect of heated water on the biological environment. This concern has led to the development of a number of alternatives to once-through cooling. Before looking into these we shall want to ask what effect added heat has on the biological residents of the cooling-water source.

## 14.2 BIOLOGICAL EFFECTS OF ADDED HEAT

To the conservationist, addition of heat to water often becomes "thermal pollution." To the ardent proponent of power development it has been "thermal enhancement" or even "thermal enrichment," on occasion. We shall adopt here the more noncommittal term *thermal addition* for the general case of added heat. Whether added heat enriches or pollutes is very much a matter of circumstances, including which biological entities are under study. It seems reasonable to state that thermal pollution has occurred when added heat produces effects which are detrimental to other uses of the water. The problem then becomes one of determining whether the heat is detrimental in some way.

The effect of added heat on water has been studied for many years. Recently this study has intensified, but there is very much we do not yet know. This will no doubt be an area of extensive research in the years ahead. In the meantime we have no clear

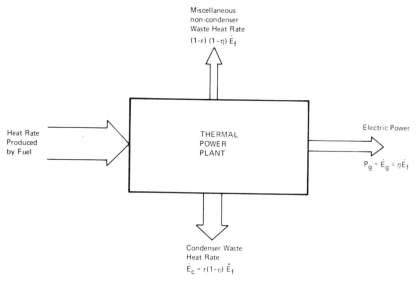

**Figure 14–1.** Heat Rates in a Thermal Power Plant.

and unambiguous answer to the question, "Does added heat cause unacceptable levels of thermal pollution?"

Added heat has a number of complex effects on the water itself. In general as water is heated there is a tendency toward:

1) Decreased oxygen capacity
2) Increased chemical reaction rate
3) Stratification, or formation of layers of water at different temperatures
4) Increased viscosity

Heat addition affects aquatic life in many ways, some direct and apparent, some far less obvious. The life of both plants and animals is affected. Plant life, which uses sunlight and nonliving components of the water for nutrition, becomes food for aquatic animal life. But temperature affects the life of important plants such as algae. As temperature is changed some forms become more dominant, some decline. The result can be a major change in the ecology of the source of the cooling water. Plants are only a part of the complex aquatic ecosystem. Other important members of the system are bacteria and fungi, phytoplankton, zooplankton, and fish. All have varying tolerance to temperature change.

To consider the effects of temperature in more detail we center our attention on fish, usually the most apparent residents of the water source. Heat addition can affect fish in a number of ways.

First, death of fish can be directly related to heat addition. Fish have maximum allowable *temperature* limits, and maximum allowable *temperature change* limits. Laboratory studies have given us some answers to the questions of temperature tolerance of certain fishes. Table 14–1 summarizes a part of one such study.(2) The water temperatures given are for survival of 50% of the test fish over 24 to 133 hours. Results of such tests give no final answers to temperature limits for fish, but they do provide a start in this highly important study. Outside of the laboratory we have some data on fish kills in reported incidents. One study lists 18 kills reported to the Federal Water Pollution Control Administration between 1962 and 1969.(3) The total number of fish killed exceeded 700,000, with a worst-case kill of over 300,000 fish at Sandusky, Ohio in 1967.

Second, increased heat may interfere with spawning. Spawning is affected by temperature in two ways. First, fish depend on temperature as a signal for migration and spawning. Temperature is a kind of seasonal yardstick. Second, eggs will not hatch above a certain temperature, depending upon the species of fish.

Third, fish suffer internal biological effects from added heat. Changes in temperature cause changes in a number of the fish's bodily functions, such as respiration, food intake, activity level, growth rate, and lifespan.(4)

Fourth, fish may be killed through indirect effects. As we saw above, fish are only a part of a complex aquatic ecosystem. Changes in that system may lead to the death of the fish. Particularly important are factors such as reduced oxygen, changes in food supply, an increase in toxic substances, or a decrease in resistance to such substances, and changes in the stratification and light penetration of the body of water.

## TABLE 14–1

### Minimum and Maximum Temperatures for Certain Freshwater Fishes

| Species | Acclimated to °F | Minimum Temp. °F | Hours | Maximum Temp. °F | Hours |
|---------|---------|---------|---------|---------|---------|
| Largemouth Bass | 68.0 | 41.0 | 24 | 89.6 | 72 |
|                 | 86.0 | 51.8 | 24 | 93.2 | 72 |
| Bluegill | 59.0 | 37.4 | 24 | 87.8 | 60 |
|          | 86.0 | 51.8 | 24 | 93.2 | 60 |
| Channel Catfish | 59.0 | 32.0 | 24 | 86.0 | 24 |
|                 | 77.0 | 42.8 | 24 | 93.2 | 24 |
| Brook Trout | 37.4 | — | — | 73.4 | 133 |
|             | 68.0 | — | — | 77.0 | 133 |

Finally, competitive replacement by other species may occur. Since some fish are more active or more adaptable to a given temperature, a change in temperature may change the dominant species. Cold water species such as trout may be forced out of a system as warm water species begin to dominate.

There is much more which can be said about harmful thermal effects on aquatic life.(5,6) We turn our attention now to some beneficial aspects of heat addition to water.

The fact that aquatic life changes its functional characteristics can in some cases be used to advantage. Major interest exists today in accelerating growth of shellfish and some fish species by exposing them to a temperature at which growth is most rapid. This permits more rapid harvesting of edible fishes.

Most of the effects of temperature elevation on aquatic life are presently considered to be undesirable. In addition, there are a number of areas in the country in which sufficient water is not available for once-through cooling. These two factors have led in recent years to significant new efforts toward finding alternative ways to cool condenser water. In the next section we discuss once-through cooling and some of its major alternatives.


## 14.3  HEAT DISSIPATION TECHNIQUES

There are a number of available schemes for cooling condenser water. The four general classes are:

1) Once-through cooling
2) Cooling ponds
3) Cooling towers
4) Heat transfer to other systems

There are a number of ways of operating each of these so that the total number of possible schemes is well over 20. We shall avoid most of the variations on each scheme and discuss only the most common forms of each.

In all schemes it is necessary to dissipate or spread out the heat. Eventually the heat is diffused over a sufficiently large part of the earth so that its effect is not apparent. Excess heat does not accumulate on the earth; it radiates out into space.* The difficulty is not with the amount of heat added, but rather with its concentration. Hence each proposed scheme must provide a mechanism for dispersing this concentrated heat with as few adverse side effects as possible.

In the once-through cooling scheme, water withdrawn from a river, lake, bay or ocean is run through the condenser with a temperature increase of perhaps 10° to 25° F, and is then returned to the source. This scheme is sketched in Figure 14–2.

A number of factors must be considered in designing a once-through cooling system. The water must be sufficient to meet the required flow rates as given by Equation 14–6. If the source of cooling water, sometimes called a *heat sink*, is a river, the minimum river flow rate should be somewhat larger than Q in the equation. The greater the flow rate of the river, the greater is its potential to disperse or spread the heat quickly as the heat moves downstream from the plant. If the heat sink is the ocean, the intake and discharge tubes must be sufficiently far apart that no significant part of the heat discharged is present at the intake tube. This effect will depend on such factors as tides and ocean currents.

Once-through cooling is used very extensively in the United States at ocean, river, lake and bay sites. Opposition to this form of cooling has arisen at all these types of sites. Although the ocean is potentially an almost infinite source of mixing and dispersing heat, the effects near the discharge point may be harmful or disastrous to local marine life, including kelp beds, fish populations, and other forms of ocean life. Essentially the same problem limits the use of rivers and lakes, except that here, if the body of water is small, a large part if not all of the body may increase in temperature.

* There is a balance between heat received from the sun and heat radiated into space. This balance is not affected by local additions of heat.

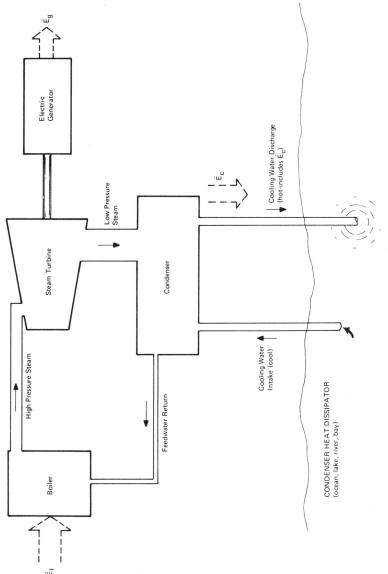

**Figure 14–2.** Once-Through Cooling.

333

The possible damage to aquatic life is one of the factors which has led to the search for an alternative to once-through cooling. The second factor is that it is not always convenient or desirable to place a plant near a large natural source of cooling water. Hence we need some other ways to cool condenser water.

The first obvious alternative is to build our own small lake or *cooling pond*. There is then no question of disturbing an existing natural body of water. In fact it may even be possible to develop a desirable new water facility, at higher than normal temperatures, suitable for water sports and warm water fish. The disadvantage of the pond is that its methods of getting rid of its heat (principally evaporation and radiation) are fairly slow, so that relatively large ponds are required. A common rule of thumb is about one to two acres per megawatt of installed capacity. That means about 1,000–2,000 acres (two to three square miles) for a large modern 1,000 MW plant. This is a rather large area which may not be available at many sites.

One technique for decreasing the amount of required pond area is to build a mechanism into the pond which sprays water into the air and increases the water area available for evaporation. This forms a so-called *spray pond*.

If a large natural body of water is not available and a pond is not desirable, we try to find a system which does what a pond does but in less space. One such system is a *cooling tower*.(7,8) We limit our discussion here primarily to *wet cooling towers*. In the wet cooling tower the heated condenser water is delivered to an open-top tower, pumped up 20 to 100 feet, and allowed to "rain" down to the floor of the tower as air moves upward through the tower. This greatly increases the surface exposure of water to air and increases the evaporation (and a little bit of radiation) enough to dissipate the required heat. The principal byproduct of the cooling tower is water vapor. This system is sketched in Figure 14–4.

There are two important types of wet cooling towers. Both are shown in Figure 14–5. One is a forced or induced draft

tower in which air motion is caused by a mechanical fan placed
either on top of the tower (induced) or on the bottom sides
(forced). The second is the natural draft tower. It requires
sufficient height—about 400 feet—that a flow of air from
bottom to top occurs naturally. Both types are used in the
United States. The latter type is becoming increasingly popular. The forced or induced draft tower is relatively small
(75–100 feet high), and is made of wood. The natural draft
tower is a massive (usually concrete) structure perhaps 400 feet
high and nearly as wide. These brief descriptions give all of the

**Figure 14–3.** A hybrid of cooling techniques. For years the Sacramento River
was used for once-through cooling of the Pittsburgh Plant in California. When
a new 790 MW unit (stack on the left) was added in 1972, water pollution
control laws prohibited further use of the river for cooling. Pacific Gas and
Electric Company built a long U-shaped spray pond (above and to the left of
the stacks) for the new unit. Note also the oil off-loading pier and the oil
storage tanks. (Courtesy of Pacific Gas and Electric Co.)

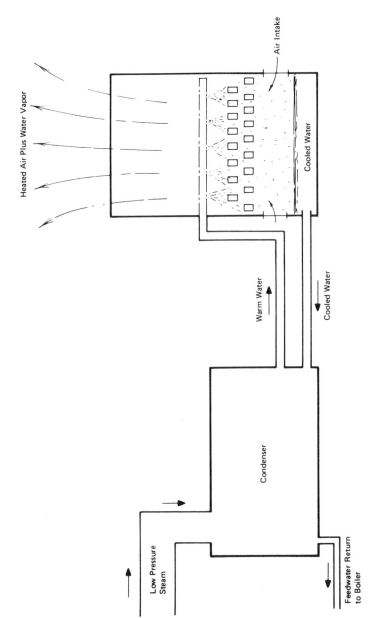

**Figure 14-4.** Cooling Tower System.

Heated Air Plus Water Vapor

Air Intake

Cooled Water

Warm Water

Cooled Water

Condenser

Low Pressure Steam

Feedwater Return to Boiler

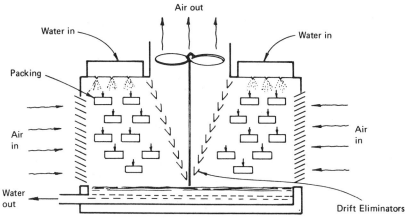

a) Crossflow Induced Draft Tower

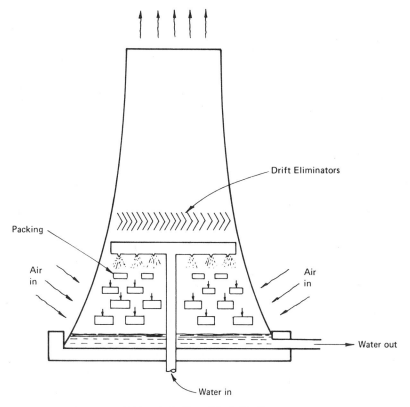

b) Hyperbolic Natural Draft Wet Tower

**Figure 14–5.** Wet Cooling Towers.

337

basic ingredients for analyzing the advantages and disadvantages of each.

Aesthetically, the smaller tower is almost certainly preferable because of its low profile. The natural draft tower has a fundamentally pleasing hyperbolic shape but its massiveness usually makes it far out of proportion to its surroundings. In terms of capital costs, the natural draft tower is much more expensive than the smaller tower. However, maintenance and operation costs (which include the cost of electric power to run the fans) are much greater for the forced or induced draft towers. The trade-offs evident here are sufficiently balanced so that it is not clear which tower is in general more desirable, and both forms are being adopted.

One of the major disadvantages of the wet cooling tower is its water loss due to evaporation. An alternative approach is to keep the cooling water inside heat-radiating pipes in the tower so that it is not exposed to the air. This saves water loss from evaporation, but it also cuts down the efficiency of the cooling system, and increases its cost significantly. This so-called *dry cooling tower* has not been developed extensively to date. However, growing water shortages in some areas and possible environmental effects of wet towers may lead to increased interest in dry towers.(9,10,11)

The final method for dissipating condenser heat is one which is being viewed with a great deal of interest at this time. This is the general technique of using the waste heat for some useful purpose. It has been proposed that waste heat be used for heating offices and homes, increasing agricultural yields by using warm water for irrigation, salt-water desalination plants, sewage treatment plants, and a variety of other processes. Such proposals seem very attractive and in fact many of these things are actually being done on at least a small scale. Whether development along such lines will be extensive is not clear. Effort no doubt will be directed toward such goals.

## 14.4  MAKE-UP WATER

We have saved for a separate section one problem common to ponds and wet towers, because it is a difficulty which will almost certainly be increasingly serious as time goes on. At first glance the use of ponds or towers seems particularly attractive from the standpoint of water use because the same supply of water appears to cycle continually from condenser to cooler, back to condenser, etc. Unfortunately, however, there are water losses and they are not, in general, insignificant. Whether the cooler is pond or tower there are three important sources of loss of water:

1) Evaporation (1–3%)
2) Drift (0.1–0.5%)
3) Blow-down (1–3%)

Evaporation is the basic mechanism for the removal of heat from the water. We can get a rough idea of the resulting water loss with some simple calculations. Suppose that the cooling scheme must remove 20° F of temperature increase before the water is re-used. Recall again that one BTU increases the temparature of one pound of water by one degree F. Thus each pound of cooling water must lose 20 BTU. But one pound of water requires roughly 1,000 BTU to evaporate. Therefore, if all of the heat is carried off by evaporation, about one of every 50 pounds of water (or 2%) must evaporate.

Drift is the process by which small water particles (not vapor) are carried off by the air. This can usually be reduced to acceptable limits by tower design.

Blow-down is a process of flushing out and discharging the water supply in the system periodically. It is necessary because evaporation leaves behind solids which tend to concentrate in the water system. The frequency of this flushing process depends on the degree of contamination of the source of water.

It is apparent from the above that a non-trivial percentage (perhaps two to four percent) of the circulating water is continually being lost and must be replaced from a source of make-up water. The magnitude of this demand is evident from the following example. (For more detail see Reference 12.)

*Example 14–5*

Consider a 1,000 MW nuclear power plant with an efficiency of 33% and a condenser $\Delta T = 15°$ F (as in Examples 14–3 and 14–4). If the water loss is three percent, calculate the required water flow rate of make-up water. From Example 14–4 we have a condenser flow rate $Q = 1.41 \times 10^6$ ac.-ft./yr.

Make-up flow rate: $Q = 0.03 \times 1.41 \times 10^6$

$$= 42,300 \frac{\text{ac.-ft.}}{\text{yr.}}$$

$$= 58.5 \text{ cfs.}$$

In many dry regions this is a significant amount of water which may even be a crucial determining factor in a site location decision.

The loss of water inherent in wet tower systems is the primary impetus for the development of dry cooling towers. The dry tower concept is severely handicapped by the fact that its heat loss mechanisms are much less effective than evaporation. The result is that dry towers must be much larger and more expensive than wet towers.

## 14.5 THE ECONOMICS OF COOLING SYSTEMS

There is no general agreement about costs of alternative cooling methods. These figures depend on such variables as plant size, site location (including environmental conditions), and the status of the economy. It is possible, however, to indicate some approximate cost levels which at least suggest relative costs with some accuracy. Table 14–2 is a summary of values reported in the recent literature.

Once-through cooling, where it is possible, is almost certain to be the most economical solution. Ponds and wet towers, both mechanical and natural draft, compete fairly evenly on an economic basis; certainly all three appear commonly in practice. Selection is often made on grounds other than economic.

### Example 14–6

Find the added cost in mills/KWH if a natural-draft wet tower is used with the fossil-fuel plant described in Table 8–2. Assume that the cost is $10 per KWh.

In this case we consider only the fixed charge (14.5%) on $10, and neglect the maintenance costs. Yearly fixed charges per kilowatt are:

$$0.145 \times 10 = \$1.45$$

This represents an increase of 2.3% over the $62.65 total annual capacity cost. This of course implies a 2.3% increase in the fixed energy cost, which was 13 mills/KWH. This increase is 0.3 mills/KWH. Total energy costs were 17.85 mills/KWH. 0.3 represents a 1.7% increase in energy cost.

### TABLE 14–2

#### Costs of Cooling Water Systems

| System | Fossil ($/KW) | Nuclear ($/KW) |
|---|---|---|
| Once-Through | 2–6 | 3–8 |
| Cooling Ponds | 5–8 | 7–12 |
| Mechanical Draft Wet Tower | 5–10 | 7–13 |
| Natural Draft Wet Tower | 6–14 | 8–20 |
| Mechanical Draft Dry Tower | 20–50 | 30–65 |

## 14.6  COOLING SYSTEMS AND THE ENVIRONMENT

Perhaps no power plant environmental problems are as complex or difficult to resolve as those of the cooling system. Alternatives to once-through cooling are themselves largely a response to an inadequately-understood threat to the environment. In their turn, the alternatives have an impact which is not easily assessed. In this section we describe some of the environmental concerns without in any way attempting to make a general statement about which system is "best." That question can be approached only in the particular and not in the general.

The problems of once-through cooling have been discussed to some extent earlier in this chapter. Heat added to natural waters tends to change the ecological balance. This may result in either subtle or catastrophic effects on marine life. There also may be some desirable effects, such as increased growth rates of some food fish.

Cooling ponds do not affect an existing natural body of water. However, they do have the disadvantage of taking up a fairly large amount of land (perhaps one to three square miles). Often this land is not available on the market. In other situations it may be available, but removing the land from use as land may be considered environmentally undesirable. Warm water ponds of this size may also cause significant local weather changes such as the development of fog banks during certain times of the year. Ponds can be effectively developed in some areas as multi-use facilities. Their temperatures immediately suggest warm-water fish breeding, and warm-water sports, including fishing, swimming, sailing.

Wet towers have the disadvantage of releasing large amounts of water vapor into the air, with possible local meteorological effects such as fogging, or icing of nearby roads.(13) In addition, towers release to the atmosphere other undesirable particles or gases present in the cooling water. Natural draft towers, which can be as much as 400 feet high, are considered to be aesthetically undesirable in many sites.

Dry towers do not release water vapor. They do release warm air which could have minor local effects, and they are somewhat larger than wet towers.

As we said earlier, there is no "best" solution. We are faced here with the problem of dispersing to the environment a large concentration of heat. The effect which each method has depends on many variables. Only when these are considered fully for a particular site can a choice be made. And still that choice must be made in the midst of much uncertainty.

Before closing this chapter we turn briefly to the question of costs and environmental benefits. At first it may seem that cooling towers are added to a plant only for environmental reasons. Their cost would then represent an internalizing of the cost of preventing water pollution. However, the situation is not quite that simple. Thermal power plants require some kind of cooling system to operate, quite apart from environmental concerns. Hence a certain basic portion of cooling costs must be assigned to plant operation. If a more sophisticated system is added to protect the environment, only the incremental costs beyond the base cost should be charged to the environment. If a plant is sited in a normally dry region, for other than environmental reasons, the cost of a water-conserving cooling system likewise cannot be attributed to environmental concerns. None of this affects the final cost of energy to the consumer, but only the question of whether or not the added cost is a part of "cleaning up the environment."

In this chapter we have reviewed the major existing methods for cooling condenser water. New concepts are continually arising, and may play important future roles in waste heat management.(14)

## REFERENCES FOR CHAPTER 14

1. National Academy of Engineering, *Engineering for the Resolution of the Energy-Environment Dilemma*, Washington, D.C., 1972.

2. Federal Power Commission, *Problems in Disposal of Waste Heat from Steam-Electric Plants*, Federal Power Commission Staff Study, 1969.

3. S.C. Bloom, *Heat—A Growing Water Pollution Problem*, in *Environment Reporter*, Monograph No. 4, The Bureau of National Affairs, May 1, 1970.

4. J.R. Clark, "Thermal Pollution and Aquatic Life," *Scientific American*, March, 1969, pp. 19–28.

5. P.A. Krenkel and F.L. Parker, *Biological Aspects of Thermal Pollution,*, Vanderbilt University Press, 1969.

6. W.S. Lee *et. al.*, *Environmental Effects of Thermal Discharges*, The American Society of Mechanical Engineers, New York, 1970.

7. R.D. Woodson, "Cooling Towers," *Scientific American*, May, 1971, pp. 70–78.

8. J.B. Dickey and R.E. Cates, "Managing Waste Heat With the Water Cooling Tower," The Marley Co., Kansas City, Missouri, 1970.

9. H. Heeren and L. Holly, "Dry Cooling Eliminates Thermal Pollution-II," *Combustion*, November, 1972, pp. 17–28.

10. R.E. Holmes and S.J. Basham, Jr., "A Dry Cooling System for Steam Power Plants," *Proceedings of the Intersociety Energy Conversion Engineering Conference*, Boston, Mass., August 3–5,1971.

11. J.P. Rossie *et. al.*, "Cost Comparison of Dry-Type and Conventional Cooling Systems for Representative Nuclear Generating Plants," R.W. Beck and Associates for the U.S. Atomic Energy Commission, Washington, D.C., March, 1972.

12. P. Leung and R.E. Moore, "Water Consumption Determination for Steam Power Plant Cooling Towers," *Combustion*, November, 1970, pp. 14–23.

13. G.F. Bierman *et. al.*, "Characteristics, Classification and Incidence of Plumes from Large Natural Draft Cooling Towers," *Combustion*, October, 1971, pp. 25–31.

14. J.A. MacFarlang *et.al.*, "Rejection of Waste Heat from Power Plants Through Phased-Cooling," *Combustion*, pp. 6–12, February, 1975.

## GENERAL READING FOR CHAPTER 14

1. *Cooling Towers*, American Institute of Chemical Engineers, New York, 1972.

   This is a very good set of papers on cooling-tower problems. They are technical papers, but many of them can be easily read and understood by persons without technical expertise.

2. National Academy of Engineering, *Engineering for the Resolution of the Energy-Environment Dilemma*, Washington, D.C., 1972.

   Pages 103 to 150 give a very good technical and general survey of cooling problems covering all points discussed in this chapter. An extensive list of references is included.

3. D.A. Berkowitz and A.M. Squires, *Power Generation and Environmental Change*, M.I.T. Press, Cambridge, Mass., 1971.

   This book has five papers on waste heat problems in addition to groups of papers on fossil-fuel power, hydro-electric power, and nuclear power.

4. P.A. Krenkel and F.L. Parker, *Biological Aspects of Thermal Pollution*, Vanderbilt University Press, 1969.

   This is an excellent set of general readings on engineering as well as biological effects of heat addition.

5. P.H. Cootner and G.O.G. Lof, *Water Demand for Steam Electric Generation*, The Johns Hopkins Press, Baltimore, 1965.

   This is a very good engineering and economic analysis of cooling systems. It is appropriate only for the advanced student or practicing engineer.

6. Reference 11 above.

   This is an excellent review of cooling tower costs. Much of it can be read with value by any reader of this text. Some parts, however, are more technical, and will be of interest to the engineer with a background in thermodynamics. Much detail on the factors which contribute to tower cost is given.

## PROBLEMS FOR CHAPTER 14

*General Problems*

14.1. Water flow rates are clearly of great importance in cooling problems. Such flow rates may be expressed in cubic feet per second (cfs), gallons per minute (gpm) or acre-feet per year (afy). Make a table which shows how these measures are related.

14.2. Consider a large, modern, 1,400 MW coal-fired steam plant with an efficiency of 40%. If the condenser temperature change is 20°, calculate the condenser cooling water flow rate in cfs, gpm, and afy. (Q = 1,350 cfs = 607,000 gpm = 977,000 afy)

14.3. Repeat Problem 14.2 under the assumption that the plant is nuclear and has an efficiency of 33%. (This is the kind of first-order calculation that a siting engineer would have to make in considering plant-type and water availability.) (Q = 2,050 cfs = 921,000 gpm = 1,485,000 afy)

14.4. For the plant described in Problem 14.2 find the make-up water flow rate in cfs if the water loss in the cooling system is 3% of the condenser water flow.

14.5. Assume that the plant described in Problem 14.3 uses a natural draft tower with a water-loss of 2.5%. How large a lake would have to be created if make-up water were to be stored for one year's use? Assume an average lake depth of 50 feet and give your answer in square miles. (1.16 sq. mi.)

14.6. Write an equation for the miscellaneous non-condenser waste heat rate. Call it $\dot{E}_m$, a function of r, $\eta$, and $P_g$. Calculate $\dot{E}_m$ for Problem 14.2. (Assume r = 0.85.)

14.7. Repeat Problem 14.6 for the five cooling systems given in Table 14–2. Make a table of total energy costs and the percentage increase from each particular system.

## Advanced Mathematical Problems

14.8. Write an equation for the cooling water flow expressed in gallons/KWH for a given $\Delta T$, r, and $\eta$. Calculate this flow for $\Delta T = 15°$ F, r = 0.95, and $\eta = 0.34$. (50 gal./ KWH)

14.9. Suppose that $P_g$ varies with time and cooling water varies proportionately. Write an equation for the total number of cubic feet of water required to cool a plant with a power output of $P_g(t)$. Let t be expressed in hours.

14.10. Assume that of all the electric energy produced in the United States in 1971 80% was produced by fossil-fuel plants using once-through cooling, and having an average efficiency of 33%. What was the average flow rate in cfs? Compare this with the flow rate of the Mississippi River.

## Advanced Study Problems

14.11. Write a short paper on the history of the dry cooling tower and its prospects for future use.

14.12. Write a paper on the effects of heat on one specific aquatic plant or animal.

14.13. It is often suggested that waste heat should be put to some useful work, such as heating, irrigation, etc. After doing some research on this topic, discuss situations in which such utilization may be feasible and some of the problems associated with it.

# 15

## ENERGY CONSERVATION

*They are as sick that surfeit with too much,*
*As they that starve with nothing.*

Shakespeare

There was born about 1970 a new ethic—an ethic of energy conservation as a necessity of life, if not a way of life. The *idea* is not new, of course. It is at least as old as Thoreau, and probably has no identifiable origin. But as a major driving force it came into being near the beginning of this decade. In its first years it was nurtured by a few environmentalists, sometimes labeled preservationists, sometimes conservationists. It grew and was fed by an increasing realization of fuel shortages and problems associated with generating energy. It reached its maturity with the Yom Kippur War of October, 1973, and the aftermath of

349

that war. By 1975 it had gained its legitmacy in the eyes of the nation. Today, energy conservation is national policy. It is accepted and urged upon us by virtually every sector of government, industry, and private interests.

We need to ask some questions about energy conservation. Why should we conserve energy? How do we effect conservation? In what sectors or activities can energy be conserved? What is the future of energy conservation? The purpose of this chapter is to answer these questions.

## 15.1  WHY CONSERVE ENERGY?

Actually there are a number of reasons why we might choose or be required to conserve energy.

1) Personal sense of excess use of energy
2) Scarcity of energy
3) Desire to save money
4) Response to urging of the government

Many people feel that they use more energy than is necessary for a reasonable quality of life. They reduce their use of energy perhaps to move away somewhat from the mechanical-industrial world. They may be motivated by a sense that they can lead simpler lives and perhaps develop a greater control over their lives. These motivations are internal, and they are sometimes almost religious in nature and intensity.

Scarcity of energy forces limitation or conservation of energy. The result is usually not a voluntary reduction, but it does have the same basic effect of decreasing energy use. If energy is scarce or somewhat unavailable for some period, use is reduced. This was the case with gasoline in the first quarter of 1974, at the height of the Arab oil embargo. It is also the case when the government deliberately withholds or limits energy availability —through rationing, for instance.

The desire to save money can lead to energy conservation. As the price of gasoline rises, car use decreases, and there is an increased tendency to purchase smaller cars, which use less gas. As electricity and heating fuel prices rise, homeowners tend to cut back on use by various conservation measures.

It is possible for the government to urge reduced use of energy. The recent call to turn thermostats down to 68° was a somewhat successful temporary measure. It seems unlikely that urgings of this nature, where no sanctions exist, will result in substantial savings. A somewhat more formal governmental urging was the legal reduction of automobile speed limits to 55 mph.

Hence there are several kinds of motivations—social and economic, political and technical—which lead to reduced energy use. Next we ask what types of actions, individual or public, can cause energy conservation.

## 15.2   CONSERVATION APPROACHES

Before we consider in Section 15.3 the specific actions which can save energy, we briefly look at some general principles or issues.

First we should be aware that there are differing effects which conservation can have on our lives. We arbitrarily suggest three types of conservation activities.

1) Activities that save energy and have no apparent disadvantages

2) Activities that save energy but have some minor associated disadvantages

3) Activities that save energy and have major associated disadvantages

In the first category are activities such as house insulation in many situations in which energy is saved, and the homeowner saves more money on his energy bill than he loses on the cost of the insulation. In situations such as this, the homeowner has everything to gain and apparently nothing to lose. Such situations should be identified and well-publicized.

In the second category are a wide variety of situations where energy is saved but some relatively small disadvantages occur. A fairly small increase in gas prices is an example. The cost goes up a little but not enough to have major consequences. In many cases where disadvantages occur, money is saved. Then the consumer must determine the value of the energy and money saved compared with the disadvantage. Turning off house lights is inconvenient, but it saves energy and money. Driving at 55 mph instead of 70 mph is inconvenient, and it costs time. Hanging clothes out to dry is considered to be inconvenient by many. And there are a number of other examples.

In the third category are very serious reductions of energy that could cause major changes in people's standards of living. Severe shortages could close factories and lead to widespread unemployment. Food shortages could occur, with resulting threats to health. Major fuel shortages could halt much of the complex transportation system upon which our economy depends.

In conclusion, it seems reasonable that we should actively seek conservation activities in the first category, learn to live at least for some time with the second category, and do as much as possible to avoid the third.

A second general principle of energy conservation is to be wary of accepting solutions just because they seem to be common sense. (Remember: Common sense is that which convinces us that the earth is flat.) For example, for some time there was a suggestion that every effort should be made to avoid using electric appliances whenever possible. Hence, the electric shaver was out. But then a number of simple studies showed that it takes more energy to fill a basin with hot water for a lather shave than to run an electric razor for a couple of minutes. A dishwashing machine may use less energy than a human dishwasher using lots of rinse water. In summary, it is not always obvious that energy will be saved in a given situation, and careful study is often required before any conclusions are possible.

## 15.3 SPECIFIC CONSERVATION MEASURES

In this section we could not hope to list all of the ways in which energy might be conserved. There are far too many conservation measures. Also, many such lists have been prepared, and they are available to the reader. (See, for example, References 1,2 and 3.) Instead we list some representative examples from each of the four major use sectors: transportation, residential, commercial, and industrial.

1. *Transportation*
   a. Purchase light-weight, low power automobiles. They require less energy to build than larger cars, and less energy to operate.
   b. Drive less by carpooling, using a bicycle, public transportation, or by walking. Eliminate unnecessary trips.
   c. Operate automobiles more efficiently by decreasing speed, minimizing braking, and using radial tires.
   d. Keep automobiles in good operating condition.

2. *Residential*
   a. When buying a new house or renovating an old house, specify wall and ceiling insulation and storm windows particularly in very cold or very hot regions. Consider other energy-saving features such as heat pumps, solar energy systems, appropriate house color for the climate, efficient heating and cooling units, and efficient built-in appliances.
   b. When buying new appliances, select units with low energy use. Large frost-free refrigerators and freezers

require more energy than smaller units and units without the frost-free feature. Large color TV requires more electric power than small black and white models. If you need an air conditioner, buy the most efficient model. Eventually, appliances will probably carry power demand data so that the consumer can consider energy demand (operating costs) as well as the initial cost.

   c. Since most of the energy in the home is used for heating and cooling, keep the heating thermostat as low as comfort permits, and the cooling thermostat as high as possible. Use drapes to let in heat during the winter and keep it out during the summer.

3. *Commercial*

   a. Construction of buildings should be designed to minimize operating energy losses. Insulate buildings. Consider use of windows carefully. Avoid overlighting buildings. Use flourescent light when possible.

   b. Reduce lighting loads. Reduce heating and cooling. Check facility to locate sources of unnecessary energy use. Turn off lights at night after closing.

4. *Industrial*

   a. Seek energy-efficient techniques for industrial processes, particularly energy-intensive processes such as steel production and aluminum reduction.

   b. Use recycled raw materials where energy savings are possible.

   c. Use total energy systems where possible, using waste heat from one process for other lower-level heat stages of the process.

Again, the above examples do not begin to exhaust the possibilities. But they do suggest general ways in which energy, and therefore money, can be saved. The reader should note that these measures could be divided into three general categories, or rules.

1. Buy devices which require as little energy as possible to build and to operate.

2. Do not operate devices unless it is necessary.

3. When device operation is necessary, restrict operation as much as possible, and operate as efficiently as possible.

With these rules, a list of do's and don't's for a specific activity, and a little bit of common sense, the reader should find it possible to save substantial and important amounts of energy and money.

## 15.4  THE FUTURE OF ENERGY CONSERVATION

What is the future of the energy conservation ethic? For some, conservation is a lifetime activity. For others it is a holding action, an expediency necessary to reduce the demand-supply gap until new sources of energy supply can be developed. It seems likely that factors such as rising prices and recurring shortages will slow the energy growth rate. Statistics released in April of 1975 indicated that energy use in the United States actually decreased by 2% from 1973 to 1974. Is this a one-time phenomenon, related to the weak economy, rising prices and gasoline shortages, or is this the beginning of a real move to cut energy use? We cannot be sure of the answer, and that uncertainty will greatly complicate the task of energy planners and suppliers.

It seems reasonable to this writer that man will eventually have to curb his growing appetite for energy. The time seems right to start practicing a new energy-use ethic. As we do so, however, it will be necessary that we seriously try to anticipate the problems which will be associated with the limiting of energy use, not only for the next few years, but for the generations to come.(4)

## REFERENCES FOR CHAPTER 15

1. "The Energy Challenge—What Can We Do?" Energy Conservation Research, Malvern, Pa., 1974.
2. "Energy Conservation Handbook—For Light Industries and Commercial Buildings," U.S. Department of Commerce, Superintendent of Documents, U.S. Government Printing Office, Washington, D.C., 1974
3. "Tips for Energy Savers," Federal Energy Administration, Washington, D.C., 1974.
4. A. Daniel Burhans, "The Steady State," *The Center Magazine*, January/February, 1975.
5. R.S. Carlsmith, "Energy Conservation and the Environment," ORNL-NSF-EP-77, Oak Ridge National Laboratory, Oak Ridge, Tennessee, September, 1974.
6. M. Corr and D. MacLeod, "Getting It Together," *Environment*, Vol. 14, No. 9, November, 1972.

## PROBLEMS FOR CHAPTER 15

*General Problems*

15.1. From Table 2–1 make a list of the devices or appliances which you have in your home. In Column A alongside the list, give the energy use of each device. In column B give the energy use of devices which are not absolutely necessary for life support, or which you would rather not give up. In column C give the energy use of devices which are critical to the sustaining of life. Add the three columns. Can you save energy in your house? At what cost? With what value?

15.2. Make a list of five devices or actions that could save you energy and money and that you feel would not decrease your lifestyle.

15.3. Assume that a major energy shortage struck the United States. What major energy uses should be cut first?

15.4. Review Example 4–3. How much more than $140 could you afford to spend on this house before the capital costs and operating savings just cancel?

## Advanced Study Problems

15.5. Read Reference 6 and use it to make an analysis of the types of activities that can save energy through sharing.

15.6. Read at least three books on steady state economies; then discuss the relation of energy savings to such economies.

15.7. Write an essay which discusses moral issues relating to the conservation of energy.

15.8. Select a major company in your area. Find out if it has a conservation program. If it does, find out what actions have been taken, what results they have had, and what their motivation has been.

# 16

# THE ENERGY INDUSTRY

*Men that hazard all*
*Do it in hope of fair advantages.*

Shakespeare

Man has always used energy, but never in so many ways and with such sophistication as he does today. Almost all our activities depend in one way or another on a continuous and dependable supply of energy.

The energy industry is a very large and complex group of companies or organizations concerned with supplying energy to meet man's needs or desires. We shall include within our discussion private companies, public utilities, and those governmental agencies which control, regulate, and guide the development of the energy industry.

We start with a description of some of the major types of companies or organizations which supply, convert, or handle energy. We then consider the role that government plays in the process of providing man with energy. Energy marketing is considered briefly. We discuss the electric energy industry in some detail because it is fairly well organized, and its objectives and methods are clear. Finally, we close with some general thoughts on the energy industry and its relationship to its customers.

## 16.1  TYPES OF ORGANIZATIONS

A great many organizations or agencies contribute to supplying energy to consumers. They can be separated into three classes:

1) Unregulated private companies
2) Regulated private utilities
3) Public utilities or agencies

Unregulated private companies include everything from the small coal company in West Virginia, or the manufacturer of parts for electric generators, to the mighty Exxon Corporation, which has operations extending around the world and a brand new gleaming 50-story corporate headquarters in downtown New York. These companies are *unregulated* in the sense that there is no government body which regulates or controls every aspect of their activities, including profits. However, most private energy producers are certainly subject to many governmental restrictions, including taxes, operating rules, pollution standards, and price controls in some cases. The result is a mix of free enterprise and government control. Companies usually believe there is too much control; the press and the public often believe that more control is needed. We shall return to this issue in Section 16.6.

A prime example of the regulated private utility is the private power company. Such companies are franchised by state public utilities commissions (PUC) to operate as a monopoly in a specified area. Their operations, prices, and profits are closely regulated by each PUC or equivalent body. They have the advantage of the efficiency of a monopoly, but they are restrained from using that monopoly to charge unreasonable rates. It is the duty of the PUC to require that restraint, and it is the responsibility of the public to see that the PUC does its duty.

Public utilities are often formed within a city or district to provide gas, electricity, and water. On a larger scale, federal agencies such as the Corps of Engineers or the Bureau of Reclamation often build and operate electric energy plants. On a still larger scale, the Federal Government has set up very large agencies, such as the Tennessee Valley Authority (TVA), to generate large amounts of electric power. We will discuss these in more detail in Section 16.5.

As we move toward possible huge solar farms in the deserts, or very large and expensive fusion reactors, we will have to ask whether the Federal Government or private enterprise will be the developer. It may be that the risks and the magnitude of capital investment will be too great a burden for private industry.

## 16.2  THE ROLE OF THE GOVERNMENT

A number of federal and state agencies play a role in encouraging, guiding, or regulating energy development and use. The agencies which have perhaps the greatest effect on the energy industry, and on energy development, are:

1) Federal Energy Administration (FEA)
2) Energy Research and Development Administration (ERDA)

3) Federal Power Commission (FPC)
4) Nuclear Regulatory Commission (NRC)
5) Environmental Protection Agency (EPA)
6) Securities and Exchange Commission (SEC)
7) Department of the Interior
8) Public Utilities Commission (PUC)

The Federal Energy Administration was established in June, 1974 in an effort to develop and direct a coordinated energy policy for the United States. Its specific charge is to ensure that the supply of energy will continue to be sufficient to meet total energy demand. Also, in the event of energy shortages, it is charged with setting priority needs and ensuring that the shortages are borne with equity. The operations of FEA and its relations with other agencies are still evolving.

The Energy Research and Development Administration was established early in 1975 to coordinate energy research in the United States. Its birth was closely associated with the breakup of the old Atomic Energy Commission. For years critics had complained that it was a mistake for the AEC to play the dual role of developer and regulator of the nuclear energy industry. With the demise of the AEC, ERDA assumed the research and development responsibility for nuclear power. It also inherited most of its 92,000 employees from the AEC. But the intent of Congress was to develop a balanced research agency. It is anticipated that ERDA's research horizons will be quite broad as the agency evolves. ERDA has six major departments or areas of study: nuclear energy; fossil fuel energy; solar, geothermal, and advanced energy systems; environment and safety; conservation; and defense. With almost 100,000 employees and a budget of over $4 billion in 1975, ERDA has become one of the most powerful agencies in the government.

The Federal Power Commission is the major federal agency responsible for assuring that the United States has an adequate supply of electric power available at the most economical prices possible.(2) It is also charged with assuring proper use and conservation of natural resources. Besides these general responsibilities for the health of the industry, the Commission has a number of specific responsibilities. It licenses most non-Federal hydroelectric facilities, establishes accounting practices, regulates interstate rates and activities, and controls some aspects of private utility activities.

The Nuclear Regulatory Commission was established early in 1975 to assume the regulatory role of the old AEC. NRC will have the responsibility for licensing reactors and providing for radioactive waste disposal. In setting up NRC, Congress made it clear that it expected tight control of nuclear reactors. It specifically required that burden of proof for the adequacy of a license application be upon the applicant.

The Environmental Protection Agency was established to carry out the mandate of the National Environmental Protection Act (NEPA) of 1969. The most important section of NEPA, as far as the electric power industry is concerned, is Section 102, which requires the preparation of an environmental impact statement in connection with any major Federal project which would have a significant effect on the environment. Section 102 also requires discussion of all alternatives to the proposed action, and discussion of any irreversibility in the action. The courts have been strict in their interpretation of NEPA, and it appears that it will have a significant effect on the environment. It has also had the effect of increasing the time required to put a plant on line, and of restricting the siting options of the company. It will almost certainly lead to greater energy costs, since pollution control costs must be passed on to the consumer.

The Securities and Exchange Commission regulates the structure and activities of holding companies, the form of mergers of companies, issuance of securities, and various other economic and business practices of the companies in the industry. Its role in the future development of the industry is important because of the movement toward merging of companies and an increase in the number of intercompany transactions.

The Department of the Interior was established in 1849 with

the primary responsibility of conserving natural resources. These include the great fossil fuel reserves in this country. The Department has carried out estensive research in coal utilization, for example, as discussed in Chapter 5. There has been much talk in recent years of enlarging the Department and renaming it the Department of Natural Resources. At this writing (Summer, 1975) the future of the Department is not clear.

Public Utilities Commissions, often with some other formal name, exist in 46 of the 50 states.(3) About half control both public and private utilities. The other half control only private or investor-owned utilities, assuming that public utilities do not

**Figure 16–1.** A regulatory hearing. The energy industry is regulated by a wide variety of public agencies. Hearings before such agencies may concern a raise in rates or the construction of a major new plant. The utility petitioning for the proposed action must show the desirability of its plans. Hearings also provide other interested companies, groups, or the general public with the opportunity to comment on the proposed action. (Courtesy of Pacific Gas and Electric Co.)

require control. These state commissions have a very wide range of responsibilities in the various states. Typically, they set rate structures at a level adequate to insure a fair and reasonable profit to private investors. They establish accounting procedures, assure adequacy of supply and safety, and certify expansion or development of systems under their control.

In addition to the above, many other federal agencies have some interests in energy questions. A number of states have set up or are planning state energy agencies. It is not clear today

**Figure 16–2.** Electricity for farming. The flow of electricity to rural areas has made available the conveniences and economic opportunities that were once found only in the city. In the past 40 years, various government programs such as the Rural Electrification Administration and the five major Federal Regional Administrations have brought electricity to the farm. The dairy farm above receives power from the Tennessee Valley Authority. When TVA started, only three out of a hundred farms in the valley had electricity. Now practically all are electrified. (Courtesy of the Tennessee Valley Authority.)

what additional regulation is necessary, or will evolve. It certainly seems today that the tendency toward regulation and energy planning will increase for some time to come.

## 16.3  THE MARKETING OF ENERGY

The energy industry, like most industries, has for decades vigorously sold its product, encouraging increased use of energy. In the early years of the industry this was perhaps important and desirable. It educated the public to the availability and value of energy. In recent years, however, there has been increasing opposition to the promotion of energy. Most companies have either eliminated or radically changed their promotional policies.(4,5) Two factors have led to this change. The first is environmental protection pressure from persons and organizations arguing against the selling of additional energy. The second is the very real shortage of energy which is either experienced or anticipated.

Most industries today are actively promoting energy conservation. In 1971 the Consolidated Edison Company in New York initiated its "Save-a-Watt" program, urging its customers to turn off air conditioners, lights, and appliances wherever possible. The program had some success and helped New York get through a hot summer without serious power curtailment.

Although the industry may at some times promote use, and at other times discourage it, it is not free to dictate use. As Charles Luce, Chairman of Consolidated Edison, put it, "I don't think people should be free to use all the electricity they are willing and able to pay for, if that implies waste. Electricity and all other forms of energy must be used wisely and not wastefully if the earth is to remain a good place to live. But utilities cannot tell people they cannot have all the electricity they want, or decide what is wise use and what is wasteful use. That is a decision each individual must make for himself—or, possibly, that our elected officials will be forced to make for all of us."(6)

While the power industry cannot decide what is wise use and what is wasteful use, it can help citizens and elected officials make that decision by providing open and unbiased information. This educational role, which would serve the public interest in general, is perhaps the most desirable form for a new marketing task for the industry.


## 16.4   THE ELECTRIC ENERGY INDUSTRY

While most of the energy industry is rather amorphous and difficult to describe, that portion which makes up the electric energy industry has a relatively clear structure.

There are four kinds of organizations in the electric energy industry. The first is the investor-owned (private) power company. The second is the Federal agency, such as the Bonneville Power Administration, or the Tennessee Valley Authority. The third is the non-Federal agency, such as any municipal utility. The fourth is the cooperative established under the Rural Electrification Administration. Table 16–1 shows the number of each type of agency, and the percentage of the total energy produced in the United States which was generated by each in 1970.

Although investor-owned companies are few in number (about 12 percent of the total), they generate over three-fourths of the energy in the nation. Most serve the three-fold role of generation, transmission, and distribution. Such systems are said to be *vertically integrated*. Investor-owned systems are usually

**TABLE 16–1**

**Agencies in the U.S. Electric Power Industry (1970)**

| Industry Segment | Number of Agencies | Percent of |
|---|---|---|
| Investor-owned | 400 | 77.3 |
| Federal | 5 | 12.2 |
| Public (non-Federal) | 2,060 | 9.1 |
| Cooperative | 955 | 1.4 |

granted exclusive franchises from state or local government agencies, entitling and obligating them to provide adequate service to all customers in a specified area. In turn they are usually tightly regulated by some form of public utilities commission.

There are five Federal agencies: the Tennessee Valley Authority (TVA); the Bonneville Power Administration (BPA); the Southwestern Power Administration (SWPA); the Southeastern Power Administration (SEPA), and the Bureau of Reclamation. TVA and BPA were originally established during the 1930s to develop the hydroelectric potential of the Tennessee River and the Columbia River Basin. In more recent years TVA has added fossil-fueled and nuclear generating plants. BPA markets hydroelectric power generated by 33 projects of the Bureau of Reclamation and the U.S. Army Corps of Engineers. It also owns very extensive transmission networks. The remaining Federal agencies generate and transmit hydroelectric power in their respective areas. With the exception of power sold to a number of large industrial customers, most Federal power is wholesaled to other segments of the industry. Federal law requires that preference be given to public agencies in such sales.

Most of the more than 2,000 public (non-Federal) agencies are owned by cities ranging in size from millions of people down to a few hundred. Only about 35 percent (700) generate their own power. The rest buy power from other generating agencies. The small percentage which generate their own power is indicative of one of the problems associated with having many small utilities. As we have seen earlier, there are important economy of scale effects in generating electric energy. That is, the cost per KWH of energy goes down as the plant size goes up. Hence, a small plant built to serve a relatively small number of people will have relatively high energy costs. A second problem is that the existence of many small systems in a region complicates regional coordination of power flows; such coordination is important to the dependable delivery of power where it is needed. There are two solutions. One is to combine a number of small systems into one. The second is to strengthen agreements and coordination between systems in a region. As a general rule the various agencies and systems in the United States cooperate quite well. Unlike private utilities, public utilities do not pay Federal income tax, and generally do not pay local or state taxes, although they often make payments or contributions to their local governments in one form or another.

The nearly 1,000 cooperatives in the United States also vary widely in size, from as few as a hundred to as many as 35,000 members. A very small percentage (6.8 percent) generate their own energy. Cooperatives are financed by the Rural Electrification Administration (REA), established in 1935, to encourage the electrification of farm areas through loans which are available at very low interest rates. Cooperatives also pay no Federal taxes but may pay local taxes in some regions.

Elements of the electric power industry are by no means isolated. The United States has a very extensive interconnection of facilities. Some transmission line ties are strong, some weak. The major advantage of interconnections is to allow systems to sell or trade power when it is surplus in one region and in short supply in another. The United States and part of southern Canada are broken into nine regions or areas where systems are tied together. The entire network is then coordinated by the National Electric Reliability Council.(7)

One of the most important problems related to the growth of the electric power industry is the *siting* or location of new power plants.(8) This is usually an individual utility or government agency decision, though it often has important regional implications which must be considered.

The term "siting" can refer to the rather narrow process of deciding where to put an electric power plant. In this section, however, we use the term in reference to the very complex and lengthy process which starts with the realization that additional power is needed, and ends with choice of a type of plant, a location, and an analysis of benefits and costs. A number of possible sets of factors for consideration might be specified. The following list is rather arbitrary but fairly complete for our purposes. These are essentially decisions which must be made by the utility.

1) Plant size
2) Development schedule
3) Type of plant
4) Plant location
5) Location politics
6) Environmental effects
7) Participation by other utilities
8) Licensing
9) Construction
10) Operation
11) Costs

These factors are not necessarily completed one-by-one in this order. It is often necessary to come back and review one preliminary decision in the light of later considerations.

Inasmuch as this is perhaps the basic growth decision of a company, it is not surprising that the decision process involved makes use of most of what has been discussed in this book.

All industries must devote a certain amount of money to research. The amount of money spent is highly dependent on the nature of the industry, the degree of competition, and the perception of the problems facing the industry. For many years prior to about 1970, the electric power industry was perceived by many to be relatively static. Its methods were established: meeting demand was largely a question of building new plants much like the old plants. This is not to suggest that no progress took place. In fact, some extraordinarily important developments occurred in the 30 years prior to 1970 in such areas as fossil-fuel plant efficiency, nuclear power, and power transmission. Nonetheless, the changes were gradual and the percentage of revenue devoted to research expenditures was small compared with more volatile segments of the technological community. In the latter part of the 1960's a new perception of the problems faced by the industry evolved, and with it came a new interest in research and development.

Expenditures for research and development in the 1960's averaged nearly one fourth of one percent of gross revenues for the utilities. In 1969 the utilities spent about $40 million. Equipment manufacturers spent an additional $110 million. It seems very likely that utility and government expenditures will rise substantially, the former by perhaps three to four times. Various proposals have been made to tax electric energy for research. If each KWH produced in the United States were taxed at a rate of 1/4 of a mill, about $400 million would be raised each year.

There is substantial disagreement on many aspects of future research and development. One is the form of financing. A second is the form of the body which would direct research. It seems to be fairly clear that the main research interests of the electric power industry center around how electric energy is generated and distributed, rather than how it is used. It is an essential position of the industry that its responsibility is to meet demand, and not to question the nature of the demand. This appears to leave to other groups the question of efficiency of use, and perhaps even propriety of use. Whether the latter is anybody's business is a question of much controversy. We shall consider that question in the next chapter.

On January 1, 1973 the Electric Power Research Institute (EPRI) came into being. EPRI was created to conduct a coordinated research and development program, with support from all segments of the power industry. It is a major new effort on the part of the industry to meet the technological challenges of the years ahead.

EPRI's budget for 1975 was just over $100 million, distributed in four major areas of research.(9)

**Figure 16–3.** The building of the electric power industry. In the first decade of the twentieth century, 14 horses pulled part of an electric generator past a quiet river in the Sierra Nevada in California. When the stream was finally tamed and harnessed, it provided the power of 100,000 horses to the growing state of California. Man had conquered nature. In doing so, he had gained something, and he had also lost something. He weighed costs and benefits and made his decision. He can never do less. The rules may change. Perspectives may also change. But every decision must be made. (Courtesy of Southern California Edison Co.)

## TABLE 16–2

### Distribution of the 1975 EPRI Budget by Areas of Research

| Division | Percent |
| --- | --- |
| Nuclear power | 27% |
| Fossil fuel and advanced systems | 45% |
| Transmission and distribution | 18% |
| Energy systems, environment and conservation | 10% |

## 16.5 SOME THOUGHTS ON THE ENERGY INDUSTRY

For years the energy industry in the United States performed (according to its charter of the time) largely out of the public eye. Most people simply assumed that the industry was doing its job. But in the late 1960s the rules of the game changed for a number of reasons. Costs began to rise, fuel availability was questioned, and the American people developed a new interest in the environment. Then in late 1973 the Yom Kippur War and the ensuing oil embargo eliminated any last doubts that there was trouble in the energy supply business. The energy industry was thrust into the public eye. Its sins were denounced, its problems laid bare. Every industry has both, but one so long unused to public scrutiny was particularly unready for such analysis. The energy industry was denounced as the villain of the so-called energy crisis.

It is neither my interest nor my desire to defend the industry in general. However, there have been some accusations which I feel have been either illogical or unjustified.

## 16.6 HIGH PROFITS IN THE OIL INDUSTRY?

During the spring of 1974 most of the major oil companies reported large percentage increases in profits for the first quarter of 1974 compared with the first quarter of 1973. These were headlined widely in the press. In fact, the percentage increase in a profit is a meaningless number unless you know the original profit. For example, suppose that a very large company has an extremely bad year, making only one dollar in profit. The next year it also does very poorly, making a $10 profit. That is a 1,000% increase in profit, which sounds big, but is in fact meaningless. There are some measures, such as the ratio of profit to capital investment, which may be meaningful, but the percentage increase in profit has, by itself, no meaning of value.

A more difficult question is whether the profits made by oil companies in 1974 were "obscene," as suggested by some. Our present system of modified free enterprise permits oil companies to earn as much as they can. We might change that if we wished by controlling or regulating oil companies more tightly. That is, we might move away from the concept of a free energy market. That is a decision which we must make.

## 16.7   HIGH UTILITY RATES?

Electric energy rates have risen quite rapidly in most areas recently. It has been charged that these increases were excessive. There is no way to say, in general, whether rate increases have been proper. However, we do know from what we have seen in earlier chapters that both construction and fuel costs of electric energy have been rising rapidly. The causes are inflation, increased environmental protection, and rising costs of domestic and international fuels. Have the new rates properly reflected these new costs? Answering that question is one of the duties of the Public Utilities Commission or other appropriate agency.

These are just a few of the questions which have been raised in recent years. It is not suggested here that there should ever be complete agreement on the controversies over energy. It is, however, very necessary that there be general agreement on two points. First, the life which most Americans lead and desire depends in part on the availability of some energy. Second, no commodity or product, including energy, can be developed independently of consideration of its impact on society; and, such consideration will moderate development. The energy industry will no doubt be called upon to play an increasing role in effecting rational compromises between demand and impact.

## REFERENCES FOR CHAPTER 16

1. A.R. Smith, "ERDA: The New Glamour Agency," *Bulletin of the Atomic Scientists*, January, 1975, pp. 29–31.
2. *Federal Regulation of the Electric Power Industry Under Parts II and III of the Federal Power Act*, Federal Power Commission, Washington, D.C., 1967.
3. *Federal and State Commission of Jurisdiction and Regulation of Electric, Gas, and Telephone Utilities*, Federal Power Commission, Washington, D.C., 1967.
4. T.J. Galligan, Jr., "The Future Role of Marketing in the Electric Utility Industry," *Public Utilities Fortnightly*, May 10, 1973, pp. 42–44.
5. W.A. Knoke, "Changing Marketing Practices in the Electric Power Industry," *Public Utilities Fortnightly*, May 10, 1973, pp. 45–61.
6. C.F. Luce, "Can People Have the Electricity They Need?" Speech Before the Supplemental Training Program, AT&T, New York City, October 13, 1971.
7. *1971 Annual Report—National Electric Reliability Council and Its Regional Councils*, Research Park, New Jersey, April 1972.
8. *Engineering for the Resolution of the Energy-Environment Dilemma*, National Academy of Engineering, Washington, D.C., 1972.
9. N. Lindgren, "What EPRI Is Up To," *IEEE Spectrum*, April, 1975, pp. 66–69.

## GENERAL READING FOR CHAPTER 16

1. E. Vennard, *The Electric Power Business*, Second Edition, McGraw-Hill, New York, 1970.

This is an excellent, easily-read overview of the electric industry, written from the perspective of the industry. Covered are such topics as regulation, economics, forecasting, marketing, power loads, costs of power, and relations with the community.

2. *The 1970 National Power Survey (Part I)*, Federal Power Commission, U.S. Government Printing Office, December, 1971.

The National Power Survey covers the entire electric industry periodically. Most of this large report is quite readable. It also covers most of the topics covered here.

3. P. Sporn, *The Social Organization of Electric Power Supply in Modern Societies.* M.I.T. Press, Cambridge, Mass., 1971.

This is a very interesting non-technical discussion of power in different social-political environments. It is written by one of the industry's foremost spokesmen.

## PROBLEMS FOR CHAPTER 16

### General Study Problems

16.1. What types of energy are used in your community? What types of agencies or companies develop and deliver this energy?

16.2. Consider that the electric utility which services your home determines that it must add a plant ten years from today. The new plant will have 10% of the present capacity. Suggest the plant type and location which you feel appropriate. Consider as many of the planner's problems as you can. Assume a base load plant.

16.3. Determine some of the major problems which require research in the electric power industry.

16.4. If possible attend a hearing of a regulatory agency on a matter relating to energy.

# 17

## *EPILOGUE*

*I hate quotations.*

Emerson

One of the definitions of an epilogue is "speech made by one of the actors to the audience at the end of a play." Today, we are all, at the same time, both actors and audience in a drama that will have no last act. But this is my last speech here on energy and society, so even though we are at mid-play in the world, this chapter is my epilogue.

We began by searching into man's dim past. We end by looking toward futures that are even less clear. There seem to be two central questions that each of us must ask as we play our parts:

377

**Figure 17-1.** Where do we go from here? This strip-mined Ohio land produced huge amounts of coal for America's energy needs. But what happens to the land when the mammoth shovels move on? Land reclamation is an accepted fact. But the quality of the land ten years from now will depend upon the amount of money we pay for reclamation. So will the cost of energy. (Courtesy of UPI.)

**Figure 17-2.** The evolution of a species. It is a long way from man's first use of fire to heat a cave to the sophisticated—and energy-intensive—air conditioner shown above. This picture leads us to ask whether man can learn to bear the burden of the increasing side effects of a growing technology, or whether there are hidden forces which will in time limit growth. (Courtesy of Pacific Gas and Electric Company.)

1) How might we view the future?

2) How might we affect the evolution of our futures?

We might view the future in two ways. First, we might assume that our basic approaches and assumptions of the past are sound and should be extended into the future. Second, we might decide that it is time to reassess our basic assumptions and to consider alternatives that would change our methods of providing and using energy. I believe that now is the time to reassess.

We assume that increased energy means a higher standard of living. Is this assumption valid, or is there some level of use beyond which our standard of living decreases? Do all the ways in which we use energy today improve our quality of life? And, more basically, what do we mean by "quality of life"? What do we value in life? These questions require serious periodic examination. It is time now to examine them.

If an examination of our assumptions leads us to change our methods, then we must ask how each of us can affect change. In the beginning, of course, we must realize that "we" are many different kinds of people, with different motivations and with different interests as well. We are ranchers and nuclear engineers, conservationists and power-company vice presidents, drugstore clerks and textbook writers. We all have our own special reasons for making the choices that collectively constitute our *de facto* energy policy. How do we resolve our differences?

At one time I believed that we could create or evolve a system, characterized by cooperation and mutual consent, for making decisions. My belief was naive. Today I am convinced that we must continue our adversary system of settling disputes. I do not see an alternative to a fight, sometimes in court, sometimes out, between the conservationist and the energy developer.

The course for the advocate of change is clear. On the personal side he must know what individual actions he can take to change his life to fit his perspectives or beliefs. In the political arena he must have the knowledge and the enthusiasm to work for new policies and goals. It has been a primary objective of this textbook to give the reader a greater understanding upon which he can base his future decisions.

Will we solve our energy problems? Never in any final sense. But I am an optimist. I believe that a new and changing set of approaches will meet our reasonable needs and wants. Men and women have come a long way in their long lifetime. They survived because they learned to respond to new threats and challenges, and because in some mysterious way nature favored men and women with the capacity to adapt to change—even their own changes.

# INDEX

382